What's Wrong with Copying?

What's Wrong with Copying?

Abraham Drassinower

Harvard University Press · Cambridge, Massachusetts · London, England 2015

Printed in the United States of America

First printing

Library of Congress Cataloging-in-Publication Data
Drassinower, Abraham, 1962– author.
What's wrong with copying? / Abraham Drassinower.
p. cm.
Includes bibliographical references and index.
ISBN 978-0-674-74397-7
1. Fair use (Copyright). 2. Intellectual property. 3. Copyright. I. Title.
K1447.15.D73 2015
346.04′82—dc23 2014035598

To Catherine, to Noah, and to Emmett

CONTENTS

PREFACE

Current discussion of copyright law is deeply mired in issues of economic value. Authors are thus construed as commodity producers; works of authorship as intellectual widgets; audiences as consumers; and the public domain—that is, the domain of lawful yet unauthorized copying—as enjoyment of value for which payment has been waived. This book provides a systematic elucidation of copyright doctrine construing authors as speakers; works of authorship as instances of communication; audiences as interlocutors; and the public domain as a set of conditions underlying an ongoing conversation of which authors and publics are equally constituent aspects. The point is to retrieve from within copyright law a neglected appreciation of the copiousness of copying, not as the agitations of wealth-maximization, but as the reverberations of thinking as a shared activity.

I have had the extraordinary privilege of counting on the confidence, support, and patience of many during the completion of this work. My legal theory colleagues at the University of Toronto Faculty of Law are at once demanding and sympathetic, exacting and generous. I have always known that satisfying them intellectually is tantamount to meeting the highest of standards. I am particularly grateful to Bruce Chapman, Arthur Ripstein, Catherine Valcke, and Ernest Weinrib. I have been equally fortunate in regard to the scholars familiar with copyright who have contributed to my thinking through the issues in this work. I am especially grateful to Maurizio Borghi, Wendy Gordon, Ariel Katz, Mark McKenna, Margaret Radin, and Mark Rose. I benefited from discussions of earlier versions of arguments contained in the book with audiences in Argentina, Canada, England, France, Israel, Italy, the Netherlands, Peru, Spain, and the United States. It goes without saying that my students have over the years helped me to sharpen formulations and abandon dead ends.

Arnold Weinrib likely knows more about this book than he would want to know.

Michael Aronson of Harvard University Press supported an unusual project from the outset. I was, and remain, deeply appreciative of his consistently concise and direct style. Two anonymous reviewers provided extraordinarily generous and helpful comments on a draft of the manuscript. Jill Breitbarth designed a whimsical cover that cleverly captures the book's attitude to the question it poses. Marianna Vertullo saw the volume through production.

I would also like to thank my friends at Torys LLP, especially Les Viner, Andrew Bernstein, Wendy Matheson (now Justice Wendy Matheson of the Superior Court of Justice of Ontario), and Andrew Shaughnessy for the opportunity to enjoy working with them; the Social Sciences and Humanities Research Council of Canada and the Center for Innovation Law and Policy at the University of Toronto Faculty of Law for research funding; Deans Ron Daniels and Mayo Moran for their insistence and encouragement; Patrick Healy and Sarah McLeod for their exemplary research assistance with the final stages of the manuscript; and Sooin Kim and Sufei Xu of the Bora Laskin Law Library for their patience and excellence as librarians. Mary Newberry compiled a helpful index.

It is, of course, customary to thank one's family, and to gesture toward the absences that, as a result of one's absorption in the work, they had to endure. I have no doubt that, certainly during the periods of most profound immersion, it was rather my presence to which they were subjected.

Portions of "Copyright Is Not about Copying," *Harvard Law Review Forum* 125:1 (2012): 108–119 are reprinted in the introduction and Chapter 4. Portions of "Copyright Infringement as Compelled Speech," in Annabelle Lever, ed., *New Frontiers in the Philosophy of Intellectual Property* (Cambridge University Press, 2012): 203–224 are reprinted in the Introduction, Chapter 2, Chapter 3, Chapter 4, and Chapter 5. Portions of "A Note on Incentives, Rights, and the Public Domain in Copyright Law," *Notre Dame Law Review* 86 (2011): 1869–1884 are reprinted in Chapter 5. Portions of "The Art of Selling Chocolate: Remarks on Copyright's Domain," in Michael Geist, ed., *From "Radical Extremism" to "Balanced Copyright": Canadian Copyright and the Digital Agenda* (Irwin Law, 2010): 121–150 are reprinted in Chapter 2 and Chapter 3. Portions of "Exceptions Properly So-Called," in *Language and Copyright,* co-edited with Ysolde Gendreau (Yvon Blais/Carswell and Bruylant, 2009): 205–238 are reprinted in Chapter 6. Portions of "From Distribution to Dialogue: Remarks on the Concept of Balance in Copyright Law," *Journal of Corporation Law* 34 (2009): 991–1007 are reprinted in Chapter 1 and Chapter 2. Portions of "Canadian Originality: Notes on a Judgment in Search of an Author," in Ysolde Gendreau, ed., *An Emerging Intellectual Property Paradigm: Perspectives from Canada* (Edward Elgar Publishers, 2009): 139–162 are reprinted in Chapter 1. Portions of "Authorship as Public Address: On the Specificity of Copyright vis-à-vis Patent and Trade-Mark," *Michigan State Law Review* (2008): 199–232 are reprinted in Chapter 2 and Chapter 3. Portions of "Notes on the Distinction between Copyright and Patent," in *New Approaches to Intellectual Property in a Transsystemic World* (Yvon Blais, 2007): 285–297 are reprinted in Chapter 2. Portions of "Capturing Ideas: Copyright and the Law of First Possession," *Cleveland State Law Review* 54 (2006): 191–204 are reprinted in Chapter 4. Portions of "Taking User Rights Seriously," in Michael Geist, ed., *In the Public Interest: The Future of Canadian Copyright Law* (Irwin Law, 2005): 462–479 are reprinted in Chapter 2. Portions of "Notes on the Public Domain," in W. F. Grosheide and J. J. Brinkhof, eds., *Intellectual Property Law 2004* (Intersentia, 2005): 137–153 are reprinted in Chapter 1 and Chapter 2. Portions of "Sweat of the Brow, Creativity, and Authorship: On Originality in Canadian Copyright Law," *University of Ottawa Law & Technology Journal* 1 & 2 (2004): 105–123 are reprinted in Chapter 1. Portions of "A Rights-Based View of the Idea/Expression Dichotomy in Copyright Law," *Canadian Journal of Law and Jurisprudence* 16 (2003): 3–21 are reprinted in Chapter 2.

What's Wrong with Copying?

INTRODUCTION

The Horror of the Copy

This book voices concern over copyright expansion—by which I mean the widespread, naturalized common sense that copying is wrongful, whether legally or morally. Digital technology literally proceeds through copying. To browse the Internet is to copy. Yet the problem with copyright expansion is not only that it chafes against the palpitations of a digital world. The problem is deeper. It is that learning as such proceeds through copying. Culture *is* copying. To be sure, its transmission cannot be reduced to 'mere' copying but, like digital technology, it is inconceivable in its absence. We grow—as Nietzsche liked to say—by becoming our own ideals.[1] We repeat and transform, adapt and transmute meanings and messages, images and symbols. Thought itself, of which memory is but a momentous instance, is predicated on copying.

The implications of copyright expansion are thus enormous. A horror of the copy is legalized philistinism. Driven to its logical conclusion, the fetish of originality outlaws the conditions for the possibility of culture.

Myriad ways are open to grapple with these difficulties and paradoxes, dangers and anxieties. The philosopher may wish to remind us that truth is but the mind's copy of the world; the economist that a wisely crafted freedom to copy is the *sine qua non* of prosperity; the anthropologist that mimesis is of the substance of *anthropos;* and the psychologist, to permit myself one more example, that the self is but a convergence of other selves in a single locus. This book, however, takes up the matter legally: I want to argue that as a matter of law there is nothing wrong with copying.

My point is not that the wrongfulness of copying is a socio-historical construct and that, therefore, there is nothing inherently wrong with it. I have no interest in arguing that in nature, as it were, copying is lawful. I am far too persuaded that, as Aristotle taught, we live in law and in society to insist that, in nature, there is no such thing as copyright.[2] What I set out to do is to demonstrate that the assumption that copying is wrongful is a radically mistaken way to approach copyright law. Copyright expansion is a misunderstanding of copyright.

The claim is only initially surprising. The point, in essence, is that copyright law is not a prohibition on copying but rather an institutionalized distinction between lawful and wrongful copying. Not all copying, to recall a classic United States Supreme Court decision, is copyright infringement.[3] In a way, this book is nothing more than a lengthy exegesis of that well-established legal proposition. Because copyright is not a prohibition on copying, but rather a distinguishing between lawful and wrongful copying, lawful copying is part and parcel of copyright. The public domain, the freedom to copy, pulsates constitutively at the heart of copyright. A theory of copyright is thus not a theory of what's wrong with copying but a theory of how distinctions between wrongful and lawful copying are drawn. We cannot help but misunderstand copyright as soon as we approach it from the standpoint that copying is wrongful.

There are basically two ways of thinking about copyright. The prevailing account, certainly in North America and especially in the United States, finds its inspiration in the efficiencies of the great science of economics.[4] This account sees copyright law as a policy instrument designed to serve the public interest in the production and dissemination of works of authorship. The requirements of the public interest are twofold. On the one hand, the public interest requires that incentives for creativity be provided. Most would not pay for a book if copying it were lawful. Thus, if we want books, we need to protect authors, and this protection is the legal barrier to copying we call copyright. On the other hand, the public interest requires that the products of creativity be widely disseminated. If the legal barriers we grant authors were to include any and all uses of their works in perpetuity, we would likely have to pay them to engage with and develop their ideas, to quote them or cite them, perhaps even to read them. Thus, if we want to ensure that the protections we grant authors do not become dead weight, so to speak, we must calibrate them carefully. Viewed as a whole, the public interest is thus neither about incentives alone nor about dissemination alone, but rather about the balance between them. Balance is what would be most efficient from the standpoint of the public interest. The task of copyright law is none other than the achievement of this optimal balance between creators and users, authors and public domain.

I find the theory unpersuasive. To put it bluntly, I do not think it is a theory of copyright law. To be sure, there can be no doubt that it is a theory of the efficient production and distribution of works of authorship. Nor can there be any doubt that it is a theory of the role of copyright law in that endeavor. But it is a theory of copyright law as an instrument in that endeavor, and so not a theory of copyright in its own terms. Of course, we would need to discuss what a body of law's own terms are, and whether copyright indeed has any terms of its own, but for that very reason I find it unpersuasive to start from the assumption that copyright is nothing but its deployment for some purpose external to itself, by the terms of which it must be thought through and evaluated. Before rushing headlong into an instrumentalist perspective, it strikes me as equally plausible to inquire whether copyright can be conceptualized from its own point of view.

Permit me to develop a brief example. The idea/expression dichotomy is a fundamental aspect of copyright law.[5] As is well known, it is a dichotomy of protection. It provides that copyright protects expression but not ideas expressed. Thus, if you write a story about star-crossed lovers, I cannot lawfully copy your text without your permission. But I do not need your permission to write my own story about star-crossed lovers. This is true even if yours was the very first story about star-crossed lovers ever written, and even if reading your story was what inspired me to write mine. Copyright law grants you exclusivity in respect of the way in which you deal with the theme, but the theme itself remains free for the taking. That is the idea/expression dichotomy. It is a representative instance of the distinction between wrongful copying and lawful copying that pervades copyright law as a whole.

The balance or instrumentalist theory does indeed offer an account of the distinction. Wrongful copying, we might say, is inefficient copying, or—to put it otherwise—copying contrary to the public interest. The idea/expression dichotomy is an easily accessible illustration. On the one hand, the protection of expression supplies an incentive to produce works of authorship, an incentive in the absence of which such production would be precarious, as authors would find it difficult to recoup their investment in production. Thus copying expression is wrongful to the extent that it would undermine the incentive. On the other hand, the simultaneous refusal to grant protection to ideas aspires to ensure that the protection of expression remains consistent with the dissemination requirement that ideas, as the building blocks of expression, be free for the taking. Adopting another's ideas, though without copying their expression, is lawful in that it serves the public interest in both dissemination and further production. Copyright doctrine thus operates to implement an optimal balance granting each aspect of the copyright whole its proper share.

But note that the account renders both wrongful and lawful copying as contingent on the public interest. The free availability of ideas, for example, is part and parcel of copyright law only to the extent that it is deemed to be efficient. If you were to sue me for adopting the idea of star-crossed lovers in my own story, you would lose, as I would no doubt rely on the idea/expression dichotomy to respond to your claim. From the standpoint of the balance theory of copyright, you would lose not because your claim is an affront to my freedom as an author, but because of an assessment, encapsulated in the idea/expression dichotomy, that it would be inefficient to have me pay you a royalty. The free availability of ideas is on this view contingent on a calculation that the social costs involved in having me pay you a royalty are too high relative to the social benefits in the form of greater incentives to authors that my payment would provide. The exclusion of ideas from copyright protection is thus the outcome of a cost-benefit analysis. Having authors charge for use of their ideas is just too expensive for society as a whole. The costs involved in the transaction would outweigh its benefits. It follows, of course, that if we were to come up with an efficient way of demarcating ideas and licensing their use, we would then have to consider reevaluation—if not abandonment—of the idea/expression dichotomy as a doctrine fundamental to copyright.

This is not at all surprising. Because instrumentalism construes copyright doctrine as an instrument of the public interest, demonstrable inconsistencies between copyright doctrine and the public interest must be resolved in favor of the latter. From an instrumentalist point of view, this is entirely obvious, almost trivial. To be sure, the suggestion that ideas may be somehow subject to copyright is bound to seem counter-intuitive, and for at least two reasons. One is that ideas are by nature quite unruly, hardly capable of distinct segregation and demarcation, so that even the hypothetical suggestion that they may be subject to protection cannot help but fill one's head with heavy thoughts about the dead weight of transaction costs. The other reason is that we are so accustomed to construe the idea/expression dichotomy as irreducible and fundamental to copyright that the suggestion that it may be abandoned seems irreducibly foreign.

Yet that is precisely the point. Instrumentalist theory both tolerates and generates foreign suggestions of that kind because it is not a theory of copyright doctrine. The free availability of ideas is not a necessary aspect of copyright law. Rather, its presence in copyright is contingent on a calculation of its efficiency. At the theoretical level, the idea/expression dichotomy comes and goes—as does every aspect of copyright law and copyright law as a whole—with the winds of the public interest. Under the aegis of instrumentalism, the object of theoretical attention is not the lawfulness of lawful copying but its efficiency. This is why instrumentalism can conceive a copyright law devoid of lawful copying. Indeed, nothing in the instrumentalist calculus prevents the postulation of copyright expansion *as* efficiency. Of course, there is nothing necessarily wrong with that. But, as a theory of copyright law, instrumentalism is by no means a self-evident choice, certainly not an obvious starting-point to voice concerns about copyright expansion.

The language of the everyday practice of copyright law, appreciated naively, seems distant from the sophistications and precisions of the economist's preoccupation with the production and circulation of commodified value. It is a language permeated to its core with a communicative nexus between speaker and audience, author and public. A cursory inventory will suffice. The words "expression" and "idea" are more than indicative of communication, of course, but so are words such as "dramatic," "literary," "musical," "artistic," "author," "work," "work of authorship," "original expression," "creativity," "publication of the work," "performance of the work in public," "reproduction of the work," and—to enumerate three more elements in this more or less random series—"copy," "right," and "fair use." This constellation of signifiers suggests that copyright law is about original expressions created by authors, with a view to making them public or communicating them, in respect of which creations authors have rights (condensed in that magnificent nodal point of a word, "copy"), and in respect of which those with whom the author communicates, too, have claims, provided that their use of the works is fair. In short, copyright law is a construal, under the rubric of right, of the communicative nexus between authors and public in respect of works of authorship. That is the standpoint I take in this book.

Let me return for a moment to the star-crossed lovers story. There is a response, attuned to our naive intuitions, as to why granting you an exclusive right in respect of a story you wrote is just not the same as granting you a right to require me to ask you for permission to write my own story on the same topic. Briefly put, your claim to an exclusive right arising from your authorship cannot be inconsistent with my reciprocal claim to an exclusive right in respect of my own authorship. That you have written a story on a given topic cannot possibly entitle you to any and all stories on that topic. Your authorship is not a prerogative to control mine, as if you could treat my agency as a mere appendage subordinate to yours. On the contrary, it would seem that it is by virtue of the very assertion of your own claim to authorship that you are bound to submit to the conditions that render my own claim reciprocally possible.

Of course, this limitation on what you can claim as a matter of right in respect of your authorship is not an explanation of why your authorship gives rise to rights to begin with. We may still ask why *that* is the case—or whether it should be. But the limitation is nonetheless a statement of a condition that your authorship claim must meet if and when it is asserted. Reciprocal acknowledgment of my authorship is the *sine qua non* of the juridical intelligibility of yours.

As a copyright doctrine, the idea/expression dichotomy sifts, as it were, your authorship claim so as to render it compatible with mine. The free availability of ideas is but the rubric under which copyright law affirms and recognizes my equality as an author at the very moment at which it affirms and recognizes yours. It works both ways. It has two sides. We might say that the idea/expression dichotomy structures the interaction between the parties to a copyright action from the standpoint of their equality as authors. From this point of view, lawful copying is a necessary aspect of copyright law. It is necessary in the sense that it is nonnegotiable, regardless of any and all efficiency considerations. It is necessary because it is about the lawfulness of the copying as an aspect of the defendant's freedom as an author. It is not that the plaintiff's claim is balanced against the free dissemination of ideas, as it were in an unimaginably complex calculus of competing yet fungible interests. It is rather, more naively, that not permitting the copying would itself be wrongful, in the sense of being inconsistent with the defendant's equal rights of authorship. To the extent that it operates contrary to the irreducible lawfulness of the public domain, copyright expansion is thus a distortion of fundamental copyright principles.

I set forth in this book a rights-based account of copyright law. I tell a story about copyright law that sees it as a juridical structure affirming and recognizing the inherent dignity of authorship. I proceed on the assumption that it must be possible to understand copyright in its own terms, rather than as a manifestation of a deeper phenomenon or reality of which it is derivative. It is this assumption that permits me to take copyright doctrine seriously as the depository of insights worthy of sustained and systematic elucidation. The idea of the inherent dignity of authorship is thus a methodological wager that there is such a thing as copyright with its own animating principle; that it has a story to tell; that the story emanates from copyright doctrine; and that authorship and the public domain are central to that story.

The account is neither descriptive nor normative. I do claim to provide a description of copyright doctrine. But this description is not an uncritical justification of existing copyright doctrine. It is rather an account of fundamental features of copyright doctrine as a coherent whole. It weaves together salient components from a single point of view. Precisely as such, the description is inseparable from the claim that aspects of existing practice at odds with the coherence of copyright are unjustified or unjustifiable. But at the same time, the normative import embedded in the account is not rooted in a deployment of normative claims external to copyright. The norms juxtaposed against existing copyright are themselves derived from the requirements of elucidating copyright as a coherent whole. The account is thus a critique of existing copyright in its own terms. It is not merely a critical theory but a critical theory *of copyright.*

The central proposition I want to advance is that the subject matter of copyright law—a work of authorship—is a communicative act. A work of authorship is the subject matter of copyright law in the sense that it is what copyright protects. A work of authorship is to copyright law what objects and land are to property law, or what certain kinds of promises are to the law of contract. The central proposition I put forward is that a work is not a thing, whether intangible or otherwise, but an act whereby a person addresses others through speech. Copyright law protects the integrity of the work as a communicative act.

The proposition that a work is a communicative act grounds two further propositions. The first is that, because a work subject to copyright is a communicative act, infringement of the right attendant on the work is best grasped as a disposing of another's speech in the absence of her authorization. Bluntly put, I argue that copyright infringement is wrongful because it is compelled speech. The second proposition is that, because a work is a communicative act, rights attendant on it must (a) be consistent with the communicative rights of others, especially where such rights require copying of a work for the purposes of responding to its author's communication, and (b) be confined to specifically communicative uses of the work. In respect to (a), for example, neither appropriation art nor fan fiction is actionable to the extent that it is an instance of authorial engagement in its own right. In respect to (b), the use of copies of works as thumbnails to facilitate the operations of digital search engines, for example, is lawful because it does not amount to the use of a work for its communicative significance.[6] In neither case does the unauthorized use compel the author to speak.

Thus, copyright doctrine protects not an author's absolute rights over her work, as if the author had some kind of despotic dominion over her speech as an imagined object of ownership, but only such rights as are consistent with both the nature of the work as speech and the structure of the dialogue of which the work is but a part. The affirmation of the author as a speaking being contains a limitation of her juridical entitlement. The concept of the work as a communicative act traverses both the justification and the limitation of copyright. The theory of authorship is inherently a theory of the public domain.

The most far-reaching implication of this communicative approach concerns the status of unauthorized reproduction of copyrighted materials for personal use purposes. The definition of the work as a communicative act carries with it a definition of the right attendant on the work as an exclusive right to recommunicate the work, to present it to the public. Because a work is a communicative act, to reproduce a work is to recommunicate it. Thus, it is not copying as such that is wrongful as a matter of copyright law. It is rather reproduction in the service of public presentation that captures the mischief copyright law targets. In short, I propose that "publication" rather than "reproduction" is the central organizing principle of copyright law. There is nothing wrong with copying *per se.* Copying for personal use purposes is not an act within the purview of an author's copyright. Uploading, but not downloading, is unlawful.

The first chapter of the book, "The Poverty of Value," presents a critique of the balance model of copyright law. The gist of the argument is that the balance model cannot produce an explanation of the way in which copyright law construes the formation of an author's copyright. Originality is a cardinal criterion of copyrightability. It guards the entrance into copyright territory. It distinguishes between copyrightable and uncopyrightable subject matter. For example, an ordinary white-pages phone directory is not subject to copyright protection. Nor is a novel mousetrap. Neither the directory nor the mousetrap originates in an act of authorship. Neither is original in the requisite sense. It is the work of authorship, not the labor of fact-collection, or the inventiveness of an invention, that gives rise to copyright protection. Thus, originality grants copyright protection to some but not all instances of economic value. It is therefore literally constituted as a distinction between kinds of value that, as such, cannot be generated out of the concept of value itself. Something more than calculations and predictions in respect of the circulation of valuable intangible commodities in society is required to make sense of the operations of copyright law. As a quantitative exercise, value-balancing cannot ground the qualitative distinctions that are part and parcel of the meaning and function of originality. Because it is focused on the production and distribution of value, the balance model of copyright law cannot elucidate the specificity of the authorship requirement standing at the threshold of copyrightability.

To be sure, the balance model will seek to remand the distinction between copyrightable and uncopyrightable subject matter to the concept of the public interest, adducing that the protection of facts or inventions under copyright law is contrary to the public interest. This appeal to the pubic interest, however, relocates but does not resolve the problem. It remains true that the concept of value, even if posited as social welfare, cannot distinguish poems from directories, or plays from mousetraps. A lover desperately seeking a lost phone number would confirm that directories are frequently more valuable than the best romantic poetry—yet poems, not directories, invariably trigger copyright protection. Along the same lines, an epidemiologist would warn that readily available statistical information about infectious disease far outweighs the social benefits of limericks, to say nothing of the effects that, from an epidemiological point of view, a chronic absence of mousetraps would have on the public's welfare. To put it otherwise, nothing in the concept of the public interest as value-maximization explains the recurrent and entirely uncontroversial copyright proposition that terrible and tasteless poetry, but not the collection of otherwise unavailable and highly important public interest information, or the creation of costly and invaluable inventions, merits copyright protection. The balance model, quite literally, cannot get copyright off the ground. The point is not so much that the calculations required to conclude that facts or inventions ought not to be subject to copyright are unimaginably complex or indeterminate. The point is that a balancing operation specifically and exclusively preoccupied with copyright subject matter presupposes, rather than generates, the principle of originality as a condition of its own intelligibility. In the absence of such a principle, one could hardly fail to point out that "the man who originated a workable system for producing and marketing paperbacks was more deserving than the authors of many sorry books put out in paperback which rest comfortably in copyright."[7] The balance itself neither does nor can tell us what to put on it. Value-balancing neither triggers copyright nor, therefore, presides over its fundamental operations.

The critique proceeds not abstractly but through exegeses of landmark case law. Methodologically, this procedure retrieves the insufficiencies of the balance model from a confrontation between the concept of balance and one of the pivotal tasks that concept is deemed to accomplish in copyright jurisprudence; namely, explaining the distinction in law between facts and works. The critique is not a disembodied confrontation between the balance model and yet another model vying for dominance, as if copyright practice were the plaything of the theoretical imagination. Rather, the critique advances as an elucidation of landmark decisions and of distinctions, in the absence of which originality in particular, and copyright law in general, would be unintelligible as juridical constructs. The point is to let originality speak for itself.

The second chapter, "Originality as Speaking in One's Own Words," accomplishes two tasks. It formulates the central proposition that a work of authorship is a communicative act and proposes on its basis that "dialogue," rather than "balance," is a more appropriate metaphor to guide copyright interpretation. I develop the concept of the work as a communicative act from within an analysis of the principle of independent creation at the heart of originality doctrine. The principle of independent creation provides that where two (or more) authors coincidentally create identical works, neither is an infringement of the other. On the contrary, each generates its own separate copyright.[8] Because independently created, each is an original work. Originality is not novelty. What matters for copyright purposes is not that an author says something new but that she speaks in her own words.

I draw two observations from the principle of independent creation. The first is that copyright law protects a work of authorship not as an object of ownership (for otherwise the identity of independently created works would render one of them a trespass on the other) but as an act of communication. It is because each of the seemingly identical works is rather an independent act of authorship that, notwithstanding the identity, copyright law grasps them as giving rise to two distinct copyrights. The second observation is that copyright law grants authors rights in respect of their works only where such rights are consistent with everyone else's equal authorship. If your authorship gives rise to rights, then so must mine, even if (or perhaps especially when) our works are seemingly the same. The principle of independent creation thus recognizes, as an equality matter, acts of authorship *per se*. An author is always among other authors. She speaks in a juridical context ensuring conditions for dialogue.

The chapter proceeds to illustrate and confirm the structural impact of the principle of independent creation by revealing its force in both the idea/expression dichotomy and paradigmatic aspects of the defense of fair use or fair dealing.[9] In a manner analogous, though not equivalent, to the free availability of ideas, fair use or fair dealing provides that the unauthorized use of another's expression is lawful where reasonably necessary to one's own authorial engagement. Originality, idea/expression dichotomy and fair use or fair dealing thus manifest the same theme. Fair use or fair dealing is of the same order as the principle of independent creation and the idea/expression dichotomy. The limitations that paradigmatic aspects of fair use or fair dealing impose on an author's copyright are neither exceptions nor countervailing weights reflecting extraneous interests, but rather specifications in the systematic articulation of the principle of independent creation. Lawful yet unauthorized copying of another's expression is constitutive of the very core of copyright law. It affirms and confirms the equal authorship of each and all. Thus, the chapter offers speech, equality, and dialogue in place of value, efficiency, and balance as guideposts for copyright interpretation.

The third chapter, "The Work as a Work," examines two related questions. The first is about the status of unauthorized use in the absence of the defendant's authorship. For example, if unauthorized copying for the purpose of criticism or review is lawful because it involves the defendant's authorship, what is to be said about Internet browsing, which, in the absence of the browser's authorship, involves the making of temporary copies technically required to display a webpage on a computer screen? Is Internet browsing wrongful? The second question is about the meaning of "reproduction" in copyright law. The proposition that unauthorized yet lawful copying is constitutive of the very core of copyright destabilizes copying as the mischief that copyright targets. Copying is not wrongful *per se*. What, then, is the mischief of copyright law? What is a wrongful copy?

The chapter delves into the classic authority of *Baker v. Selden* in order to develop answers.[10] It finds in *Baker* the holding that, because a work is a communicative act, it follows that (a) infringement requires recommunication, and that (b) therefore merely technical noncommunicative uses are not actionable. In *Baker,* the plaintiff had devised a novel accounting system and authored a book explaining its operation. The book contained accounting forms designed by the plaintiff. The plaintiff used these forms in his book as illustrations to help explain the operation of the system. But these very same forms were also necessary to the actual operation of the system itself. The defendant reproduced the forms for the purpose of operating the system. The Court focused its reasoning on the dual function and meaning of the forms as (a) illustrations used in the explanation of the system, and (b) accounting tools necessary to the operation of the system. It held the defendant's technical use of the forms as an accounting tool did not and could not infringe the plaintiff's copyright in the forms considered as aspects of the explanation offered in the plaintiff's book. The defendant used the forms as a tool but not *as a work,* and was therefore not liable in copyright.

I show that we learn from *Baker* that it is not as a pattern of ink on a page, so to speak, but only as a communicative act that a work falls within the purview of copyright law. *Baker* thus turns on a crucial distinction between the work as a communicative act and its material form as its physical embodiment. Use of the physical embodiment for noncommunicative purposes does not give rise to liability. The use of a work's material form is not a use of the work. The chapter thus finds in *Baker* a classic and profound affirmation of the foundational principle of independent creation: because multiple and distinct works can occupy the same material form, a work cannot be equated with its material form. On this basis, the chapter distinguishes *Baker* from the idea/expression dichotomy and from the doctrine of merger.[11] It also proposes that recent case law finding use of digital copies of works in Internet search engines lawful on the grounds of fair use is misguided. The merely technical use of the material form of a work as a search-tool is certainly lawful. But it is not a fair use. Rather, it is a *non*use of the work. Therefore, it is not subject to fair use analysis. By the end of Chapter 3, then, originality, idea/expression dichotomy, merger, paradigmatic aspects of fair use, and now nonuse—as I call it—fall within a conceptual tapestry woven out of the work as a communicative act.

The fourth chapter, "Infringement as Compelled Speech," takes up the proposition that, because a work of authorship is a communicative act, copyright infringement is a wrong to an author's autonomy as a speaking being. I adopt as a baseline the intuition that publishing unpublished work without its author's authorization is wrongful because it is an instance of compelled speech. I canvass several explanations of what the intuition brings into relief. The upshot is that the wrong to which the intuition reacts is not that unauthorized publication of unpublished work amounts to breach of privacy, misrepresentation, misattribution, or deprivation of an object of ownership. Rather, the problem with unauthorized publication of unpublished work is that it ignores the author's irreducible prerogative whether to publish or not. As unauthorized, the publication forces the author to speak.

The chapter takes issue with Samuel Warren and Louis Brandeis's thesis, in their celebrated piece, "The Right to Privacy," that the law of unpublished works is actually privacy law masquerading under another name.[12] Examined through a privacy optic, the act of voluntary publication may indeed amount to a deprivation of protected subject matter—a kind of voluntary disclosure that deprives the published content of its privacy. From a copyright perspective, however, publication neither can nor does deprive a work of its originality. An author does not deprive herself of the prerogative to publish by virtue of having exercised it. That an author has already published her work does not mean that we can (re)publish it for her.

To put it otherwise, a ventriloquist is not any less of a ventriloquist because he compels me to say what I have already said, or what I would have in any case said or repeated of my own volition. The problem is not in the content of what he makes me say. Rather, it is that he removes my choice whether to speak. He disposes of my speech in the absence of my authority. The intuition as to the wrongfulness of unauthorized publication of unpublished work thus goes to the fact that the publication is unauthorized. That the publication is also of unpublished work is of secondary significance. Infringement of the right of first publication is therefore not a wrong distinct from copyright infringement generally. The chapter thus shows that, flowing from the concept of the work as a communicative act, the author's prerogative whether to speak or not is the normative thread that holds unpublished and published works under the single rubric of copyright law.

Chapter 5, "The Public Domain as Dialogue," takes on a twofold task. On the one hand, it addresses concerns that to affirm copyright under the rubric of right is to shortchange the public domain. It is as if (so the concern goes), having enshrined the author's entitlement as a matter of inherent dignity, a rights-based account cannot coherently limit that entitlement in light of the public domain. On the other hand, the chapter addresses a parallel impression that instrumentalist accounts of copyright law are theoretically superior precisely because, free from the encumbrances of right, they can, indeed, provide adequate foundation for the public domain. The chapter sets out to reverse this remarkably pervasive set of associations. It argues (a) that the public domain in instrumentalist thinking is unstable because it is posited as a contingent calculation of its efficiency, and (b) that rights-based thinking advances not only the author's copyright but also, and therefore, the public domain as necessary matter of inherent dignity. In short, the image of the author as speaker engaged in dialogue opens up immanently toward the public domain far more naturally and amicably than does the image of the author as value-originator ensnared in transaction costs. Following an inquiry into the history of the remarkable set of associations that this chapter takes as its theme, I conclude the sketch of the public domain as dialogue by arguing that, understood from a rights-based perspective, the idea/expression dichotomy entails the lawfulness of any and all unauthorized copying for personal use.

Chapter 6 is entitled "Copyright and the System of Rights." Each of the previous chapters is a moment in a progressive elaboration of the concept of the work as a communicative act permitting us to grasp authors and users as equally integral coprotagonists on the copyright stage. Thus, so-called exceptions to copyright infringement, such as fair use or fair dealing, for example, are rather immanently driven implications of a work as the speech of an author. This final chapter raises questions not about intra-copyright relations between authors and users, but rather about encounters between copyright and other recognized juridical interests. Are the claims of a plaintiff as author under copyright law, for example, superseded by those of a defendant as citizen under constitutional guarantees of freedom of expression? Is that an "exception" to copyright infringement? What is the relation between authors and citizens in liberal democracy?

Chapter 6 seeks to locate the copyright system within the larger system of rights of which it is a part. My aim is to specify the assumptions that must be made for the questions to arise meaningfully from a rights-based perspective. I identify four kinds of copyright limitations, of which only one can be regarded as a true exception. There are (a) subject matter limitations, (b) scope limitations, (c) miscellaneous exceptions, and (d) exceptions properly so-called. "Exceptions properly so-called" are instances where copyright claims run into claims recognized in other juridical orders such that the resolution of the ensuing conflict calls for parameters beyond or outside the copyright order. It is as if exceptions properly so-called were crossroads wherein the language of copyright encounters other juridical languages, demanding thereby efforts of translation, modes of juridical analysis able to examine relations between heterogeneous claims of right. I suggest by way of conclusion that "proportionality" is the name we give to those efforts of translation. Under the rubric of proportionality, exceptions are starting-points: provocations to understand the relatedness of plural regimes as aspects of a comprehensive system of rights. The book thus concludes with an evocation of departure.

Four coordinates inform and pervade my reflection as a whole. The first is Edgar Allan Poe's "The Purloined Letter." This is the story of an investigation in the course of which Poe's perspicacious C. Auguste Dupin casually remarks: " . . . over-largely lettered signs and placards of the street, escape observation by dint of being excessively obvious."[13] What we seek hides on the surface. Copy*right* tells us that it is about right. This book takes it at its word. The second coordinate is Jorge Luis Borges's "Pierre Menard, Author of the *Quixote*." A single text is the home of more than one work: "Cervantes' text and Menard's text are verbally identical," Borges writes, "but the second is almost infinitely richer."[14] A work is not in the visible letters that carry it, but in the arch between author and public that traverses its meaning. Menard is, *par excellence,* the great copyright hero of independent creation. The third coordinate is Sigmund Freud's concept of identification.[15] This, too, is a story. It teaches that, like Oedipus, the self seeks itself through the crucible of its forgeries of others. The horror of the copy is thus but an exaggeration of our autonomy, an understatement of our community. The fourth and final coordinate is Immanuel Kant's brief essay, "On the Wrongfulness of Unauthorized Publication of Books."[16] It sets forth the thought that the work of an author is the speech of a person. No one can doubt that, as lawyers, we need Kant to make sense of Poe, Borges, and Freud.

1

The Poverty of Value

An author's work is not subject to copyright unless it is original. Originality is thus a cardinal criterion of copyrightability. It is the central category through which the law of copyright frames the formation of an author's exclusive right to her work.[1]

This chapter examines the originality requirement in order to prepare the ground for the proposition that the subject matter of copyright law—an original work of authorship—is a communicative act. An original work is not a thing—whether intangible or otherwise—but an act whereby a person addresses others through speech. From the very outset (that is, at the level of the formation of the right), copyright law construes authors as speakers, originality as a speaking in one's own words, and works of authorship as instances of speech in an ongoing conversation.

An author's work responds to those before her and addresses those who follow her. It arises from, and is directed toward a network of communicative acts of which it is irretrievably a part. It is not a metaphysical object or intangible commodity but a nodal point of an author's interaction with others in and through speech.

The chapter prepares the ground for this view of the work as a communicative act by showing that the prevailing account of copyright law (that is, the instrumentalist or balance model of copyright) does not and cannot provide an adequate understanding of the originality requirement. The instrumentalist or balance model sees copyright law as a policy instrument designed to encourage and facilitate the production and distribution of works of authorship in the marketplace. Accordingly, the model focuses on the implementation of a balance between the creation and dissemination of works of authorship conceived as information commodities. It construes works not as instances of speech but as instances of economic value. Thus it ignores, in favor of its value, the specificity of the author's speech as such.

The basic problem with the model is that not any and all value sounds as a matter of copyright law. The fundamental function of the doctrine of originality in the structure of copyright law is to distinguish copyrightable from uncopyrightable subject matter. Originality guards the entrance, so to speak, into copyright territory. It grants copyright to some but not all instances of economic value. It is thus literally constituted as a distinction between kinds of value. Precisely as such, originality cannot be generated out of the concept of value itself. As a quantitative category, value cannot ground the qualitative distinctions that are part and parcel of the very meaning and function of originality. Value cannot capture the specificity of authorship.

There is no doubt, of course, that works of authorship can and do have market value. My point is not that works of authorship are valueless, but that it is not as instances of value that originality grants them entrance into copyright territory. Originality is not about value *per se.* It is about authorship. This is why, framed as it is as an inquiry into the production and distribution of value, the instrumentalist or balance model cannot provide an understanding of originality.

Originality is the *sine qua non* of copyright protection. Our understanding of originality therefore pervades and permeates our understanding of all aspects of copyright. The encounter between speech and value as ways to understand originality is thus a deeper struggle about the concepts and metaphors in and through which we construe copyright law as a whole. From this point of view, the burden of this first chapter is a heavy one. It is to adumbrate a landscape in which, throughout the rest of this book, copyright will gradually come into relief as a juridical order addressing aspects of the interaction between human beings as speaking beings, rather than as a mechanism designed to supervise and facilitate the production and distribution of intangible commodities. The struggle over originality is a struggle between copyright visions.

From Labor to Authorship

The concept of originality has recently undergone significant transformation in both the United States and Canada. In 1991, in *Feist Publications Inc. v. Rural Telephone Service Co. Inc.*, the Supreme Court of the United States unambiguously rejected "sweat of the brow" in favor of "creativity" as the governing originality standard in United States copyright law.[2] Similarly, in 2004, in *CCH Canadian Ltd. v. Law Society of Upper Canada*, the Supreme Court of Canada unambiguously rejected sweat of the brow in favor of "skill and judgment" as the governing originality standard in Canadian copyright law.[3] Both judgments present themselves as definitive resolutions of a then ongoing historical struggle in each jurisdiction between sweat of the brow and creativity schools of originality.[4] Appreciation and awareness of divergences between *Feist* ("creativity") and *CCH* ("skill and judgment") need not obscure their convergent rejections of sweat of the brow jurisprudence. In neither jurisdiction is the sweat of an author's brow in the production of her work any longer sufficient to qualify for copyright protection.[5]

The sweat of the brow standard provides that labor or industry, even in the absence of creativity, is sufficient to make out a finding of originality. For example, the labor invested in the collection of the information making up a simple, alphabetically arranged phone directory, gives rise to copyright protection. The directory is an "original" work of authorship in the sense that it was not copied from another work. The fact that the production of the directory can be characterized as a merely mechanical or automatic collection of factual material does not preclude the directory's copyrightability. Mere labor is sufficient to generate copyright. Precisely because collecting facts requires labor, facts are not immune to copyright protection. On the contrary, the protection of factual works is but an instance of copyright protection conceived as protection from the injustice of a person's misappropriation, through copying, of value produced by another. To refuse copyright in the name of a higher originality standard is to deprive copyright of its efficacy in respect of misappropriation.[6]

By contrast, the creativity standard, as its name indicates, provides that a finding of originality is impossible in the absence of creativity. An original work must be not only not copied, but also minimally creative. As a merely mechanical or automatic arrangement of preexisting material, a simple phone directory lacks originality. It is public domain material regardless of the labor invested in its production. It can be copied with impunity. The loss or harm that the producer of the directory would sustain were another person to copy it and offer it for sale in the same market would not be an actionable wrong under copyright law. The directory's value is insufficient to ground its copyrightability. By the same token, a poem's creativity grounds its copyrightability even in the absence of value. From the standpoint of the creativity standard, the movement away from the sweat of the brow standard is thus a movement from labor to authorship as the defining category. Copyright arises as a right inhering in authorship as distinct from any and all other kinds of labor. To grant copyright on the basis of labor alone, such as the labor involved in fact collection, is to run afoul of basic copyright categories.[7]

CCH offers skill and judgment rather than creativity as the standard of originality in Canada. Nonetheless, *CCH* expressly points out that "concerns [raised in *Feist*] about the 'sweat of the brow' doctrine's improper extension of copyright over facts also resonate in Canada."[8] Thus, whatever their differences (to which we shall return briefly), *Feist* and *CCH* share a set of family resemblances in which (a) raw facts or data are not subject to copyright protection, (b) misappropriation of the value of another's mere labor through unauthorized copying is not the mischief copyright law targets, and (c) public domain considerations (e.g., the free availability of facts) are constitutive of the definition of originality; that is, in both *Feist* and *CCH,* the public domain impinges not only on the limitation but also on the very formation of an author's copyright.

Perhaps the deepest of family resemblances between the two judgments is a conception of the purpose of copyright law as a balance between authors and users—a balance, as it is often put, between the incentive to create and the imperative to disseminate works of authorship. While the author's right to exclude others from certain uses of her work provides encouragement for creation, the limits that copyright law imposes on protection ensures that recognition of the author's interest remains consistent with further creativity. The operations of copyright doctrine are thus conceived as mediating a perennial tension between incentive and dissemination, seeking to implement a balance granting each aspect of the copyright whole its proper share. "[C]opyright assures authors the right to their original expression," says *Feist*, "but encourages others to build freely upon the ideas and information conveyed by a work."[9] "When courts adopt a standard of originality requiring only that something be more than a mere copy or that someone simply show industriousness to ground copyright in a work," *CCH* states, "they tip the scale in favour of the author's or creator's rights, at the loss of society's interest in maintaining a robust public domain that could help foster future creative innovation."[10] In both *Feist* and *CCH*, the concept of balance captures a manifold structure that refuses copyright protection to facts, denies that the misappropriation of value through copying is the mischief that copyright law targets, and affirms the public domain as integral to copyright jurisprudence. In respect of originality in particular, both *Feist* and *CCH* dismiss the sweat of the brow standard in the name of the copyright balance.

Because both judgments present themselves as unequivocal dismissals of sweat of the brow jurisprudence, their discontinuity from antecedent Anglo-American and Anglo-Canadian case law is self-evident.[11] But while it is correct to emphasize the innovative dimension of either judgment, it would be incorrect to forget that they settled an ongoing struggle between originality schools, and that therefore elements of the side that emerged victorious were themselves present in the shared yet conflicted United Kingdom copyright tradition from which each seeks to differentiate itself. The continuity between *Feist* and *CCH* and the copyright tradition should not be underestimated.[12] Moreover, just as it is to be expected that elements of the victorious side were already present in the copyright tradition, it is equally to be suspected—contrary to first impressions—that elements of the defeated side, albeit in altered or disguised form, remain operative in *Feist* and *CCH*.

I argue in this chapter that the rise in *Feist* and *CCH* of an alternative to sweat of the brow jurisprudence is not as unambiguous as it may first appear. More precisely, I argue that the concept of balance is insufficient to ground the doctrinal shift from sweat of the brow to creativity or skill and judgment. *Feist* and *CCH* thus display a tension between the doctrinal shift they propose and the vision of the purpose of copyright law in the name of which they propose it. The result is that the affirmation of creativity or skill and judgment as originality standards hovers over a justificatory vacuum. The chapter thus brings into relief the necessity of an alternative interpretation of the purpose of copyright law.

To begin with, following brief overviews of *Feist* and *CCH,* I analyze two classic and foundational United Kingdom authorities on originality, *University of London Press, Ltd. v. University Tutorial Press, Ltd.* and *Walter v. Lane.*[13] My purpose in doing so is twofold. First, I want to find in these two classic authorities traces of the struggle between sweat of the brow and creativity schools, and hence to appraise the presence in each of these authorities of an alternative to the traditional sweat of the brow standard. Second, I expect to learn from that exercise what some of the fundamental presuppositions and implications of the shift from sweat of the brow to creativity or skill and judgment must be. I hope in this way to deepen our understanding of the relationship between *Feist* and *CCH* and the copyright tradition they criticize, and to asses, therefore, the significance of *Feist* and *CCH* for the development of that tradition in the direction of a clear (or at least less conflicted) movement away from sweat of the brow jurisprudence.

The upshot of the analysis is that sweat of the brow jurisprudence is rooted in a principled and deliberate refusal to distinguish between the generality of labor (i.e., "sweat") and the specificity of authorship (i.e., "creativity" or "skill and judgment"). Accordingly, it grants copyright protection to compilations of facts because it sees no significant distinction for copyright purposes between the labor of fact compilation and the work of authorship. A phone directory is as worthy of copyright protection as a poem. The refusal to distinguish is principled and deliberate in the sense that it both posits and presupposes a vision of the purpose of copyright law as a remedy for the misappropriation through copying of value created by another. The transition away from sweat of the brow jurisprudence thus requires a distinction between labor and authorship able to elucidate the specificity of the latter.

With that distinction in mind, the chapter now underlines in more detail that *Feist* and *CCH* posit the transition away from sweat of the brow to creativity or skill and judgment by reference to the copyright balance. Because it is focused on the production and distribution of value, however, the concept of balance cannot generate, in spite of *prima facie* appearances, the requisite distinction between sweat and creativity, or labor and authorship. Nothing in the idea of balancing value, or in that of value itself, can account for a consistent practice of refusing copyright to phone directories while granting it to poems. Creativity or skill and judgment are but ways of making distinctions of that kind, of including novels and excluding mousetraps, of distinguishing between copyrightable and uncopyrightable subject matter. Thus the concept of the copyright balance cannot generate creativity or skill and judgment as originality standards because, on the contrary, it presupposes them as the principle that makes the balance intelligible as a copyright-significant balance to begin with. Literally preposterous, the effort to put the cart before the horse cannot help but be counterproductive: the unequivocal doctrinal thrust toward the specificity of authorship in *Feist* and *CCH* nonetheless becomes enmeshed and submerged in a value-centered vision of the purpose of copyright law.

Deployed in the name of balance, originality is doctrine devoid of vision; practice devoid of theory. Analysis of the transition from sweat of the brow to skill and judgment reveals the need for an alternative conception of the purpose of copyright law. It reveals, as we shall see in Chapter 2, that copyright is best grasped from the standpoint of speech rather than value.

Feist Publications v. Rural Telephone

In *Feist*, the US Supreme Court denies copyright protection to an alphabetically arranged phone directory on the grounds of lack of originality. This denial takes place through the Court's dismissal of the sweat of the brow standard. The Court offers two related yet conflicting reasons for its dismissal.

On the one hand, the Court defines the originality requirement as an authorship requirement. Facts are not subject to copyright because facts do not "owe their origin to an act of authorship."[14] The sweat of the brow standard is untenable to the extent that, in granting copyright to facts, it runs contrary to the authorship requirement. The Court's insistence on this requirement could not be more forceful. The Court enshrines it as the "most fundamental axiom of copyright law," the "*sine qua non* of copyright," a "bedrock principle of copyright," the "touchstone of copyright protection" the "very premise of copyright law," "the essence of copyright," and "a constitutional requirement."[15] In the widest and deepest of senses, there is no such thing as copyright in the absence of originality, where originality is unequivocally defined not as the investment of industry, sweat, labor, or value, but as "an act of authorship."[16]

Of course, the Court points out that protection of labor invested in the collection of factual information "may in certain circumstances be available under a theory of unfair competition."[17] Yet it adds immediately that to grant protection on this basis alone "distorts basic copyright principles."[18] The point runs deep. The Court does not hesitate. At stake is not some kind of regret that sweat of the brow jurisprudence is inconsistent with copyright, as if protecting the fruit of one's labor or effort were in and of itself either justified or desirable. On the contrary, the Court's point is, emphatically, that a juridical order premised on protecting labor or effort is just not cognizable as copyright law.

Value invested in and created through the collection of factual information is and remains public domain material. It may be used with impunity. This is no mere unforeseen eventuality. It is part and parcel of the definition of copyright: "It may seem unfair that much of the compiler's labor may be used by others without compensation. As Justice Brennan has correctly observed, however, this is not 'some unforeseen byproduct of a statutory scheme.' It is, rather, 'the essence of copyright,' and a constitutional requirement."[19] Originality is "constitutional" of copyright, not only in the sense that it is mandated as a requirement of copyright protection by the United States Constitution, but also in the sense that it is constitutive of the intelligibility of copyright as a distinct juridical order.[20] The "act of authorship" requirement is literally radical. It goes to the root of copyright as such.

On the other hand, notwithstanding this constitutive status, the Court derives the authorship requirement from the constitutional imperative to promote the "Progress of Science and useful Arts."[21] In so doing, the Court demotes authorship from its axiomatic standing to that of a derivative category. Authorship now appears not as a "bedrock principle" but as an instrument parasitic on the public interest in progress. "The primary objective of copyright," the Court writes,

> is not to reward the labor of authors, but "[t]o promote the Progress of Science and useful Arts." To this end, copyright assures authors the right to their original expression, but encourages others to build freely upon the ideas and information conveyed by a work. This principle, known as the idea/expression or fact/expression dichotomy, applies to all works of authorship. As applied to a factual compilation, assuming the absence of original written expression, only the compiler's selection and arrangement may be protected; the raw facts may be copied at will. This result [i.e. that "much of the fruit of the compiler's labor may be used by others without compensation"] is neither unfair nor unfortunate. It is the means by which copyright advances the progress of science and art.[22]

Thus, in this iteration, the Court's dismissal of the sweat of the brow standard is less an affirmation of the constitutive role of authorship than an assertion that copyrighting facts contravenes the public interest. Not the authorship requirement but rather the progress of science and art presides over the turning away from sweat of the brow jurisprudence.

This reduction of authorship to the public interest in progress is puzzling in at least two central respects. First, nothing in the concept of the public interest, or in that of the progress of science and arts, necessitates the conclusion that copyrighting facts is unwarranted. On the contrary, it is equally plausible that the absence of copyright for facts undermines—contrary to the public interest—incentives to discover, collect, and compile fresh facts.[23] That progress can do without protection of admittedly mechanical efforts to collect and compile those facts is by no means self-evident. My point is not that copyright ought to protect facts. My point is that a theory of copyright protection rooted in the public interest in progress has no conclusive basis to exclude facts from its purview. It cannot account for the rejection of the sweat of the brow standard in favor of the creativity standard. On this basis alone, the deployment of the concept of progress in *Feist* falls short of its intended target.

Second, the demotion of the authorship requirement from a bedrock principle to a derivative category stages the return, as it were, of a persistent image of the author as mere laborer rather than creator. To see this, we need to recall that the Court's initial formulation of the radically constitutive status of authorship reads as a (re-)definition of authorship. From this point of view, the creativity school is an insistence that, because the mere labor of fact collection is not an act of authorship, it is therefore unworthy of recognition under copyright law. The sweat of the brow school distorts copyright as a juridical regime to the extent that it reaches beyond the regime's proper limits. Thus, as we noted, facts are denied copyright protection not because the public interest demands that denial but because facts do not "owe their origin to an act of authorship."[24] There is no authorship in the mere labor of fact collection, and it is this absence of authorship, not the public interest, that orients and determines the analysis.

Once the logic of progress appears on the scene, however, it is not the absence of authorship, but the limiting force of the public interest that assumes the central role. But while this force is summoned in support of the redefinition of authorship as creativity, it has the opposite effect. The logic of progress proclaims triumphant that (a) not authorship but the public interest in progress is the "primary objective of copyright," and that therefore (b) authorship is to be relegated to a "secondary consideration." In other words, the logic of progress assumes that, if authorship were to remain untrammeled, it would swallow up the public interest in progress into the centripetal vortex of its *prima facie* entitlement to the products of its labor, the sweat of its brow. This assumption is what governs the assertion that authorship is secondary. The relegation of authorship to the level of a secondary consideration thus presupposes—and therefore revives—the definition of authorship that *Feist* is intended to debunk.

The irony could not be more striking: the landmark decision enshrining the creativity of authorship in United States copyright law as a radically constitutive "bedrock principle" winds up demoting authorship to the level of a merely derivative category and, in so doing, retaining the sweat of the brow definition of authorship it seeks to undo. The forceful rise of authorship as creativity turns out to be but a brief prelude to its immediate downfall. *Feist* debunks authorship with the very same stroke with which it grants it constitutional status. Worse, because the logic of progress emphatically asserts the bedrock status of the principle of authorship even as it relegates it to secondary derivative status, it in fact masks the persistence of labor as a defining feature.

It is as if *Feist* suffers from a bad conscience over depriving authors of the fruit of their labor, and thus enlists nothing less than the majesty of a constitutional imperative to assuage its sense of guilt. The upshot is that, in the name of copyright balance, the creativity school achieves little more than an overlaying of itself super-structurally, as it were, over a persistent structure focused on the author as a laborer and *prima facie* entitled to the fruits of the sweat of her brow. The constitutional majesty of the countervailing principle that *Feist* emphatically asserts against the sweat of the author's brow cannot help but reveal the enduring gravitational pull of the author as laborer. Albeit constitutionally, the public domain is thereby condemned to appear negatively, as that which deprives the author of what would otherwise be hers. Not only the project of redefining authorship, but also that of anchoring the public domain affirmatively in copyright jurisprudence, is muddled and diluted in an ocean of public interest considerations.

CCH v. Law Society of Upper Canada

A similar reversal, and equally striking, besets the rejection of the sweat of the brow standard in *CCH*. Even more than *Feist*, *CCH* is worthy of consideration because it presents us not only with a rejection of the sweat of the brow standard, but also with a significant expansion of the fair dealing defense in Canadian copyright. Anglo-Canadian fair dealing, a close cousin, or sibling perhaps, of American fair use, specifies situations in which use of a work subject to copyright in the absence of the copyright holder's authorization is lawful.[25] Because fair dealing is about permissible yet unauthorized use, it is more often than not regarded as an exception to an author's exclusive right to her work. In a single judgment, then, *CCH* narrows originality and both deepens and widens fair dealing, holding unambiguously that fair dealing is not an exception to an author's copyright but a user's right.[26] The judgment thus restricts entrance into copyright territory and, moreover, constrains the prerogatives of those who gain admission. Put another way, *CCH* enfranchises users in the copyright universe. For that reason alone, *CCH* is and remains the most explicit judicial affirmation of user rights in the world.[27] To be sure, the "user rights" terminology is perhaps specific to the Canadian context, but the concept of copyright law as a juridical order involving both authors and users is certainly familiar in common law jurisdictions, and by no means unfamiliar in civil law ones. *CCH* thus provides a particularly helpful context in and through which to construe the formation and the limitation of authorial entitlement from a single point of view.[28]

In *CCH,* publishers CCH Canadian, Thomson Canada, and Canada Law Book sued the Great Library at Osgoode Hall in Toronto, operated by the Law Society of Upper Canada. The Great library ran a photocopying service from which members of the Law Society, the judiciary, and other authorized researchers could request photocopies of materials. The materials were copied by library staff and delivered in person, by mail, or by fax to the requesters. The publishers' action against the library alleged infringements of copyright resulting from the photocopying service, and also from usage by library patrons of self-service photocopiers provided by the library.[29] The Court held, *inter alia,* that the publishers' materials were original works subject to copyright protection and that the library successfully made out the defense of fair dealing for research purposes with respect to the photocopying service.[30] In the course of its reasoning, the Court defined originality as "skill and judgment" rather than sweat of the brow and defined fair dealing as a user's right, which is not to be interpreted restrictively.[31]

The concept of copyright as balance in large part mediates the Court's dismissal of sweat of the brow jurisprudence. The Court refuses to take sides in the ongoing battle in Canadian copyright law between sweat of the brow and creativity schools. It posits, instead, a third standpoint, for which "skill and judgment" is the hallmark of originality. The Court arrives at skill and judgment through its rejection of what it sees as two extremes equally incompatible with a balanced copyright. On the one hand, because it would bring facts within the purview of copyright, and hence operate contrary to the preservation of a "robust public domain," the traditional British sweat of the brow standard is said to be too author-centered and "too low" a standard. On the other, the American creativity standard formulated in *Feist* is said to be too public-centered and "too high" a standard, favoring the public interest at the creator's expense. In the Court's construal, the creativity standard would require novelty or nonobviousness, "concepts more properly associated with patent law than copyright law." In this vein, the Court formulates the skill and judgment standard as "workable, yet fair": an in-between truly attuned to the dual purpose animating the copyright balance. A skill and judgment copyright is a balanced copyright.[32]

The difference between skill and judgment in *CCH* and creativity in *Feist* is at best elusive, at worst nonexistent. This impression is reinforced by the peculiar and surprising fact that in *CCH* the Supreme Court of Canada clearly misrepresented and misapprehended the *Feist* creativity standard. In *Feist,* the US Supreme Court explicitly and unambiguously stated that "originality does not signify novelty," and, moreover, that the creativity standard is "extremely low."[33] Thus, it is hard to avoid the impression that, given its misunderstanding of the creativity standard, the Supreme Court of Canada happens to occupy with the phrase "skill and judgment" the very same space inhabited by the United States Supreme Court by virtue of its treatment of "creativity" in *Feist.*[34] Otherwise, one would have to credit the Supreme Court of Canada with the mysterious achievement of having found a significant mid-point between zero and "extremely low."

Scrutiny of *CCH* will confirm and develop two observations already available from the analysis of *Feist.* First, the transition away from sweat of the brow to creativity or skill and judgment is inadequately premised on the concept of balance. The historical struggle between doctrinal schools of originality has not been overcome. It has become transmuted into a struggle between doctrine and purpose, copyright practice and copyright theory. The doctrinal push toward authorship (i.e., creativity or skill and judgment) encounters a justificatory framework preoccupied with the production and distribution of value (i.e., balance). The result is a conflicted jurisprudence in which an authorship paradigm incipient at the doctrinal level protests against a value paradigm entrenched at the theoretical level.

Second, because *CCH* is a reflection on the roles of both authors and users under copyright law, it reveals with particular clarity that shortcomings in the justification of author rights are also shortcomings in the justification of user rights. *CCH* intimates that the path toward an integrated copyright law is in the elaboration of the authorship paradigm rather than the value paradigm. Taking user rights seriously requires taking authorship seriously. The public domain can thus arise not as an imposition on authorship but both vigorously and immanently as an unfolding of authorship itself. More precisely, as we shall see in Chapter 2, authorship and public domain are mutually constitutive and inextricable aspects of a copyright law that, anchored on speech rather than value, is conceived not as balance but as dialogue.

A fuller and nuanced appreciation of the intertwining dynamics at play in the treatment of originality in *CCH*—and also in *Feist*—requires greater familiarity with the images, contexts, and assumptions of the copyright tradition to which it responds. With that in mind, I want at this point to postpone more detailed analysis of *CCH* to make room for a brief, yet helpful excursus on the *University of London Press* and *Walter* cases mentioned at the outset.

University of London Press v. University Tutorial Press

Briefly stated, the facts in *University of London Press* pertinent to the originality question were as follows. In September of 1915, Professor Lodge and Mr. Jackson were hired by the University of London to set entrance examinations in mathematics. It was a condition of their being hired that copyright in the examination papers vested in the University. Together they set three examination papers: one in arithmetic and algebra, a second in geometry, and a third in more advanced mathematics. (Accordingly, the Court referred to the first two papers as "elementary," in contrast to the third paper in more "advanced" mathematics).[35] The University then assigned the copyright in the examinations to the plaintiff, University of London Press. The Press published the examination papers. But, having obtained copies of the examination papers from students who had taken the examinations, the defendant, University Tutorial Press, also published the examination papers. University of London Press sued for copyright infringement.

In a famous passage, the Court defined "originality" as follows: "The word 'original' does not in this connection mean that the work must be the expression of original or inventive thought. Copyright Acts are not concerned with the originality of ideas, but with the expression of thought, and, in the case of 'literary work,' with the expression of thought in print or writing. The originality which is required relates to the expression of the thought. But the Act does not require that the expression must be in an original or novel form, but that the work must not be copied from another work—that it should originate from the author."[36] This passage involves three closely related propositions worth parsing. Two of these propositions tell us what originality is not, and one tells us what it is.

The first proposition is that originality is not novelty of thought. It is trite copyright law that to express an old or familiar idea anew in one's own words is to be original for copyright purposes. Originality is not about *what* the work says—whether novel or otherwise—but about *how* the work says it. It pertains not to content but to form, not to idea but to expression.

The second proposition is that originality is not about novelty in expression. While it is true that originality pertains exclusively to expression, this does not mean that the expression must itself be novel. This is aptly captured in the defense of independent creation. As Justice Learned Hand put it, "if by some magic a man who had never known it were to compose anew Keats's Ode on a Grecian Urn, he would be an 'author,' and, if he copyrighted it, others might not copy that poem, though they might of course copy Keats's."[37]

The third proposition is already contained in the second. What is required for originality is not that the expression be novel in the sense that it has never been composed by anyone else before, but that it be not copied from another work—i.e., that it be original in the sense of being the author's own product. One does not cease to have said something in one's own words just because, coincidentally, another person happens to have used those very same words. The coincidence, however unexpected or unlikely, does not make one's expression any less one's own. It is this sense of "one's own"—that of the origins or pedigree of the expression—that originality recognizes. Original means independently created.

Having described the originality standard, the Court in *University of London Press* proceeded to apply it to the facts of the case. Peterson J. pointed out that Professor Lodge and Mr. Jackson had proved that they had themselves thought of the questions they had set. They had notes or memoranda proving that they had themselves come up with the questions—i.e., that they had not copied them. The examination papers were therefore original within the meaning of the *Copyright Act*.[38]

The Court then moved on to consider four objections to its holding. Three of them are directly relevant to our present purposes. In essence, the Court's response to these objections was that they are all rooted in a misunderstanding of the meaning of originality. In particular, the objections misunderstand the crucial proposition that originality does not mean novelty. Examining these objections is instructive because, in the course of its response to them, the Court's reasons appear to give rise to a struggle between two distinct views of originality. One of these views is consistent with the Court's manifest formulation that "original" means "not copied from another work." The other view announces, as it were in latent form, the proposition that "original" means—to use the Court's own words—involving "selection, judgment and experience."[39]

The first objection dealt with by the Court was that, in composing the examinations, the authors "*drew* upon the stock of knowledge common to mathematicians."[40] The Court replied that drawing from the common stock of knowledge does not preclude originality. Originality is not novelty, otherwise "only those historians who discovered fresh historical facts could acquire copyright for their works."[41] The objection is thus untenable in that it suggests that originality turns on the novelty of the information conveyed in a work. The work of Professor Lodge and Mr. Jackson met the originality standard because they did not copy from the common stock; they only drew upon it. While *copying* from the common stock is indeed inconsistent with originality, *drawing* from the common stock does not preclude originality.

The second objection was that the examination questions set by Professor Lodge and Mr. Jackson were questions in "book work"—that is, "questions set for the purpose of seeing whether the student has read and understood the books prescribed by the syllabus."[42] This objection is but a version of the first; namely, that a work is not original if it draws from another. The Court therefore responds by affirming once again the proposition that originality is not novelty and that drawing from another work does not preclude originality. To be sure, the objection here is not that the examiners drew from the common stock but rather that they drew from the specific books prescribed by the syllabus. Still, the answer is basically the same in that it restates that original means not copied: "the questions set are not copied from the book."[43]

Yet the passage in which the Court responds to the "book work" objection gives us reason to pause:

> Some of the questions, it was urged, are questions in book work, that is to say, questions set for the purpose of seeing whether the student has read and understood the books prescribed by the syllabus. But the questions set are not copied from the book; they are questions prepared by the examiner for the purpose of testing the student's acquaintance with the book, *and in any case it was admitted that the papers involved selection, judgment, and experience.* This objection has not, in my opinion, any substance; if it had, it would only apply to some of the questions in the elementary papers, and would have little, if any, bearing on the paper on advanced mathematics.[44]

The Court's additional remark that the papers involved "selection, judgment and experience" is puzzling. The remark is at best unnecessary and at worst counter-productive. It is unnecessary in that, on the view that original means not copied from another work, the papers would be original even if they had involved no selection, judgment, and experience. The Court does not need to assert that the papers involved "selection, judgment, and experience" in order to find them original.

The remark is counter-productive in that the criteria of "selection, judgment, and experience" are not necessarily consistent with the "not copied from another work" criterion. Ordinary phone directories, to once again refer to the classic example, can be both "not copied from another work" *and* involve no "selection, judgment, and experience" in their production. Peterson J. himself raises the possibility of works of such a kind when he comments that the "book work" objection "would only apply to some of the questions in the elementary papers, and would have little, if any, bearing on the paper on advanced mathematics." It is as if Peterson J. were saying that if originality were about "selection, judgment, and experience," the "elementary papers" could be denied protection. Thus the comment seems to be some kind of concession on Peterson J.'s part that the originality determination is easier in respect of the paper on advanced mathematics because it is easier to characterize that paper as involving "selection, judgment, and experience." Paradoxically, then, Peterson J. invoked the admission that the papers involved "selection, judgment, and experience" as a response to the objection that the papers lacked originality, yet in so doing he in fact wound up raising the spectre of a standard of originality that at least some of the papers in issue could have had some difficulty meeting.

The Court's treatment of the third objection, however, consolidated the proposition that "selection, judgment, and experience" are not necessary for originality. The third objection was that "the questions in the elementary papers were of common type."[45] That is, even if the advanced examination were to be regarded as original on the grounds that its production involved "selection, judgment, and experience," the elementary examinations could not be so regarded because they were of "common type." Note that the objection here was not that the elementary examinations *drew* from the common pool of relevant information, but rather that they *were* common, too common—so the objection goes—for the Court to hold that their production involved anything other than copying from the commons. Whereas *drawing* from the common in the absence of copying likely involves "selection, judgment, and experience," *being* common or ordinary is not clearly the result of anything other than purely mechanical or automatic repetition.

Nonetheless, the Court dismissed this objection. The Court once again affirmed the proposition that original does not mean novel—that to be original is simply to be not copied from another work. Thus, the Court insists that the elementary examinations, even if common, were not copied from other papers, and therefore, they were original within the meaning of the *Copyright Act.* What is original as a matter of copyright law may well be common, even ordinary, like the questions in the elementary examinations: "I suppose that most elementary books on mathematics may be said to be of a common type, but that fact would not give impunity to a predatory infringer. The book and the papers alike originate from the author and are not copied by him from another book or other papers."[46]

In the wake of the suggestion that "selection, judgment, and experience" may have a role to play in the determination of originality, the Court's insistence that original means not copied may seem slightly less persuasive. Yet it is precisely this insistence that renders the judgment a classic "sweat of the brow" authority. The word "original" did not find its way into the English *Copyright Act* until 1911. At the very least, this represented an opening, not seized by the *University of London Press* Court in 1916, to introduce criteria such as "selection, judgment, and experience" into the copyrightability determination. Had the Court done so, it could have of course reached the same result it actually did. It could have held that the elementary papers, too, involved "selection, judgment, and experience," even if to a lesser degree than the paper in more advanced mathematics. Such an interpretive path would have inevitably brought with it a distinction between mere products and works, as well as between producers and authors. Thus, products lacking "selection, judgment, and experience" would not have been regarded as works of authorship subject to copyright protection, and the requirement of originality would have arisen—however slightly—as a more robust way of guarding entry into the world of copyright. If not the elementary examinations in issue in the case, some products—such as ordinary phone directories—would be refused entry, and by implication, some producers would be denied the status and fruits of authorship. The Court's refusal in 1916 to take up this opportunity is all the more telling in light of the introduction of the word "original" into the *Act* in 1911. The refusal is nothing less than a self-conscious decision to affirm an understanding of copyright inimical to any rendering of originality premised on a distinction between production and authorship, between the labor of mere production and the specific work of authorship.

The Court's decision to steer away from narrowing the meaning of originality in response to the 1911 legislative amendment had at least two related determinants. On the one hand, the Court relied on precedents evidencing a wide conception of copyrightability. Before discussing the originality issue, the Court discussed the question whether the examination papers could be regarded as "literary work" within the meaning of the *Act*. "Under the Act of 1812, which protected 'books,'" Peterson J. wrote, "many things which had no pretensions to literary style acquired copyright; for example, a list of registered bills of sale, a list of foxhounds and hunting days, and trade catalogues; and I see no ground for coming to the conclusion that the present Act was intended to curtail the rights of authors."[47] If a list of foxhounds and hunting days is worthy of copyright protection, and its producer is therefore an author within the meaning of the *Act,* then it is understandable that elementary examination papers, and Professor Lodge and Mr. Jackson, must also be worthy of the same status. Peterson J. found no reason to hold that "originality" should be given a more restrictive meaning.

On the other hand, the Court derived inspiration from a particular conception of the purpose of copyright law. Famously, Peterson J. concluded his examination of originality as follows: "The objections with which I have dealt do not appear to me to have any substance, and, after all, there remains the rough practical test that *what is worth copying is* prima facie *worth protecting.* In my judgment, then, the papers set by Professor Lodge and Mr. Jackson are 'original literary work' and proper subject for copyright under the Act of 1911."[48] David Vaver makes an important point when he remarks that: "As a legal invitation, this is too crude to be overtly accepted. Taken literally, it begs all questions of copyrightability, infringement, and substantiality."[49] In *University of London Press,* the question was whether copying by the defendants amounted to a wrong to the plaintiff. Naturally, the answer to this question required a determination whether the material copied was subject to copyright. After all, no wrong can be found in the absence of a right. It was precisely in order to determine whether a right obtained that Peterson J. examined the issue of originality. Thus, even if only under the guise of a "rough practical test," inferring the existence of the copyright from the fact of copying is at best puzzling. The procedure raises a presumption that copying is wrongful, yet before any determination as to whether an exclusive right to copy obtains to begin with. The presumption is as odd as would be one establishing that, in negligence cases, damage suffered by a plaintiff is worthy of compensation, yet before reaching a determination as to whether the damage caused was reasonably foreseeable (i.e., negligently caused). Just as, in the law of negligence, not all damage caused by the defendant is actionable, so in the law of copyright not all copying amounts to copyright infringement. The maxim that "what is worth copying is prima facie worth protecting" threatens to collapse any viable distinction between harm and wrong, between mere loss and actionable injury.

A more sympathetic rendering of the maxim would point out that the Court seems concerned with the unauthorized transfer of value from plaintiff to defendant as a result of the defendant's act of reproduction. The defendant could not have denied that what he copied was worth copying—his very act is an affirmation of that proposition. It does not lie in his mouth, so to speak, to deny the appropriation of value involved in his act.[50] The fact of copying thus permits us to deploy against the defendant the inference that the material produced by the plaintiff is worth copying—i.e. that in the defendant's own view there is value to be taken. The defendant has after all copied the plaintiff's examination papers in order to publish them in a book of his own, in the expectation of selling that book to students interested in studying previous examinations.

The first "worth" in the maxim "what is worth copying is prima facie worth protecting," then, is about *value*—it is literally about the worth of the material copied. But the second "worth" in the maxim is about *entitlement*. It is less about the value of the plaintiff's product *per se* than about the plaintiff's legally recognized right to exclude others from that value. It is not about the worth of the material, but about whether that material is, so to speak, worthy of legal protection as a matter of copyright law.

As a whole, then, the maxim conveys an affinity between value and entitlement, between the production of value and the entitlement to exclude others from benefits to be derived therefrom; in a word, between origination and copyright protection. From the point of view of this affinity, the purpose of copyright law is to prevent defendants from reaping where they have not sown. Copyright guarantees plaintiffs the value generated through the sweat of their brow.

Peterson J.'s classic judgment is a decision to opt for a standpoint for which originality as a matter of copyright law is a proxy for value-origination, and for which the purpose of copyright law is to remedy the misappropriation of that value. The decision is also a refusal to distinguish the labor of value-production from the specific work of authorship. From this viewpoint, the question whether any given value is properly the subject matter of copyright law is to be decided not through an investigation of the specificity of authorship but rather through an interpretation of particular categories of subject matter listed in the statute. Thus, for example, copyright protects not works of authorship, but—to use the language of the *Act* of 1812—the value of "books": whether these are the writings of Robert Louis Stevenson, registered bills of sale, a list of foxhounds and hunting days, trade catalogues, examinations in elementary mathematics, ordinary phone directories, or the poems of Lord Byron.

Walter v. Lane

The opening lines of Lord Halsbury's classic judgment in *Walter* eloquently capture the sweat of the brow approach to originality:

> I should very much regret it if I were compelled to come to the conclusion that the state of the law permitted one man to make profit and to appropriate to himself the labour, skill, and capital of another. And it is not denied that in this case the defendant seeks to appropriate to himself what has been produced by the skill, labour, and capital of others. In the view I take of this case I think the law is strong enough to restrain what to my mind would be a grievous injustice. The law which I think restrains it is to be found in the Copyright Act, and that Act confers what it calls copyright—which means the right to multiply copies—which it confers on the author of books first published in this country.[51]

The affirmation of the normative significance of the sweat of the author's brow generates a vision of copyright law as a remedy for the grievous injustice of misappropriation. Copyright is there in order to preclude reaping by those who have not sown.

Walter involved several public speeches delivered by the Earl of Rosebery. Journalists attended the speeches and reported them verbatim in the *Times* newspaper. Sometime after publication of the reports of the Earl of Rosebery's speeches, the defendant published a book that consisted of reports of the very same speeches, preceded by short notes. It was admitted that these reports were taken from the reports in the *Times*. The *Times* sued for copyright infringement, asserting copyright in the verbatim reports of the speeches.

Five judgments were delivered. Four (Earl of Halsbury L.C., Lord Davey, Lord James of Hereford, and Lord Brampton) found in favor of the plaintiff. Lord Robertson dissented.

In *Walter*, the Court of Appeal had found in favor of the defendant on the grounds that the reporters were not "authors" for copyright purposes. To *produce* a verbatim report of a speech is not to *author* a work subject to copyright. In Lord Halsbury's view, however, the Court of Appeal's judgment was based on too narrow and misleading use of the word "author." Whatever the word "author" means in some ordinary or general sense, the word "author" within the meaning of the *Act* could not exclude the producers of a verbatim report such as the one in the case at hand. Lord Halsbury relied on the directory cases, which hold that ordinary phone directories are subject to copyright protection.[52] "If the producer of such a book [i.e. a phone directory] can be an author within the meaning of the *Act*," he writes, "I am unable to understand why the labour of reproducing spoken words into writing or print and first publishing it as a book does not make the person who has so acted as much an author as the person who writes down the names and addresses of the persons who live in a particular street."[53] Lord Halsbury's reliance on the directory cases displays an insistence, echoed by Peterson J. in *University of London Press,* that no meaningful distinction can be drawn for copyright purposes between producers and authors, and, by that same token, between products and works. Once again, what is at stake is not "authorship" in any special sense, but rather the "grievous injustice" involved in the misappropriation of another's effort—in reaping where another has sown.

Before moving on to Lord Robertson's dissent, I want to comment briefly on Lord James's judgment. Lord James's view is of interest at this point because, while he agrees with Lord Halsbury as regards the result, he nonetheless reaches that result from the standpoint of a distinction between production and authorship. Lord James frames the issue by stating that the report of the speech is "something different" from and beyond the speech itself.[54] The question is whether this difference represents a "something" of which any one can be regarded as "the author" within the meaning of the *Copyright Act*.[55] Lord James finds this mysterious "something" in what he calls the "reporter's art."[56] Taking down the words of a speaker, and certainly of a rapid speaker, Lord James points out, is "an art requiring considerable training."[57] In fact, reporters less skilled are "deficient in this quality of accuracy."[58] It is on the basis of this quality that Lord James concludes that "a reporter of a speech under the conditions existing in this case is the *meritorious producer of the something necessary to constitute him an 'author'* within the meaning of the Copyright

Act."[59] Thus, although Lord James applies an authorship standard, he nonetheless concurs with Lord Halsbury at the level of the result. Lord James finds the features of authorship in the verbatim reports.

In his dissent, Lord Robertson restricts the meaning of "authorship" even further than does Lord James. Nothing but literal accuracy, Lord Robertson notes, is required to produce the verbatim reports in question.[60] The reporter of a speech is a good reporter by virtue of a contribution of a purely negative kind. The good reporter "does not interfere, but faithfully acts as a conduit."[61] The merit of the verbatim reports, says Lord Robertson, is that "they present the speaker's thoughts untinctured by the slightest trace of colour of the reporter's mind."[62] Thus, Lord Robertson's view is that the very merit of the reports is what indicates that the reports are not copyrightable. The rival of a good stenographer is the phonograph, and it is hard to see, says Lord Robertson, "how, in the widest sense of the term 'author,' we are in *the region of authorship.*"[63] Lord Robertson's judgment is thus premised on an affirmation of the specificity of the work of authorship, and, therefore, on a distinction between mental products *per se,* and the specific works of authorship.

As regards the directory cases on which Lord Halsbury relies, Lord Robertson insists that they are not inconsistent with his affirmation of the specificity of authorship. Thus Lord Robertson admits that there are cases that apply the words of the *Act* to "very pedestrian efforts of the mind," such as furniture catalogues and timetables.[64] Still, he insists that even such pedestrian efforts of the mind nonetheless exhibit "structure and arrangement on the part of the maker."[65] In the end, Lord Robertson's view is that "the recording by stenography the words of another is in a *different region* from the making up a timetable." "I do not say it is [a] lower or higher [region]," he is careful to add, "but in a different plane, *because there is no construction.*"[66]

Thus, if Lord Halsbury does not require anything more than the undifferentiated and unspecified labor of production, and Lord James requires, in addition, the application of a "skill" of some kind, Lord Robertson requires not the application of just *any* skill, but the application of *a particular skill or faculty he identifies with "authorship":* "The word 'author,'" he writes, ". . . seems to me to present a criterion consistent with the widest application of the Act to all who can claim as embodying their own thought, whether humble or lofty, the letterpress of which they assert the authorship."[67] Whatever else he might be, a stenographer is not an author, and copyright is about authorship.

Whereas Lord Halsbury affirms a view of copyright concerned with the origination and protection of value, Lord Robertson affirms a view of copyright concerned with the specificity of authorship. This tension *between* the two judgments appears internalized as a tension *within* Peterson J.'s judgment in *University of London Press*. It is as if the intervening insertion of the word "original" into the *Act* had compelled Peterson J. to gesture, albeit unnecessarily and counter-productively, toward "selection, judgment, and experience" in his discussion of the distinction between elementary and advanced examinations. Lord Halsbury was far less ambiguous: "[I]f I have not insisted upon the skill and accuracy of those who produce in writing or print spoken words," he wrote, "it is not because I think the less of those qualities, but because, as I have endeavoured to point out, neither the one nor the other are conditions precedent to the right created by the statute."[68] The principled and deliberate refusal to distinguish between producers and authors, the labor of production and the work of authorship, is as clear as it is unmistakable. It is not the specificity of authorship but the value it produces that is ultimately at issue.

CCH Revisited

University of London Press and *Walter* provide helpful background to assess the effort to dismiss sweat of brow jurisprudence in *CCH*. It will be recalled that in *CCH* the Supreme Court of Canada affirmed the skill and judgment originality standard by invoking a vision of the purpose of copyright law as a balance between the incentive to create and the imperative to disseminate works of authorship. It was in terms of this balance that the Court dismissed both the sweat of the brow and the creativity standards as extremes of which the skill and judgment standard is the appropriate mean—in between inappropriately "low" and inappropriately "high" alternatives. But neither the metaphor of balance, nor that of a continuum from "low" to "high," provide sufficient basis to explain or justify the shift from sweat of the brow to skill and judgment. The result of this justificatory vacuum is truly striking. In *CCH*, the skill and judgment rhetoric of a copyright model centered on the specificity of authorship coexists with the generation and distribution of benefits rhetoric of a copyright model centered on the origination of value. If *University of London Press* exhibited traces, however slight, of an internalized struggle, so to speak, between Lord Halsbury and Lord Roberston, *CCH* manages to reconstitute the tension in altered form: a vision of copyright fundamentally preoccupied with the balancing of value presides over a doctrinal shift in the direction of authorship.

Nothing about the concept of copyright as a balance necessarily entails the proposition that the sweat of the brow standard is too low. On the contrary, many regard the sweat of the brow standard as appropriate from the standpoint of copyright law as a balance between authors and users, ownership and access.[69] After all, the vision of copyright law as a balance is by no means novel. In 1785, in *Sayre v. Moore,* for example, Lord Mansfield famously formulated the task of copyright law as one in which "[w]e must take care to guard against two extremes equally prejudicial; the one, that men of ability, who have employed their time for the service of the community, may not be deprived of their just merits, and the reward of their ingenuity and labour; the other, that the world may not be deprived of improvements, nor the progress of the arts be retarded."[70] The sweat of the brow standard is part and parcel of a centuries old tradition that, at least nominally, devoted itself to finding an in-between "two extremes equally prejudicial." To be sure, there can be no doubt that in *CCH* the Supreme Court of Canada presents its dismissal of the sweat of the brow standard in the name of the copyright balance. But a bare assertion that the traditional originality standard is too low is surely insufficient in an historical and jurisprudential context that has always aspired to that balance precisely through that standard. The same is true of the Court's dismissal of the creativity standard as too high. Once again, a bare assertion is simply insufficient in light of the adherence to that standard in the name of a balanced copyright in United States copyright jurisprudence.

Moreover, even if we were to accept that varying originality standards can somehow be understood and classified as more or less conducive to the achievement of a balance between authors and public, it seems clear that the degree to which any given standard would either promote or be consistent with the balance in question would depend crucially on one's construal of other copyright doctrines, such as, for example, fair dealing.

The Court of Appeal in *CCH,* for example, addressed in its reasons the relation between originality and fair dealing in this light. It suggested that the interaction between originality and fair dealing as central copyright doctrines, not either one in isolation, is to be considered as instrumental in achieving the requisite balance.[71]

In other words, conclusions about the role of the originality standard in the achievement of the copyright balance cannot possibly be persuasive in the absence of more integrated assessments of its combined and concurrent action in light of other copyright doctrines. Because the Supreme Court's dismissal of the sweat of the brow standard in *CCH* takes place in the absence of any such integrated assessment, it cannot help but remain at best unpersuasive, and at worst short-lived and precarious (the same can be said of the Court's dismissal of the creativity standard). While *CCH* did deal extensively with fair dealing, it did not deal explicitly with the balanced and integrated interaction between originality and fair dealing. It seems *prima facie* clear that a decision, such as *CCH,* that both narrows originality and widens fair dealing in the same breath must do more than merely invoke the copyright balance and assert without more ado that the sweat of the brow standard is too low, or that the creativity standard is too high.

Finally, even if we were to assume that originality standards can (whether in isolation or along the lines of more integrated assessments) be correlated with certain outcomes at the level of the copyright balance, there is no self-evident reason to believe that these correlations would be industry neutral. That is, it is entirely plausible, perhaps even probable, that one originality standard may be more conducive to "balance" in one industry or field of activity (such as phone directory production), and another in another industry or field of activity (such as sculpture or painting).[72] In short, the Supreme Court's holding that the sweat of the brow and creativity standards are inadequate may well be correct, but unfortunately the Court has hardly provided any reasons for its holding.

To be sure, these criticisms of the use of the balance metaphor are not unassailable. The observation that the idea of balance has been used to support more than one version of originality need not mean that, appropriately constructed, the idea of balance cannot yield meaningful support for a particular originality standard. Similarly, the fact that neither *CCH* nor *Feist* offer integrated assessments of the concurrent operations of copyright doctrines need not mean that no such assessment is possible. And finally, it is not implausible that, once industry-specific considerations are, so to speak, put on the balance, the general viability of a certain originality standard, subject to modifications in specified circumstances, can be advanced.

There are deeper reasons, however, to remain suspicious of the use of the concept of balance as an anchor for a definitive move away from sweat of the brow copyright jurisprudence. The point is not so much that the concept of balance has not yet managed to produce the required justification. More than that, the point is that it is inherently unable to do so.

Considering the metaphor of a continuum from "low" to "high" in terms of which originality standards can somehow be meaningfully classified will help us see this clearly. The image of the continuum presupposes that the sweat of the brow standard requires less of authors than the skill and judgment standard, and that, in turn, the skill and judgment standard requires less than does the creativity standard. It is by no means clear, however, what it is that these standards share, so as to make it meaningful to place them in a continuum moving from less to more, or—for that matter—in any kind of continuum. It may be that what the Court has in mind in *CCH* is that the sweat of the brow standard is "lower" in that the requirements it imposes for admission to the world of copyright protection are such that any work qualifying under the other two standards would also qualify under the sweat of the brow standard, whereas the reverse is simply not true. Similarly, it may be that what the Court also has in mind is that any work qualifying under the creativity standard would also qualify under the skill and judgment standard, whereas the reverse, again, is simply not true. Nonetheless, this continuum image—assuming that it informed the Supreme Court's decision in *CCH*—is radically insufficient. It does nothing by way of providing reasons for the view that there is a shared something at all underlying the so-called continuum, or by way of providing a description of what this shared something is.

Consider the Court's conclusions regarding the nature of "originality." The text of the judgment suggests that the Court does indeed have in mind a kind of creativity continuum moving from "none" (sweat of the brow), through "enough" (skill and judgment), to "more than enough" (creativity):

> For these reasons, I conclude that an "original" work under the *Copyright Act* is one that originates from an author and is not copied from another work [i.e. sweat of the brow]. That alone, however, is not sufficient to find that something is original. In addition, an original work must be the product of an author's exercise of skill and judgment. The exercise of skill and judgment required to produce the work must not be so trivial that it could be characterized as a purely mechanical exercise. While *creative works will by definition be "original" and covered by copyright,* creativity is not required to make a work "original."[73]

Thus, whereas the sweat of brow standard is too low in that it would admit a "purely mechanical" yet "not copied" product into the world of copyright, the creativity standard is too high in that, as the Court puts it in this context, it "implies that something must be novel or nonobvious—concepts more properly associated with patent law than copyright law."[74] The Court, then, appears to affirm the following three propositions:

1. Sweat of the brow, skill and judgment, and creativity are part of a continuum of which creativity is the highest form.
2. This highest form must be ruled out as an originality standard because it requires novelty or nonobviousness, which are associated with patent law, not copyright law.
3. Creative works will by definition be original and covered by copyright.

The problem with these propositions is that if proposition (2) is true, then proposition (3) is false. Proposition (2) defines creative works as novel or nonobvious. Proposition (3) asserts that such works will by definition be covered by copyright. But that is simply not true. Patentable subject matter is indeed novel and nonobvious. But it is trivially true that such subject matter is *not* as such—and certainly not "by definition"—subject to copyright protection.

The point is not that patentable inventions are in some sense not sufficiently creative. Nor is the point that inventions do not involve skill and judgment in their production. The point, rather, is that the production of a patentable invention, even where such exercise is significant and cannot possibly be characterized as purely mechanical, is qualitatively distinct from the production of a work of authorship. The invention of a mousetrap, for example, no doubt requires creativity and/or skill and judgment. But a mousetrap is not a literary work, and an inventor is not an author. It is as absurd to place these human faculties in a continuum as it is to suggest that an author is less creative than an inventor, or that Lord Byron is somehow better at compiling phone directories than your local telephone company. It seems far more fruitful to regard these activities as distinct, to refrain from regarding them as belonging in a continuum moving from low to high, and to attempt the elaboration of the specificity of each.

Consider a mousetrap. Its invention requires skill and judgment or creativity of a certain kind. We do not say, however, that we should put the mousetrap on the copyright balance in order to make determinations about the rights of the inventor to preclude others from using it, and the rights of users to use it freely. On the contrary, we know very well that mousetraps do not get on the copyright balance to begin with. The copyright balance makes determinations in respect of works of authorship, but not in respect of inventions. There is a difference between a mousetrap and a poem, and it is self-evident that while poems get on the copyright balance, mousetraps do not. This appears trivial, but it is not. It is of the essence of the problem of originality in copyright. The doctrine of originality makes determinations regarding what gets on the copyright balance to begin with. Mousetraps do not get on because they do not exhibit the *requisite* skill and judgment or creativity. This does not mean that mousetraps are not the result of skill and judgment or creativity of some kind. But that is irrelevant. What is relevant is that mousetraps do not exhibit the skill and judgment or creativity specific to a work of authorship subject to copyright. Determinations as to what gets on the balance are prior to the balancing of the relative entitlements of authors and users in respect of the subject matter in issue.

In other words, the originality standard is not the result of the balancing process. Rather, it is prior to and independent of that balancing. The standard of originality specifies what kind of weights or values get on the balance to begin with. The skill and judgment or creativity specific to authorship is the irreducible "principled fulcrum" or "most fundamental axiom" that defines and orients the copyright balance.[75] Any effort to derive this fulcrum or axiom from a higher order category is ultimately counterproductive. The reason that the standard of originality cannot be generated out of the concept of the copyright balance is that the concept of the copyright balance presupposes the standard of originality. Originality is, rather, the fundamental principle that makes the *copyright* balance—as distinct from, for example, the patent balance—possible in the first place.

One more example will help to drive the point home. Consider once again the classic case of an ordinary, alphabetically arranged phone directory. Whereas the sweat of the brow standard grants copyright on the basis of the labor invested, the creativity or skill and judgment standards deny copyright on the basis that the specific kind of labor recognized in copyright law (i.e., creativity or skill and judgment) is absent. The important point to observe is that sweat of the brow and skill and judgment (or creativity) are not just indices of different distributions of weight or value on the copyright balance. Rather, they are radically distinct visions of the purpose of copyright law. The sweat of the brow standard affirms a view of copyright law on the basis of what we might call a misappropriation paradigm—that is, a paradigm that grants copyright in the products of a person's mental effort so as to preclude others from reaping where they have not sown. Its target is the "grievous injustice" of misappropriation. By contrast, the skill and judgment or creativity standards are focused not on the misappropriation of value *per se* but rather on the misappropriation of the plaintiff's authorship, defined as an exercise of skill and judgment or creativity. Copyright is not about any and all value but about the specific value of authorship. In other words, the skill and judgment or creativity standards affirm a view of a copyright on the basis of a paradigm that necessarily rests on (a) a distinction between kinds of value, and (b) an affirmation of the specificity of authorship. Because this paradigm is an affirmation of the specific value of authorship, we may regard it—at least in this respect—as an authorship paradigm, to be distinguished from the misappropriation paradigm.

Once we appreciate the difference between sweat of the brow and skill and judgment or creativity as a difference between copyright paradigms, we can see once again the radical insufficiency of the concept of balance to account for the transition from sweat of the brow to skill and judgment or creativity. The transition necessarily requires a distinction between kinds of value, between mere sweat, on the one hand, and skill and judgment or creativity, on the other. But nothing in the concept of balance can ever make that distinction. A balance weighs values placed on it. It does not, and cannot, make distinctions between different kinds of values. It is as capable of balancing the costs and benefits of the production and dissemination of mousetraps and phone directories, as it is capable of balancing the costs and benefits of the production and dissemination of poems. And that is as it should be. But that is also why the bare concept of balancing is as compatible with sweat of the brow jurisdictions as it is with skill and judgment or creativity jurisdictions. It simply cannot tell us which originality standard to adopt. Because it reduces everything to mere values or quantities to be placed on the balance, balancing cannot make the qualitative distinctions between kinds of value that the transition from sweat of the brow to skill and judgment or creativity requires. This is why the invocation of balance in *CCH*—and of progress in *Feist*—is bound to remain woefully unsatisfactory.[76] The concept of balance cannot bear the weight of the distinction it is asked to ground. It cannot tell us which originality standard to adopt any more than a compass can tell us where we want to go.

The difficulty is not merely that the rejection of the sweat of the brow standard hovers over a justificatory vacuum. More deeply than that, the difficulty is that, because it retains characteristic features of the misappropriation paradigm, the image of balance gravitates contrary to the landmark affirmation of the skill and judgment or creativity standards. Of course, it is abundantly clear that, by rejecting the sweat of the brow standard, we cast off the presumption, characteristic of the misappropriation paradigm, that authors are *prima facie* entitled to the value they originate. On the contrary, the value authors generate is now *ab initio* taken up and metabolized through the operations of the copyright balance. The application of copyright doctrine in any given case is but a way to determine who should get the generated value, whether it should fall within the domain of the author, or that of the user. In the absence of a presumption in favor of the author's entitlement, instances in which that value falls outside the reach of the author's copyright no longer require special justification, as if they were mere exceptions to be narrowly construed. But what is altered in this decision to remove the presumption in the author's favor is only the default distribution of value between authors and users, ownership and access. To be sure, we need not scoff at that redistribution. Yet we should also keep its limitations in mind. The assumption, also characteristic of the misappropriation model, that authorship as a matter of copyright law is essentially about value-origination remains intact throughout the redistribution, perhaps even strengthened through its canonization under the banner of distributive balance. Viewed as nothing more than redistribution, the transition from sweat of the brow to skill and judgment or creativity falls short of its own requirement: to distinguish between kinds of value and to affirm the specificity of authorship. The author remains a mere producer of unspecified value.

Otherwise put, the sweat of the brow standard is composed of two related, yet separable aspects. One is that the author is entitled—or at least *prima facie* entitled—to the value she originates. The other, implicit in the first, is that the author is an originator of value. Grasped from the standpoint of the concept of balance, the shift from the sweat of the brow standard to the skill and judgment or creativity standards dislodges the first aspect (that the author is entitled to the value she originates) but retains the second (that the author is an originator of value). Thus, while the victory of the skill and judgment or creativity schools of originality sets the stage for a redistribution of value from author to public, it falls short of presenting a challenge to the very concept of the author as value-originator. If, for example, we were to assume for the sake of argument that the concept of the author as value-originator is the essential aspect of the sweat of the brow standard, then, paradoxically, the shift to the skill and judgment or creativity standards is not so much a defeat as a distillation of the sweat of the brow standard. The dislodging of the author's *prima facie* entitlement amounts to an ever more pristine entrenchment of the concept of value, rather than a distinction between kinds of value, as the central concept in copyright law.

Under the tutelage of the concept of balance, the debunking of the sweat of the brow standard is grasped not as an affirmation of the authorship paradigm, but rather as the evolution of the misappropriation paradigm into a value paradigm of copyright law. The value paradigm is, as it were, the misappropriation paradigm *manqué*. It retains the primacy of the concept of value, yet without the assumption that the value in question is *prima facie* the author's. To the extent that the value paradigm cannot itself distinguish between kinds of value, however, this emancipation of value from the trappings of authorial entitlement is not as profound as it may first appear. In the absence of an elucidation of the specific value of authorship, the transition to the skill and judgment or creativity standards is fated to remain incomplete. On the one hand, the transition rejects, and stands for the rejection of, the copyrightability of ordinary phone directories and mousetraps. Yet, on the other, devoid of an account of the specificity of authorship, the transition is unable to ground that very rejection in anything other than radically indeterminate concepts such as "balance" in *CCH* or "progress" in *Feist.* Under the rubric of value, copyright law cannot account for itself as a legal affirmation of the specific value of authorship. In short, the image of the copyright balance produces and reproduces its recurrent shortcomings: it reveals itself as an apotheosis of mere and sheer value, radically unable to ground the intelligibility of that value as subject matter specific to copyright law.

The insufficiencies of the concept of balance go beyond the failure to provide a foundation for the transition from sweat of the brow to skill and judgment or creativity. The concept is also insufficient, albeit in a different sense, when it comes to the integration of authors and users as aspects of a single system called copyright. The metaphor of balance cannot help but suggest a related constellation of understandings and construals, including a construal of authorship as value-origination, of the "work" as an instance of value, of the public domain as a depository of commodities to be freely consumed by users, and, no less importantly, of the expansion of the public domain as a decrease in the price that the public must pay for the production of works of authorship. It seems natural enough to suppose, for example, that by narrowing originality and widening fair dealing in a single stroke, the *CCH* decision more than likely improves the lot of users at the expense of authors. But that is precisely the point: once the metaphor of balance is assumed as the integrating mechanism holding authors and users together, integration properly so-called can never occur. And that is because once value-balancing is the ordering mechanism, then the relation between authors and users is but a perennial struggle for value, such that the claims of authors are but minimizations of the value-entitlements of users, and similarly, the claims of users are but minimizations of the value-entitlements of authors. The upshot is that successful haggling about price masquerades as the foundation of a truly public domain. The failure to elucidate authorship as anything other than value-origination generates an impoverished vision of the public domain as nothing other than a realm of commodified dispute resolution.

To be sure, the struggle for value between authors and users is a sociological fact, and an obvious one at that. The problem, however, is that once copyright law is understood as a balance preoccupied with sheer and mere value, it cannot account for itself as a practice providing the basis for a specifically juridical resolution of that struggle. Framed as a balance, copyright law becomes nothing more than a distributive mechanism, on the one hand designed to achieve a balance between authors and users, yet on the other unable to make the qualitative distinctions necessary to get the entire balancing process going in the first place. In the absence of a principled fulcrum, copyright law is more the field of a struggle for value, and even a source of contested weapons in that struggle, than a juridical practice elucidating the conditions for the possibility of its resolution. Copyright becomes enmeshed and submerged, as it were, in the very sociological facticity of the struggle for value it aspires to order.

Under the rubric of balance, then, the transition from sweat of the brow to skill and judgment or creativity is not only unjustified and incomplete. It is also counterproductive. Because it frames the struggle between authors and users as a matter of mere and sheer value, the value paradigm obscures and precludes the possibility of an alternative understanding of copyright law as an ordering of the juridical relationship between authors and users. It is not distributions of value within the value paradigm, but rather the conceptual poverty of the value paradigm itself, that is at issue.

From Distribution to Dialogue

The critique of sweat of the brow jurisprudence in *Feist* and *CCH* reproduces a juncture evocative of that faced by Peterson J. in *University of London Press* in 1916. In 1916, in the wake of the introduction of the word "original" into the English *Copyright Act* in 1911, Peterson J. opted to affirm an affinity between value-origination and entitlement as the organizing principle of copyright law. Thus he rejected "selection, judgment, and experience" as relevant criteria in the originality determination, and concluded his examination of originality with the maxim that "what is worth copying is prima facie worth protecting." Almost a century later, *Feist* and *CCH* unambiguously affirm the creativity and skill and judgment originality standards. This is by any account a decisive movement away from the sweat of the brow standard. Yet this movement at the level of doctrine has not yet crystallized at the level of principle. With the creativity and skill and judgment standards, *Feist* and *CCH* alter the *prima facie* default distribution of value, but do not question the very concept of the author as a value-originator. It is only that the author is now, in the name of balance, entitled to less of that value.

Faced with this juncture, it is perhaps only natural to seek to retain the vision of copyright law as a mode of governing the origination and distribution of value. When this option is followed, the task is to distinguish the specific kind of value or values to which copyright applies. This is what the idea of balance is intended to accomplish. It enlists for this task not only the concepts of creativity and skill and judgment, but also the entire arsenal of copyright doctrines that separates out different kinds of values and reserves protection for only some of them. Thus, for example, the idea/expression dichotomy refuses protection to ideas, regardless of their value, and regardless also of the creativity or skill and judgment, if any, that their production may have involved. Similarly, fair use or fair dealing represent a refusal to grant protection for the use of copyright subject matter in respect of certain purposes. These are decisions to retain the definition of the author as a value-originator, yet to curtail in light of the public interest the value-amount to which the author is entitled. They are decisions to distribute value toward users rather than authors.

The basic difficulty with this option is that it does not have at its disposal the tools necessary to make the distinctions it requires. It cannot account for the doctrinal operations it deploys precisely because, as distinctions between kinds of value, those operations irretrievably presuppose concepts other than value itself. Thus, limitations imposed on the author's entitlement cannot help but appear super-structurally grafted onto a persistent structure driven by the gravitational force of the author's entitlement as value-originator. The transition from sweat of the brow to creativity or skill and judgment jurisprudence gives way to a most striking of reversals, whereby the public domain in the name of which the transition is initiated becomes little more than some kind of taxation scheme—a superficial layer, as it were, reserving or extracting value to which authors would be otherwise entitled.

The alternative option is to accept the unambiguous affirmation of creativity and skill and judgment as an invitation to elaborate the specificity of authorship. To follow this option is to pursue relentlessly the logic implicit in the transition from sweat of the brow to creativity and skill and judgment, and thus to take on the task of setting forth copyright doctrine in general and originality in particular not as a mechanism designed to distribute the value of a work but as an elucidation of its distinctive nature. It is only in this way, I think, that we can hope to grasp copyright subject matter not as an instance of unspecified value but—to use the language of copyright law—as *the work of an author.*

2

Originality as Speaking in One's Own Words

The insufficiencies of balance as a metaphor structuring copyright interpretation resolve themselves into two related observations. One is that the category of value cannot account for the specificity of authorship. The value paradigm cannot ground the basic distinction between sweat of the brow and creativity or skill and judgment as originality standards. The other is that the twin construal of authors as value-originators, and of works as instances of value, generates a view of copyright limitations as externally imposed takings of value that would otherwise remain the author's. Authors and users burden each other's holdings, so to speak, in a precarious truce involving juxtaposed yet unmediated considerations. The metaphor of balance is but a juridical euphemism for what is otherwise well known as the "copyright wars" besetting contemporary copyright theory and practice.[1]

The purpose of this chapter is twofold. First, I want to unfold from within established copyright doctrine a concept of the work of an author as a communicative act. Second, I want to deploy that concept to develop an understanding of copyright law not as a balance but as a dialogue between authors and users. By conceiving the work as a communicative act, this understanding opens up a rendition of the public domain not as a countervailing weight burdening the author's claim, but rather as an irreducible condition of the audience's entitlement to respond to and participate in the ongoing conversation of which the author is but a part. Authors and users thus appear not as contenders for value but as mutually constitutive aspects of copyright as a single juridical whole.

A characterization of the work as a communicative act cannot be posited out of thin air. Accordingly, this chapter develops the concept of the work as a communicative act from within an analysis of the principle of "independent creation" at the heart of originality doctrine. I have chosen that principle as a starting point for two reasons. First, given that I offer the communicative construal of the work with an eye to supporting and developing a grasp of the public domain as integral to the copyright system, it would be appropriate if the construal were to arise from premises already embedded in the way in which copyright law frames the formation of the author's right. Analysis of the formation of the right would thus ground the understanding of its scope and limitation. I start with independent creation because it is there that copyright itself starts.

Second, independent creation is constitutive of copyright in a manner that is decisively absent in patent. Analysis of the principle of independent creation provides quick and fruitful access into the specificity of copyright vis-à-vis patent, a work vis-à-vis an invention. To compare and contrast originality in copyright and novelty in patent—that is, authorship and inventorship—is to reveal features of authorship not otherwise accessible. I start with independent creation because it can help us broach the specificity of a work of authorship.

Thus, independent creation is an optimal starting point because it catalyzes insights into the nature of a work, the formation of the right attendant on it, and the limitation of that right. To anticipate, what we will find is that the limitation of the copyright in and to a work is but an elaboration of the nature of the work as a communicative act. Copyright scope tracks copyright subject matter. Precisely as communicative, a work of authorship contemplates the tradition from which it arises, the audience to whom it is addressed, and the public domain to which it is ultimately destined.

Two propositions permeating this chapter as a whole will first arise through our analysis of independent creation. One is that the work of an author is not a thing—whether intangible or otherwise—but an act; specifically, a communicative act. Copyright is less a property right than a right inhering in persons as speaking beings. The other is that authors have exclusive rights in respect of their works only where such rights are consistent with everyone else's equal authorship. As a matter of copyright law, an author is and must be an author among others. She speaks in a context that ensures conditions for dialogue.

The chapter proceeds to illustrate and elaborate the structural significance of these two propositions in and through examinations of fundamental copyright doctrines; namely, the idea/expression dichotomy and paradigmatic instances of the defense of fair use or fair dealing. The idea/expression dichotomy is inseparable from the doctrine of originality. It provides that not originality *per se* but rather original *expression* is at stake in copyright law: ideas, even if original, are "free as the air to common use."[2] An author's claim to exclusivity in respect of her original expression—i.e., her work of authorship—thus leaves ideas expressed therein freely available for others to express or develop anew. The exclusion of ideas from copyright protection thereby reinforces and refines the concern with equal authorship that we will find embedded in the principle of independent creation.

Similarly, the defense of fair use or fair dealing—the copyright limitation *par excellence*—provides that unauthorized use of an author's expression is lawful in certain circumstances, paradigmatically including (as we will see in more detail) circumstances where such use is reasonably necessary for another's work. For example, author A may lawfully use for the purpose of criticism or review author B's expression without authorization. There are circumstances, that is, in which expression itself is free as the air to common use. Fair use or fair dealing thus extends beyond ideas, to original expression, the constitutive concern for equal authorship. While fair use or fair dealing is not restricted to situations involving the defendant's own authorship, it is those situations that I analyze in this chapter, leaving for subsequent chapters the analysis of lawful unauthorized use in the absence of the defendant's authorship.

This chapter thus offers speech, equality, and dialogue in place of value, efficiency, and balance as signposts to guide copyright interpretation. The chapter concludes with a juxtaposition of the subject matter of copyright law (i.e., a work of authorship) and the subject matter of trademark law (i.e., a trademark). This juxtaposition of works and trademarks complements the chapter's opening comparison of works and inventions. The chapter thus underlines by way of conclusion the specificity of copyright in the great intellectual property triptych of patent, copyright, and trademark. In so doing, it brings further into relief the construal of a work as an instance of speech in an ongoing dialogue, and confirms that dialogue is a metaphor more appropriate than balance to structure copyright interpretation.

Independent Creation

"Originality" and "novelty" respectively denote cardinal requirements of copyrightability and patentability. An author's work is not subject to copyright protection unless it is *original.*[3] Similarly, an inventor's invention is not subject to patent protection unless it is *novel.*[4]

This familiar distinction highlights the equally familiar observation that whereas the law of patent—through the novelty requirement—focuses on an inventor's contribution to existing knowledge, the law of copyright—through the originality requirement—focuses not on an author's contribution to existing knowledge, but rather on the form in or through which the author communicates her thinking. Expressing an old idea in one's own words is sufficient to give rise to a finding of originality for copyright purposes. It is patent, not copyright, that requires novelty. If patent law is concerned with *what* an inventor contributes, copyright law is concerned with *how* an author says what she says. What matters is not that the author says something new, but that she speaks in her own words. Not the content of an author's speech, but the *very speaking itself* is at issue in copyright law.

Nowhere is this focus on the "very speaking itself" clearer than in the defense of independent creation. The defense of independent creation provides that a defendant cannot be held liable in copyright if he can show that his work, though identical to the plaintiff's, was independently created. Independent creation of two identical works gives rise not to a finding of infringement, but to a finding that two independent copyrights arise over two distinct works. As the United States Supreme Court put it in *Feist Publications Inc. v. Rural Telephone Service Co. Inc.:* "Originality does not signify novelty; a work may be original even though it closely resembles other works so long as the familiarity is fortuitous, not the result of copying. To illustrate, assume that two poets, each ignorant of the other, compose identical poems. Neither work is novel yet both are original and, hence, copyrightable."[5] Thus, it is true not only that copyright law is indifferent to the novelty or lack thereof of the idea expressed in a work. Copyright law is equally indifferent to the novelty or lack thereof of the form of expression itself. Neither idea nor expression need be novel. Copyright has nothing to do with novelty.

What must be shown to make out the claim that a work is original, then, is not that the work is new or unique but rather that the author came up with it—that she did not copy it. In *University of London Press Ltd. v. University Tutorial Press Ltd.,* Petersen J. stated that an original work is a work "not . . . copied from another work."[6] Post-*Feist* and post-*CCH,* that is no longer accurate. An ordinary phone directory resulting from independent fact collection (i.e., not copied from another work) is not original for copyright purposes. In Canada, as we know, an original work requires "skill and judgment."[7] In the United States, the requirement is that the work display "creativity."[8] An original work of authorship is copied neither from another work *nor from the world.* Census-takers, *Feist* points out, do not originate figures: "they copy these figures from the world around them."[9] Similarly, in arranging names alphabetically, the producer of an ordinary phone-directory says nothing in her own way. She "lets the facts speak for themselves."[10] But she herself remains, so to speak, speechless. Thus copyright law refuses her a hearing.

The principle of independent creation establishes, then, that the mere coincidence that my expression happens to be identical to someone else's previously existing expression does not make my expression any less my own. Because novelty is not in issue, there is no requirement that there be differences between my expression and the art that precedes it. The originality inquiry is not about a work's relation to other works.[11] It is about the relation between author and work. It is literally about origination, about source. The determination that a work is original is a confirmation of the work's origins. The origin of a work—its origin*ality*—is its source. Identical poems coincidentally composed by two poets are nonetheless original because each is an independent creation.

Things are different in the law of patent. There is no defense of independent invention in patent law. Patent law focuses on the result rather than the source. The operative inquiry is the novelty of this result. The question here is not, "Did this come from or originate with the inventor?" Instead, the question is, "Is this new," or, "Is this something that was previously unavailable to the public?"[12] If the answer is yes, the invention satisfies the novelty requirement. If the answer is no, there is no invention. The novelty determination is made through a comparison of the invention and the prior art.[13] Novelty is a relation between the inventor's product and other preexisting products, between present and past. The patent application of a second inventor who comes up with something previously available, must fail for lack of novelty, even if she is an "independent inventor." Patent lawyers express this by saying that the invention is "anticipated" in the prior art.[14]

We can summarize the point as follows. There is no such thing as a "second" inventor in patent law—one cannot invent something already available. But copyright operates with a different concept of priority. In copyright, there *is* such a thing as a second author. More precisely, one is an author even if one produces something already available. This is because authorship in copyright is about speaking in one's own words, whereas inventorship in patent is about contributing to the prior art.

Of relevance here is an intriguing story by the great Argentinean writer, Jorge Luis Borges, about a fictional novelist named Pierre Menard, whose greatest work consisted of nothing less than two chapters and a fragment of a third chapter of Miguel de Cervantes's *Don Quixote.*[15] In his 1956 story, Borges unequivocally affirms that this work of Menard's, identical to parts of Cervantes's, is "perhaps the most significant of our time."[16] Borges acknowledges that "such an affirmation seems an absurdity," but he insists that "to justify this 'absurdity' is the primordial object of this note."[17]

The task that, in Borges's account, Menard had set for himself when he began writing the *Quixote* in the twentieth century is truly astonishing: "He [Menard] did not want to compose another *Quixote*—which is easy—but *the Quixote itself.* Needless to say, he never contemplated a mechanical transcription of the original; *he did not propose to copy it.* His admirable intention was to produce a few pages which would *coincide*—word for word and line for line—with those of Miguel de Cervantes."[18] Aside from the important question of whether Borges manages to justify the "absurdity" to which he devotes his story, we cannot fail to observe that, *assuming Menard succeeded in his task,* the result, though identical to Cervantes's, would be an original creation for copyright purposes.[19] Borges in fact manages to ascertain the differences between the identical texts of these two works: "The contrast in style," he writes, "is also vivid. The archaic style of Menard—quite foreign, after all—suffers from a certain affectation. Not so that of his forerunner [Cervantes], who handles with ease the current Spanish of his time."[20] The identity of the works is a coincidence, and need not deprive Menard of the status that the title of Borges's story, "Pierre Menard, Author of the *Quixote,*" rightly attributes to him.

The originality standard in copyright is perfectly consistent with the view that, although he composed a work that had already been written, Menard was nonetheless an author. It goes without saying that the same cannot be true in patent law. To produce anew a previously available invention is to fail the standard of novelty.

One might be tempted to object that the defense of independent creation, by its very nature, addresses only anomalous or exceptional circumstances. The defense of independent creation, however, does not operate in accordance with foreign standards. Independent creation is of the essence of originality in copyright law. The defense of independent creation illustrates the fundamental proposition that originality is about origination, and that the inquiry into originality is an inquiry into source—not an inquiry into the difference between a work and preexisting works. The defense of independent creation does not depart but rather derives from the *principle* of independent creation at the heart of originality. Originality is nothing other than independent creation. This is why, not merely a defense, a finding of independent creation is a finding of a distinct copyright.

To be sure, the substantial similarity or identity between newly created work A and preexisting work B may function as both the motivation and the foundation for the owner of work B to allege infringement.[21] Such similarity or identity, however, cannot in and of itself give rise to liability. The plaintiff must additionally show that the defendant copied the work or at least that the defendant had access to the work.[22] Where the defendant makes out a defense of independent creation, the defendant succeeds in precluding the very similarity or identity that gives rise to the plaintiff's claim from maturing into a finding of infringement. The defense of independent creation reduces the similarity or identity of the works to the level of a mere coincidence. It reminds us that the role of substantial similarity between the works is to contribute to a presumption—rebuttable upon a finding of independent creation—that the source (or origin) of these works is the same (i.e., that the defendant copied).[23] Once again, the defense of independent creation is but an assertion of the fundamental proposition that originality is about source, and that the comparison between works is only an aspect of the inquiry into source. If the identity between the works were determinative, we would be operating with concepts drawn from patent law, where the comparison between products, regardless of source, is sufficient to find infringement or anticipation.[24]

Of course, two independently created yet identical works *look* the same. But this does not mean that they *are* the same in the eyes of copyright law. Seeing through the mere appearance of identity is fundamental to understanding copyright. As a copyright matter, the works are different because each of them originates in an independent act of authorship. Textual identity is not originative identity. To be duped by the appearance of identity is but to misunderstand the fundamentals of originality. Once we focus on the distinct authorship of each of the works, their so-called identity collapses. It is at best a remarkable coincidence. It is at no point a denial of their juridical difference as independent acts of authorship.

While it is true that copyright protects the form of expression, it is important to observe that this does not mean that copyright protects expression as some kind of proprietary object—whether intangible or otherwise—exclusively held by its author. If that were the case, identical expression, even if independently created, would amount to a trespass on the author's exclusive holding of her work as an object of ownership. Thus, the defense of independent creation is intelligible only if we posit the work as an act of authorship rather than as the reified result of an act of authorship. A work is not a thing but an act: at issue is the *work* not as a noun but as a verb. An author does not hold her expression as an object of ownership to the disposition of which she has exclusive rights. Copyright infringement is neither conversion nor theft.[25] It is less a matter of disposing of an object than of repeating or reproducing an act of authorship without authorization. This is why to infringe the right attendant on the work is to repeat it or to reproduce it—i.e., to copy it—but not to create it independently. Either we insist on grasping the work as a communicative act, or we jettison the defense of independent creation from copyright doctrine.

To summarize, the defense of independent creation entails that the apparent identity between two independently created works is juridically irrelevant, and that, notwithstanding that identity, two copyrights arise over two distinct works. This distinction between the two seemingly identical works is possible only to the extent that we resile from the works as objects of ownership—as things—and focus on the works as acts of authorship. Viewed as things, the seemingly identical works do indeed look identical. It is only as independent acts of authorship that the two works embodied in identical material form can be construed as radically distinct. What is juridically significant as a matter of copyright law is the "very speaking itself," regardless of the novelty of either its content or its form. What gives rise to distinct copyrights for independent authors of so-called identical works is that—albeit identically—each speaks in her own words. Originality *is* this "speaking in one's own words." To be an author is to speak in one's own voice.

Thus, that independent creation is also a defense should not obscure its fundamental role in structuring originality, and, moreover, in structuring originality as a relation between equals. The defense of independent creation makes available the foundational principle of independent creation to the defendant in a copyright action. Precisely because she claims her work as originating in her, a copyright plaintiff cannot deny the equal juridical significance of the defendant's own origination, even if the work that originates in the defendant happens to be identical to or substantially similar to the plaintiff's work. The defense of independent creation thus ensures that the plaintiff's right to her expression is consistent with the defendant's equal right to the *defendant's* own original expression. The plaintiff has a right to her expression only to the extent that her right does not intrude upon the defendant's equal right to *his* expression. It is but an insistence on this limit. If an author has a right to her original expression, then so must everyone else, including the defendant in any given copyright action. The defense of independent creation thus encapsulates the juridical equality as authors of the parties to a copyright action. As soon as the law of copyright grants an author rights in her expression, the law of copyright also requires that the author submit to every other person's equal right in *his* original expression. The defense of independent creation affirms the parties' equal entitlement to original expression.

Of course, this equality of the parties is their equality not as owners but as authors. The defense of independent creation cannot be adequately understood as some kind of trump or exception to an author's otherwise proprietary entitlement to her work. It is not as if the author owns her work, except where her ownership conflicts with the defendant's equal ownership of the products of *his* authorship. Independent authors whose works happen to be identical do not somehow share the same resource. Independent creators are not co-owners. Precisely because independent creation gives rise to two independent copyrights over two distinct works, what we have in these seemingly identical works is not some kind of mutual restriction on a single proprietary holding, but rather an insight into what each independent creator holds as a matter of copyright law. The defense of independent creation affirms the defendant's authorship *in the very same way in which it affirms the plaintiff's.* As much as the plaintiff's originality, the defendant's defense is rooted through and through in independent creation. Each speaks in her own words. Each holds her work not as a thing but as an act, not as an object of ownership but as a work of authorship. The principle that grants juridical status to an author's authorship also renders it consistent with the authorship of everyone else. At stake is not an external limitation of the plaintiff's claim but rather the principle holding plaintiff and defendant together as parties to a legal action centered on the authorship of each and both. Independent creation shows us unequivocally that copyright law engages the author not as a self-contained atom but rather as an author among authors. So radical is this insistence to construe an author among others, and only among others, that copyright law grants rights only on condition that we learn to hear, even if in the very same words, the speech of another. This is precisely what Borges does with the words of the *Quixote.*

The nature of copyright subject matter as a speaking in one's own words thus defines the scope of the right to which it gives rise. Copyright scope is not an artificially imposed limitation but rather an immanently driven determination of copyright subject matter itself. The limits of copyright follow from the nature of its subject matter as speech. There are indeed two senses in which, as a copyright law matter, the authorship of each is necessarily mediated and therefore limited through the authorship of all. The first is that the rights attendant on a work of authorship are and must be consistent with the authorship of each and all. Precisely as speaker, an author cannot claim rights that stand in the way of another's speech. Independent creation is the first of a set of doctrinal moments—which we will presently examine—whereby copyright law ensures the universality of the principle of authorship.

The second is that not only the rights attendant on a work, but rather the work itself is a relation between persons. Precisely as speech, a work necessarily implicates its addressee. An author is not only someone who says something. She is also thereby someone who addresses others. Expression is expression toward another. An interpersonal relation is thus at the heart of copyright subject matter. More precisely, copyright subject matter *is* a relation between persons. Rights in respect of that subject matter therefore contemplate lawful claims of use inhering in those it addresses. The work is a relation between author and public. The universality of authorship is thus a fundamental ground of user rights in copyright law.

Comparison of copyright and patent, a work of authorship and an invention, can once again help us broach this aspect of the problem. To begin with, the observation that copyright *subject matter* is an interpersonal relation should be sharply distinguished from the quite different proposition that copyright *law,* as a legal regime, is a relation between persons—that is, an author's exclusive right to summon the authority of the state to preclude others from doing certain acts with respect to the author's work. What I am trying to emphasize here is not that copyright is a legal relation, but rather that the subject matter of this legal relation—i.e., the author's work—is itself a relation between persons.

Patent, like copyright, is also a legal relation. A patent is an inventor's legal right to preclude others from doing certain acts with respect to her invention. Unlike a copyrightable work, however, an invention is not itself an interpersonal relation. An invention is not a mode of discourse addressed to another. In patent, a person offers the public a previously unavailable way of manipulating nature. Thus, the subject matter of patent is an act with respect to nature—that is, a relation between a person and an object.

Viewed in this light, the distinction between patent and copyright is a distinction between subject matter involving a relation between persons and objects (patent), and subject matter involving a relation between persons (copyright). Thus, whereas an inventor's patent permits him to preclude others from repeating his act in respect of nature, from operating his invention, an author's copyright permits him to preclude others from repeating his discourse, from reproducing his work. Patent law is about learning and doing things in and to nature. Copyright law is about speaking to one another. Colloquially put, the distinction between patent and copyright is a distinction between technology and culture.[26]

Note that this way of framing the distinction between patent and copyright does not mean that patent law is devoid of discourse. On the contrary, patent specifications, which both claim and define in words the scope of the inventor's right, are communications to the public disclosing the invention.[27] These communications, however, are *about* the subject matter of the right. By contrast, in copyright, the discourse *is* the subject matter of the right. The ongoing conversation through which the law of patent specifies the novelty and utility of its subject matter appears in copyright law as the very subject matter that, regardless of its novelty or utility, is worthy of our attention. This is yet another way of saying that copyright is not about the content of what is said but is rather about the speaking itself.

An inventor offers the public an instrument previously unavailable. This invention is no mere scientific discovery that increases or deepens the public's knowledge for its own sake. As a matter of patent law, the invention must satisfy both a novelty and a *utility* requirement—that which is not useful is not an invention.[28] Patentable subject matter is by definition radically instrumental. An invention is a tool—a product specifically designed to perform a function—it is not knowledge but *applied* knowledge, not science but the embodied application of scientific knowledge to practical purposes. An inventor, then, offers the public novel ways of dealing with practical problems.

Things are very different in copyright. An authorial creation is not by definition a tool. It need not perform a function.[29] It is not an embodied resolution of a practical problem. Rather, a work is a "speaking itself," a mode of discourse addressed to another. As such, an authorial creation inserts itself not into the technological space between persons and objects, but instead into the cultural space between persons. An author addresses others. It is the form of this address *per se,* neither the novelty nor the utility of its content, that copyright law deems inherently worthy of protection. Authorship as communicative act is thus the fundamental axiom of copyright law. As we are about to see, this axiom necessarily generates equally axiomatic lawful claims of use inhering in the public that authorship addresses.

Idea/Expression Dichotomy

If the principle of independent creation teaches that copyright law regards authorial speech as inherently worthy of recognition, and that, as speech, a work is addressed to another, the idea/expression dichotomy incorporates this other also as a speaker in her own right whose entitlements include the conditions for the possibility of responding to the speech of others. Each and all both address and respond to each other's authorship.

The free availability of ideas is the freedom of each and all to express or develop ideas anew. The idea/expression dichotomy is thus a condition for the possibility of authors addressing each other as interlocutors. It captures doctrinally the proposition that imprisoning ideas would construe copyright subject matter not as an intervention in an ongoing conversation but rather as the preclusion of another's speech. The liberation of ideas from copyright is but the affirmation of a work as an invitation to dialogue. Authors speak not at each other monologically but to each other dialogically. The idea/expression dichotomy teaches that the independence that independent creation enshrines juridically is the independence of participants in a dialogue. It thus elaborates upon the insight that an author is always among others. She responds and speaks to those others.

The idea/expression dichotomy is a dichotomy of protection. It provides that an author's ideas, no matter how novel, are not subject to copyright. Only her expression of those ideas is. *Moreau v. St. Vincent* puts it succinctly: "It is, I think, an elementary principle of copyright law that an author has no copyright in ideas but only in his expression of them. The law of copyright does not give him any monopoly in the use of the ideas with which he deals or any property in them, *even if they are original.* His copyright is confined to the literary work in which he has expressed them. The ideas are public property, the literary work is his own. Every one may freely adopt and use the ideas but no one may copy his literary work without his consent."[30] Unsurprisingly, the *Moreau* Court reminds us that the originality or lack thereof of the plaintiff's ideas is "immaterial."[31] Evidence bearing on that issue is "strictly speaking, irrelevant and inadmissible."[32] The plaintiff in a copyright action must show not that her ideas have been adopted by the defendant, but that the defendant has copied the plaintiff's expression.

Learned Hand J.'s judgment in *Nichols v. Universal Pictures Corporation* remains the *locus classicus* of the idea/expression dichotomy. In *Nichols,* the plaintiff was the author of a play entitled "Abie's Irish Rose." The defendant produced a motion picture play entitled "The Cohens and the Kellys," which the plaintiff alleged was taken from her own play. Following a description and comparison of the plays, Hand J. found that "[t]he only matter common to the two is a quarrel between a Jewish and an Irish father, the marriage of their children, the birth of grandchildren and a reconciliation."[33] On that basis, Hand J. ruled in favor of the defendant: "A comedy based upon conflicts between Irish and Jews, into which the marriage of their children enters, is no more susceptible of copyright than the outline of Romeo and Juliet."[34]

At no point does Hand J. contest the claim that the defendant "took" from the plaintiff. Hand J.'s point, rather, is that what the defendant took did not belong to the plaintiff, even on the counterfactual assumption that the plaintiff had indeed, as it were, created it *ex nihilo:* "We assume that the plaintiff's play is altogether original, even to an extent that in fact it is hard to believe. We assume further that, so far as it has been anticipated by earlier plays of which she knew nothing, that fact is immaterial. Still, as we have already said, her copyright did not cover everything that might be drawn from her play; its content went to some extent into the public domain."[35] What Hand J. had "already said," of course, is that copyright does not protect "ideas": "If the defendant took so much from the plaintiff, it may well have been because her amazing success seemed to prove that this was a subject of enduring popularity. Even so, granting that the plaintiff's play was wholly original, and assuming that novelty is not essential to a copyright, there is no monopoly in such a background. Though the plaintiff discovered the vein, she could not keep it to herself; so defined, the theme was too generalized an abstraction from what she wrote. It was only a part of her 'ideas.'"[36] The plaintiff's ideas are not copyrightable even though they may be said to have originated in her—and are in that sense "her" ideas—as much as her expression.[37]

Yet although the author's copyright is thus limited to her expression, it is not limited "literally to the text." Otherwise, Hand J. observes, "a plagiarist would escape by immaterial variations."To limit copyright to the literal text would be as unfair to the plaintiff as Hand J. takes it to be unfair to the defendant to grant the plaintiff a monopoly in "stock figures," "prototypes," or in "too generalized an abstraction from what she wrote."[38] The idea/expression dichotomy thus comes to place itself neither on the side of the plaintiff nor in that of the defendant, but rather between plaintiff and defendant, as the guide through which the relation of each and both to the work is legally construed.

Famously, Hand J. writes: "Upon any work, and especially upon a play, a great number of patterns of increasing generality will fit equally well, as more and more of the incident is left out. The last may perhaps be no more than the most general statement of what the play is about, and at times might consist only of its title; but there is a point in this series of abstractions where they are no longer protected, since otherwise the playwright could prevent the use of his 'ideas,' to which, apart from their expression, his property is never extended."[39] Precluding the author from laying exclusive claim to her ideas is entirely intelligible from the standpoint of the equality of the parties as authors. Assume for a moment that you use or adopt in your own work an idea drawn from another person's work, yet without copying that other person's expression of the idea. Say, for example, that you write an original play developing the idea of "star-crossed lovers." This means not that you have reproduced the text of *Romeo and Juliet* (i.e., William Shakespeare's expression of that idea), but that you have expressed the idea anew. To use in one's own work ideas drawn from another's is necessarily to exercise one's own expressive capacities. Strictly speaking, we might say that ideas *per se* cannot be copied; they can only be (re)expressed anew. This is why the copyright case law speaks not of copying ideas but of "adopting" or "using" them.[40] The lesson to be drawn from such formulations is that a plaintiff seeking to enjoin a defendant from using or adopting in the defendant's own work ideas expressed in the plaintiff's work is a plaintiff seeking to interfere with the defendant's own original expression.

Where the defendant expresses an idea in his own words, the plaintiff cannot complain of a violation of her copyright because her own claim to copyright is but an affirmation that persons have a right to their expression. What the plaintiff would have to assert in order to claim copyright in an idea is that she, but not the defendant, has rights in her expression. Yet that assertion would, of course, be inconsistent with the equality of the parties considered in their capacity as authors, as originators of copyrightable expression. The proposition that only expression is copyrightable, and not ideas, is thus rooted in the equality of the parties as authors. Just as the defense of independent creation precludes the defendant's liability even where the defendant's work is identical to the plaintiff's, so does the idea/expression dichotomy preclude the defendant's liability even where the defendant's work draws ideas from the plaintiff's. In neither case does copyright law permit the plaintiff to interfere with the defendant's entitlement to his own expression. In both cases, respect of the defendant's expression is the condition *sine qua non* of the plaintiff's own copyright. In short, copyrighting ideas is inconsistent with the principle of independent creation.

But while it is correct to emphasize that copyrighting ideas is incompatible with the definition of originality as independent expression, this does not yet explain why the law of copyright defines originality in the way it does, as pertinent only to expression, and not to idea. What, then, is it that informs the necessity to define authorship exclusively as a matter of expression rather than ideation? Why is it that copyright protects only expression?

Indeed, imagine a plaintiff who, having come up with an indisputably novel idea, complains that, even if copyrighting ideas is indeed inconsistent with the definition of originality as independent *expression,* there is nonetheless nothing in the concept of independent *creation,* or in that of the parties' equality as authors, that necessitates such a definition. Such a plaintiff may argue as follows: "I want to claim not that I have a right to my own expression but that I have a right to what originates in me, regardless of whether it is expression or idea. This novel idea here, and not only its expression, originated in me. I have no problem in acknowledging that others, too, have a right to the exclusive use of the ideas that they themselves originate. Nor do I have any difficulty in acknowledging a defense of independent ideation. Thus nothing in my claim to copyright my novel idea contradicts everyone else's status as originators of ideas, if and when they in fact come up, as I have, with a novel idea of their own. The law of copyright ought to affirm our equality not only as expressive beings but also as thinking beings, not only as beings who originate expression but also as beings who originate ideas."

It goes without saying, of course, that this plaintiff's position has no legal weight. Even if we were to assume, as does Hand J. in *Nichols,* that the plaintiff truly originated an idea *de novo,* it is abundantly clear that the law of copyright would not grant her protection of that idea.[41] But the question here is not whether the plaintiff would succeed in court. Rather, the plaintiff's objection demands that we understand why the law of copyright finds authorship in expression but not equally in idea.

The beginning of the answer lies in the observation that, considered as bare ideation, the plaintiff's thought cannot help but be legally irrelevant. This is because, as distinct from her identity as an expressive being, the plaintiff's identity as a thinking being is a matter thoroughly internal to the plaintiff, outside the purview of the plaintiff's relation to others. It is expression, not ideation, that renders thought a matter of right, that plunges thought into the field of interpersonal relations. On this view, the reason that copyright law refuses to protect ideas is that ideas can be said to enter the sphere of right, of relations between persons, only as expressed. Thus, for example, the plaintiff cannot claim an entitlement to her thoughts, or as arising exclusively from her thoughts, any more than, in the context of first possession in the world of tangible property, a plaintiff can claim that her bare intention to possess an object, in the absence of an unequivocal and publicly recognizable manifestation of that intention, is sufficient to constitute another person's obligation to refrain from using the allegedly possessed object.[42] Ideas are no more relevant in copyright than mere intentions are in the context of first possession.

As distinct from what we may call the merely subjective emptiness of bare ideation, expression is always expression toward another. An author is not someone who just thinks; she is also someone who expresses her thoughts. Not the subjectivity of thought but the interpersonality of communication is at the heart of the legal concept of authorship. One might even say that it is precisely the transition from thought to communication, inchoate intention to manifested word, that the law of copyright calls authorship. Copyright, then, is necessarily copyright in expression because only expression, not ideation, can have legal import.

While correct as far as it goes, the proposition that the interiority of ideas excludes them from copyright protection is nonetheless insufficient as an account of the idea/expression dichotomy. The difficulty is that the distinction between "idea" and "expression" in copyright law is not a distinction between "internal" and "external." Thus in *Nichols* the defendant is said to be within her rights in adopting the plaintiff's ideas, but, of course, she could have hardly adopted them had they remained merely internal to the plaintiff. On the contrary, the ideas had indeed been communicated to the defendant. This means that, while it is undeniably true that ideas can enter the world of legality only as communicated, it is equally true that not every aspect of a communication is, by that token alone, an instance of copyrightable expression. The idea/expression dichotomy bifurcates the external field of communication between people into aspects that are not subject to legal protection—i.e., idea—and aspects that are—i.e., expression. Our question is how this bifurcation is to be understood from the standpoint of the equality of the parties as authors.

What Hand J. tells us in *Nichols* is that the plaintiff's ideas are "too generalized an abstraction from what she wrote" to be worthy of copyright protection.[43] The "less developed the characters," he writes elsewhere in the judgment, "the less they can be copyrighted; that is the penalty an author must bear for marking them too indistinctly."[44] The contrast between ideas and expression is a contrast between the generality of ideas and the specificity of expression. By the same token, a work of authorship is a translation or development of general into specific, abstract into concrete, idea into expression. What matters is not the source of the idea—whether "internal" or "external." What matters is its particularization. To express is not to press out but to concretize, to move from the abstract possibilities of what one may have meant to the expressed reality of what one has said. To author is to particularize.

Thus, the idea/expression dichotomy is less about the interiority of ideas than about their generality. Even if communicated, ideas are not *per se* subject to copyright protection due to their inherent generality. Considered in their bare generality, ideas are the material but not the product of the work of authorship. This is true of ideas communicated at too high a level of generality (such as "stock figures" or "prototypes"), as well as of ideas underlying thoroughly concretized expression (such as "too generalized an abstraction" from an author's work). Authors do not author ideas; they author expressions. An author's work is the expression of an idea, and it is only as expressed, as particularized, that he can lay claim to it. Thus Shakespeare is the author of Romeo and Juliet, not of the idea of "star-crossed lovers," and this would remain true regardless of the source of the idea; that is, regardless of whether anyone before Shakespeare had either thought of or communicated the idea.

The fact that Shakespeare wrote a story about "star-crossed lovers" cannot mean that he has a claim to all stories about "star-crossed lovers." Such a claim to exclusive use at the level of bare generality would render an author's copyright inconsistent with another's equal dignity as an author. This is why copyright can arise only at the point where the plaintiff's claim to the specificity of her expression is no longer inconsistent with the defendant's claim to his original expression, to his own translation of general into particular. For it is only at that point that, having marked its subject matter with sufficient distinctiveness, the plaintiff's claim is no longer, by virtue of its inchoate generality, inconsistent with the defendant's equal claim to authorship. An author has to have said something rather than anything. As a copyright matter, authorship has nothing to do with bare ideas, whether novel or otherwise.

It is tempting to infer that the law of copyright refuses to protect ideas because ideas are not the kind of thing that can be marked with sufficient distinctiveness. Ideas, one might say, cannot be possessed or occupied. That much seems clear.[45] I do not need to rehearse here either the extraordinary difficulties attendant on demarcating a mere idea as subject to legal protection, or the equally insurmountable obstacles that would accompany any serious inquiry into the origin of something as elusive as an idea.[46] The point here, however, is not so much that ideas cannot be occupied or possessed, but rather that they cannot be occupied or possessed in their bare generality in a manner consistent with another's equal dignity as an author; that is, in a manner consistent with another's claim to his original expression. The theory of the idea/expression dichotomy is not a theory of the radical intangibility of ideas. It is a theory of the defendant's positive entitlement to speak in her own words about what the plaintiff speaks. The exclusion of ideas from the purview of copyright is thus an instance of the normativity of copyright as a relation between persons. The legal definition of the plaintiff's copyrightable work is therefore not so much—or not only—an evidentiary matter, as much as a normative exercise conducted under the rubric of interpersonality. In short, the author's copyright necessarily entails an affirmation of the equal authorship of those it seeks to obligate.

Analysis of the principle of independent creation, then, brings into relief a constellation of concepts comprised of the author as speaker, of originality as a speaking in one's own words, and of the equality as authors of the parties to a copyright action. This constellation of concepts is but a differentiation of the concept of the work as a communicative act. As communicative, the work is a speaking. Its originality flows from its being a speaking of one's own, a speaking in one's own words. As act, the work is one's own regardless of a previously existing identical work. Just because you happen to have spoken the same sequence of words, it does not follow that my coincidentally identical utterance is any less my own. The idea/expression dichotomy further elaborates this constellation of concepts by making explicit that the defendant's equality as an author entails more than the lawfulness of creating independently seemingly identical work. It also entails the lawfulness of the defendant's drawing from the plaintiff's work. That is, the proposition that the plaintiff can claim her copyright only where it is consistent with the defendant's own authorship generates both the defendant's entitlement to produce identically in the absence of copying, and the defendant's entitlement to draw from the plaintiff's work. The idea/expression dichotomy deepens the insight, embedded in the principle of independent creation, that the plaintiff's copyright neither is nor can be an entitlement to interfere with the defendant's authorship. On the contrary, the juridical status of your speaking in your own words generates my entitlement to engage your speaking in my own. Thus, the principle of independent creation necessarily entails that authorship is inconceivable in the absence of user rights.

Fair Use/Fair Dealing

Fair use in the United and States and fair dealing in Canada specify situations in which copying expression in the absence of authorization from the copyright holder is lawful. Both fair use and fair dealing construe the lawfulness of unauthorized copying by reference to the purpose of the copying involved. In the United States, fair use engages "purposes *such as* criticism, comment, news reporting, teaching (including multiple copies for classroom use), scholarship, or research."[47] In Canada, fair dealing engages "research, private study, education, parody or satire," "criticism or review," and "news reporting."[48] Central among the differences between fair use and far dealing is that whereas the purposes listed in the United States statute are illustrative (i.e., purposes "such as"), the purposes listed in the Canadian statute are said to be exhaustive. For this reason, fair dealing is often regarded as more restrictive or narrower than fair use.[49] This and other differences aside, however, what matters for the present discussion is that both fair use and fair dealing are about unauthorized yet lawful use. My interest here is not to compare and contrast fair use and fair dealing but to set forth fundamental and shared aspects of fair use and fair dealing that, continuous with the principle of independent creation and the idea/expression dichotomy, further elaborate the defendant's equal authorship within the innermost structure of copyright law.

The fair dealing provisions in the Canadian *Copyright Act* permit substantial reproduction that would otherwise be an infringement where the reproduction in question is for any of the specified purposes. Not all acts of reproduction for these purposes, however, meet the requirements of the defense. The acts of reproduction in question must be for one of the allowable purposes, but they must also be "fair." The threshold determination that the defendant's dealing with the plaintiff's work falls within the statutorily specified purposes gives rise to an inquiry into whether the dealing is fair.[50] This determination of fairness amounts to an examination of several factors pertinent to the dealing, including, in addition to the purpose of the dealing, the character of the dealing, the amount of the dealing, alternatives to the dealing, the nature of the plaintiff's work, and the effect of the dealing on the market of the work.[51]

These factors govern a determination of whether the dealing is reasonably necessary for its purpose. The fairness of the dealing is assessed in relation to the purpose used to justify the dealing.[52] Thus, for example, the permitted amount of the dealing varies in accordance with the invoked purpose. What is fair for the purposes of research or private study need not be fair for the purposes of criticism or review. The permitted amount of any given dealing is not a quantitative category. At stake is not an allowable proportion either of the plaintiff's work (as in how much of the plaintiff's work was reproduced) or of the defendant's work (as in how much of the defendant's work is made up of reproduced material). The fair amount is rather a relation between what is reproduced and the purpose of the reproduction. A fair dealing is a dealing reasonably necessary for its purpose. Thus, what transforms an otherwise infringing reproduction into a legitimate exercise cognizable under the fair dealing provisions is nothing other than the fit between the reproduction and its (allowable) purpose.[53]

Five of the eight statutorily specified fair dealing purposes necessarily involve the defendant's authorship. Criticism, review, parody, satire, and news reporting are at best difficult to imagine in the absence of the defendant's authorship. All of these purposes involve use of the plaintiff's work in the defendant's own. This is not to say that the remaining fair dealing purposes (research, private study, education) necessarily exclude the defendant's authorship. Rather, it is to highlight that use of the plaintiff's work in the defendant's is a paradigmatic instance of fair dealing.

For example, in *Théberge v. Galerie d'Art du Petit Champlain inc.*, the first of the Supreme Court of Canada's cases announcing the importance of "user rights" in Canadian copyright jurisprudence, Binnie J. describes copyright "exceptions" as follows: "Excessive control by holders of copyrights and other forms of intellectual property may unduly limit the ability of the public domain to incorporate and embellish creative innovation in the long-term interests of society as a whole, or create practical obstacles to proper utilization. This is reflected in the exceptions to copyright infringement enumerated in ss. 29 to 32.2, which seek to protect the public domain *in traditional ways such as fair dealing for the purpose of criticism or review* and to add new protections to reflect new technology, such as limited computer program reproduction and 'ephemeral recordings' in connection with live performances."[54] Fair dealing for the purpose of criticism or review, in which the defendant responds to the plaintiff's work, and uses for that purpose the plaintiff's work in her own, figures as the paradigmatic example of fair dealing.

In the US, concern with the defendant's authorship is also paradigmatic. Thus, for example, in *Campbell v. Acuff-Rose Music Inc.,* the US Supreme Court held that the fair use inquiry seeks to determine whether the defendant's use of the plaintiff's work merely supplants the plaintiff's

> or instead adds something new, with a further purpose or different character, altering the first with new expression, meaning, or message; it asks, in other words, whether and to what extent the new work is "transformative." . . . Although such transformative use is not absolutely necessary for a finding of fair use . . . the goal of copyright, to promote science and the arts, is generally furthered by the creation of transformative works. Such works thus lie *at the heart of the fair use doctrine's guarantee* of breathing space within the confines of copyright . . . and the more transformative the new work, the less will be the significance of other factors, like commercialism, that may weigh against a finding of fair use.[55]

Use of the plaintiff's work in the defendant's is not the only instance of transformative use. We will see in Chapter 3, for example, that using the plaintiff's work "with a further purpose" need not entail use of the plaintiff's work in the defendant's. Nonetheless, transformative use in the sense of use in the defendant's work for purposes "such as" those listed in the statute remains a paradigmatic instance of fair use in United States jurisprudence. Fair use for the purpose of comment and criticism, moreover, is the traditional example.[56]

This paradigmatic concern with the integrity of the defendant's authorship manifests the principle of independent creation in fair use or fair dealing jurisprudence. The plaintiff can claim only as an author among authors. Fair use or fair dealing arises as an issue when it has been found that the defendant has substantially reproduced the plaintiff's work without authorization. There is no reason, and no legal basis, to raise fair use or fair dealing where there has been no unauthorized reproduction. Grasped from the standpoint of the principle of independent creation, the function of fair use or fair dealing is to inquire into the circumstances of the unauthorized use with an eye to determining whether, in spite of the appearance of infringement as a result of the defendant's act of substantial reproduction, the defendant's work is after all his own, not truly a copy of the plaintiff's. A finding of fair use or fair dealing means precisely that the act of substantial reproduction that gives rise to the fair use or fair dealing inquiry fails to mature into a finding of infringement. The defense gives the defendant the opportunity to show that his substantial reproduction of the plaintiff's work does not negate his own authorship. From this point of view, fair use or fair dealing stands for the proposition that responding to another's work in one's own does not mean that one's work is any less one's own. The defendant who makes out the fair use or fair dealing defense is an author in her own right. It is as author that—under paradigmatic instances of the defense—the defendant is a fair user.[57]

The principle of independent creation also explains why fair use or fair dealing affirms the free availability of another's expression only where such expression is reasonably necessary to one's own. The reason is that the "fairness" in fair use or fair dealing operates bilaterally. Fair use or fair dealing must be fair to both plaintiff and defendant. This means that fair dealing must impose limitations not only on the plaintiff's copyright but also on the kinds of uses that the defendant can make of the plaintiff's work. Thus the defendant can legitimately use the plaintiff's work where the purpose of such use engages the defendant's authorship and only to the extent that such purpose reasonably requires. If fair use or fair dealing is to be "fair" in the sense of being bilaterally consistent with the authorship of each party, then the allowable purposes must be understood in this twofold manner, as purposes which on the one hand make the plaintiff's work freely available to the defendant, yet on the other specify the conditions that limit that availability. Fair use or fair dealing affirms the defendant's user right while preserving the plaintiff's authorial right. This is why the fair use or fair dealing purposes allow certain copying but do not thereby legitimate all or any copying. The fairness of the use or dealing operates as a bilateral recognition of the parties' equal claims as authors. It affirms and sustains the higher principle of independent creation to which both parties appeal and to which they must, therefore, both be subject.[58]

It is as if, through the operations of fair use or fair dealing, copyright law were saying to the plaintiff: "You have asserted rights in your authorship; you cannot now turn around and deny the defendant's authorship." Viewed in this light, the defense is not about undoing or overlooking a wrong for reasons extraneous to authorship itself. At stake is not an excuse or exception. Rather, fair use or fair dealing involving the defendant's authorship is an affirmative statement of a person's right to respond to another's work in her own. It is as if, upon hearing the plaintiff's complaint, the defendant were to say: "It is true that I have reproduced your work, but my use is not 'piratical;' it is reasonably necessary to my own work. I am equally an author." Transformative use—to invoke the United States terminology—of this kind is lawful because it evidences that the defendant is not parroting the plaintiff's work parasitically but rather responding to the plaintiff's work in her own, addressing it as the subject matter of her own authorial engagement.

The parallel between the defense of independent creation and the defense of fair use or fair dealing is worth emphasizing. Both defenses affirm the proposition that identity or substantial similarity between the plaintiff's work and the defendant's work does not *per se* give rise to copyright liability. Assume for a moment that a lay audience were to be shown two identical sheets of paper with identical text on them. It is reasonable to expect that, when asked whether the sheets are copies of each other, most members of that audience would reply affirmatively. If we were to ask the very same question to a group of copyright lawyers, however, we would likely get an answer along the following lines: "Well, it depends. There is certainly substantial similarity, or even identity, but it does not follow that we have an instance of copying. In order to show copying we would have to inquire whether there is a causal connection between these two sheets—that is, whether there was actual copying involved or whether, on the contrary, what we have before us is an instance of independent creation." The copyright lawyer is well aware that mere identity does not in and of itself give rise to liability. The copyright liability inquiry is more complex than a mere ascertaining of substantial similarity or identity between patterns of ink on sheets of paper.

The complexity is greater, but not of a different kind, in the case of the defense of fair use or fair dealing. Fair use or fair dealing precludes liability even where there is a finding of substantial similarity (or identity) *and* causal connection. If the defense of independent creation warns us away from inferring liability from mere identity, the defense of fair use or fair dealing warns us away from inferring liability even from identity *coupled with actual copying.* Thus, strictly speaking, a finding of "reproduction" (i.e., substantial similarity coupled with actual copying) is not in and of itself sufficient to warrant the inference that liability obtains. The defense of fair use or fair dealing confirms that the copyright liability inquiry is far more complex than the ascertaining of physical similarity, even where such similarity is the result of copying.

Both defenses follow from the principle of independent creation. The defense of independent creation asserts the difference between a copy and a coincidence. The defense of fair use or fair dealing asserts the difference between a copy and a comment, a parrot and a parodist. In both cases, the basic point is that the plaintiff's copyright cannot preclude the defendant's authorship. Precisely as speaker, the plaintiff cannot claim to intrude upon the defendant's own speech. Both are authors among authors, flowing from and toward an ongoing conversation.

Viewed in this light, paradigmatic aspects of fair use or fair dealing is not about undoing or overlooking a wrong for reasons extraneous to authorship itself. At stake is not an excuse or an exception—a trumping, so to speak, of the plaintiff's copyright. Rather, fair use or fair dealing is but an affirmative statement of the defendant's right to participate in the communicative network of which the plaintiff is herself a part. Because it arises from and affirms on the defendant's side the very same principle that grounds the plaintiff's entitlement, fair use or fair dealing is integral to the copyright system. As independent creation arising on the defendant's side, it is best grasped as a user's right, not an exception. To put it otherwise, fair use or fair dealing is not a super-added condition somehow grafted onto a fully constituted order. On the contrary, the fact that, procedurally, fair use or fair dealing arises as a defense should not mislead us into positing that, substantively, fair use or fair dealing is anything less than integral to the copyright system as such.[59] It does not interrupt but continues and deepens the elaboration of the dialogic principle of independent creation that also animates the doctrine of originality and the idea/expression dichotomy.

Patent, Copyright, Trademark

The distinction between patent and copyright, inventions and works, brings into relief the communicative nature of the latter. An invention is a way of doing things in and to nature, and thus a relation between persons and objects. A work, by contrast, is a relation between persons, and thus a communicative act that, as such, is addressed to others.

If the comparison of copyright and patent brings into relief the work as a communicative act, a comparison of copyright and trademark, as we shall presently see, reveals the specificity of the particular kind of communicative act at issue in a work. Like a work, a trademark, too, is a communicative act. But it is not the same kind of communication as a work. Unlike a work, a trademark addresses others as consumers rather than speakers. Study of the relation between copyright and trademark will thus confirm and deepen the appreciation of the work as speech and of copyright as dialogue.

A trademark is a distinctive signifier of source in the marketplace. It is a communicative act in the sense that it tells consumers about who brings a product to the market. A trademark owner has an exclusive right to use his trademark for the purpose of distinguishing his goods or services from those of others in the marketplace.[60] By definition, a mark that does not distinguish goods or services is not a trademark. This is the requirement of distinctiveness, which encompasses the observation that a trademark owner does not have an absolute right of use over his trademark.[61] Generally speaking, he does not have, for example, an exclusive right to use the trademark in association with significantly dissimilar goods or services in a nonconfusing way.[62] His right is not an exclusive right to any and all uses of the mark. His ownership of a trademark is rather ownership for a particular purpose. In accordance with the nature of a trademark, it is an exclusive right to use the mark as a distinctive signifier of source in the marketplace. It is an exclusive right to its specifically communicative (i.e., distinctive) use.

The communication involved is radically unidirectional. It flows from the trademark owner to the public. A trademark communicates information about the source of a product in the marketplace, but it transmits that information in the same way that a one-way traffic sign on a street provides information about the direction to drive on that street. In neither case is the information provided with the expectation that the public engage in a dialogue about it. Motorists are not expected to question or discuss the fact—communicated by the one-way sign—that the street in question is a one-way street. They are expected to follow its command. Similarly, consumers are not expected to question or discuss the fact—communicated by the trademark—that the product in question comes from the source indicated by the trademark. A trademark is not an invitation requesting a response from the public by way of a dialogue, either about the source of the product or about the product itself. On the contrary, consumers are expected to receive this information passively and to identify the product with the indicated source.

This is not to say that consumers do not, as a matter of fact, talk about trademarks, express feelings about them, analyze them in academic papers, wear them, or discuss and criticize vigorously the companies they represent or the products they provide. The point is not that consumers are mindless automatons. The point is that, *as a matter of trademark law,* where discussion or doubt arises as to a trademark's indicated source, the trademark has likely failed for lack of distinctiveness—that is, the discussion or doubt would be evidence that the trademark is no longer an effective indicator of source. It is no longer a trademark.

A trademark owner owns a mental association in the public's mind between himself and the product he offers in the marketplace.[63] Thus, for example, if A uses B's trademark to offer in the marketplace the same kind of products B offers, such that the consuming public believes or is likely to believe that A is B, then the law of trademark finds that A has infringed B's trademark rights. We may say that A has availed himself of the association in the public's mind linking B and the kind of product or products in question. By the same token, if that association is diluted or absent, then there is nothing that B can own. The subject matter of ownership has vanished. This is what happens when, for example, the trademark ESCALATOR becomes the generic term for moving staircases. The signifier "escalator" no longer indicates moving staircases that come from a particular provider. It merely indicates moving staircases; it does not distinctively *mark* them as staircases from someone in particular. The former trademark owner has lost its special relation to the term "escalator." He can no longer sue others for its unauthorized use. More precisely, when others use the term they are not presenting themselves to the marketplace as if they were the trademark owner. They are simply describing or denoting moving staircases.

The life of a trademark as such is thus rooted in its owner's control of its meaning. This is why a trademark presupposes the public to which it is directed as a passive recipient of information, not as a participant in a dialogue. Participation of the public in the determination of the trademark's meaning indicates that the trademark owner has lost the requisite control. Discussion or doubt as to the trademark's indicated source weakens and evidences the weakening of the very status of a trademark as a trademark. One can readily imagine an author smiling gleefully at an interpretation of her work that she had not at all envisaged. The richness of her words, its imprecisions and ambiguities, its capacity to carry meanings other than those intended, may well be a source of pride and pleasure for her. Things are different for a trademark owner. Evocations and ambiguities other than those strictly intended would hardly please him. Unauthorized usages that threaten the trademark as a distinctive indicator of source would drive him to hire a lawyer. Where the author smiles gleefully, the trademark owner fires off a cease and desist letter. Doing what Borges does in the Menard story with the text of the *Quixote,* demonstrating that a single text can amply be the home of multiple works, is the stuff of independent creation, the play of authorship. But it would be nothing short of maddening to a trademark owner, whose mark must be distinctively and exclusively his.

Unlike trademarks, then, works of authorship subject to copyright protection are, as a matter of copyright law, addressed to audiences engaged with and responsive to the work as such, not merely to the work as some sign that merely provides information. An author's public is not a passive recipient but a participant whose response to the work is invited and elicited. A work is an invitation to engage in dialogue. Of course, this need not mean that each and every member of an author's audience takes up the invitation. It does mean, however, that one can scarcely be surprised to find that, through the principle of independent creation, copyright law recognizes this dialogical feature of both work and audience. The defense or fair use or fair dealing contemplates, as a matter of right, the expected response on the part of the recipient. It is double-edged. It precludes the author from controlling the expected response, and it also precludes the user from merely repeating the author's work without engaging it. It limits the rights of both users and authors. It institutionalizes the dialogue that traverses the life of the work as a matter of right.

This difference between a work of authorship and a trademark as modes of communication, the former dialogical and the latter monological, can be understood as a distinction between differing relations between form and content in each body of law. True, copyright and trademark are both about form and not content. Copyright is about expression and not idea. Thus, A can express the very same idea as B in A's own words without infringing B's copyright. Similarly, trademark is about the "dress" of the product and not about the product itself. Thus, A can sell the very same product as B clothed in A's own distinctive "dress" without infringing B's trademark.

This shared aspect, however, need not obscure their difference. Copyright and trademark are both about form, but not in the same way. They are in fact about fundamentally different relations between form and content. In copyright, form is a way of explicating substance. Expression is after all just that—a way of expressing an idea.[64] An expression is an expression only where it specifies an idea—where it renders the general specific. It is a discussion, a treatment, and a rendering of the general in one's own words. In trademark, however, form is by definition unrelated to substance. It is precisely this lack of relation that makes a trademark a trademark. A trademark can neither describe the product (i.e., be clearly descriptive, such as "orange" for orange juice) nor be the name of the product (i.e., be generic, such as "beer" for beer) it presents to the market. This is why, generally speaking, the strongest of trademarks have no relation to that product (i.e., are fanciful or arbitrary, such as "Corona" for beer).[65] Thus, whereas a work is a mode of rendering the substance (i.e., the idea) to which it gives expressive life and form, a trademark is but a mode of dressing the ready-made substance (i.e., the product) it presents to the market.

This difference at the level of relations between form and content is also a difference at the level of ownership with respect to the substance at issue in each body of law. The trademark owner owns the product that he dresses through his trademark. He identifies himself as the source of the product in order to sell it. Thus, the trademark is both mark and trademark. Those who receive the communication—i.e., the consumers—have access to the substance of the communication—i.e., the product marked and offered in the marketplace—through a property transfer, a contract of sale. By contrast, an author does not own the ideas she discusses in her work. Unlike the situation in trademark, an author's audience has access to the necessarily shared substance of her communication as a matter of fact and right. Precisely because the substance of her communication is shared, it can be expressed anew by others in the absence of further transactions, whether contractual or otherwise. In short, while trademarks invite transactions in the market, works invite dialogues about ideas. This difference between trademarks and works is already contained in the familiar proposition that, whereas trademarks are indicators of source in the marketplace, works are expressions of ideas not themselves subject to ownership.

Study of the specificity of copyright vis-à-vis patent and trademark thus reveals that a work of authorship is not only a communicative act but also a dialogical one. An author is always among others. The principle of independent creation informs the doctrine of originality, the idea/expression dichotomy, and the irrevocably integral and constitutive role of fair use or fair dealing in copyright law. Inventions insert themselves into the technological space between persons and objects, offering the public novel ways to manipulate nature. Trademarks insert themselves into the commercial space between sellers and buyers, offering the public distinctive ways to identify products. Works of authorship insert themselves into the cultural space between persons, offering the public an invitation to dialogue about ideas. Fair use or fair dealing structures the legality and legitimacy of the responses that a dialogical communicative act can and does generate. It is as fundamental an aspect of the ongoing conversation as are the original works of authorship. It can be nothing other than a user's right.

3

The Work as a Work

How is it possible to be identical but not a copy? In what sense can a creation of the mind be identical to a preexisting creation, yet at the same time original?

The principle of independent creation in copyright law provides an answer. A work is not a thing but an act. Two independent copyrights can arise over seemingly identical work because each has its origin in an independent act of authorship. Both works are original, yet neither is unique. Their identity is but a coincidence, and a mere coincidence does not deprive either author of her status as an author. On the contrary, copyright requires that they encounter each other as equals. The doctrine of originality teaches as much.

The idea/expression dichotomy reminds us that the act at issue is communicative in nature. To author a work is to express an idea, to particularize the general, to speak in one's own words. Expression is expression toward another. Ideas remain outside the purview of copyright because their availability is a condition for the possibility of this other's response. Indeed, it is not so much that ideas remain "outside the purview of copyright." On the contrary, it is that their being outside the purview of the author's entitlement is precisely the way in which ideas are recognized within the copyright system. The idea/expression dichotomy is not about the exclusion of ideas from copyright. It is about the inclusion of the defendant within copyright. The principle of independent creation posits the author as always among others.

The lawfulness of paradigmatic instances of unauthorized transformative use falls squarely within this series. Unauthorized use of the plaintiff's work in the defendant's own is not use of the plaintiff's work as a work in its own right but use of the plaintiff's work as the subject matter of the defendant's own work. The defendant is using the plaintiff's work as idea, so to speak; that is, as condition for the possibility of his own work. He is equally an author. We need the language of "exceptions" for this interaction only if we start with the assumption that a work is an instance of value to which the author is *prima facie* entitled, and that therefore any unauthorized use of the work is a misappropriation (or balancing) of that value. Understood as an affirmation of the defendant's autonomous authorship, fair use or fair dealing is, on the contrary, a user's right constitutive of the core of the copyright system. It is of a status and pedigree analogous to the venerable and indisputable idea/expression dichotomy. Fair use or fair dealing falls within the same series because it is an aspect of the systematic deployment of the principle of independent creation in copyright doctrine.

This chapter responds to two related questions that arise from the foregoing observations. The first is about the status of unauthorized use *in the absence of the defendant's authorship.* Are user rights restricted to situations involving the defendant as an author? For example, if unauthorized copying for the purpose of criticism or review is a user's right because it involves the defendant's authorship, what are we to say about Internet browsing, which involves the making of temporary copies to display a webpage on a computer screen? Is browsing *prima facie* unlawful?

The second question is about the meaning of "reproduction" in copyright law. What is a copy? It is clear enough that copyright is an exclusive right to reproduce the work or any substantial part thereof in any material form. Of course, it is harder to tell what that means, or, worse, what that ought to mean. Fair use or fair dealing is an example—perhaps the example *par excellence*—of lawful yet unauthorized copying. It is about unauthorized yet noninfringing reproduction. If this were an exception to copyright infringement, things would be relatively simple. We would know that unauthorized reproduction is *prima facie* wrongful, and that fair use or fair dealing is a doctrinal mechanism to permit the defendant to appeal to considerations designed to excuse the wrong. But if fair use or fair dealing is a user's right, not an exception, it follows that it is not about *excused* wrong, but about the *absence* of wrong. Unauthorized reproduction is not *per se* wrongful, whether *prima facie* or otherwise.

Reproduction, then, is not the mischief that copyright law targets. What then, is that mischief? What, precisely, is a wrongful copy? To anticipate, it turns out that, because a work is a communicative act, to reproduce it is to recommunicate it. To copy is to repeat an author's speech as such. Uses of the work as a mere pattern of ink, so to speak, in the absence of recommunication, are not uses of the work *as a work*.

The chapter begins with a discussion of the classic authority of *Baker v. Selden.*[1] It finds in this authority an investigation of unauthorized lawful use in the absence of the defendant's authorship. More precisely, it finds in *Baker* the proposition that because a work is a communicative act, noncommunicative uses are not actionable. In the course of the discussion, the chapter differentiates the *Baker* doctrine from the idea/expression dichotomy and from the doctrine of merger, and then applies it to, *inter alia,* recent case law involving the encounter between copyright law and digital technology. The theme developed here is that merely technical reproduction incidental to the operation of digital technology cannot give rise to liability. For example, the making of digital copies of student papers for purposes of detecting plagiarism by other students is a noninfringing use of the student papers.[2] The papers are in that instance not being used for their expressive significance. The use is noninfringing because it is noncommunicative. It is not a *fair* use but a *non*use of the work as a work.

Thus, two kinds of overarching limitations of the author's copyright are entailed in the concept of the work as a communicative act. On the one hand, there are limitations captured in the proposition that, as a communicative act, a work of authorship invites and elicits responses from those to whom it is addressed. This is fair use. On the other hand, there are limitations captured in the proposition that, because the work is a communicative act, it cannot support entitlements in respect of merely technical or noncommunicative uses. This is nonuse. Because these kinds of limitations both flow from the very nature of the work as a communicative act, they are consistent with and required by the fundamental principle of independent creation. The reproductions they authorize are thus not exceptions but user rights. Reproduction is not *per se* wrongful.

The chapter concludes with the observation that the principle of independent creation entails the proposition that "reproduction" is not the mischief copyright law targets. Copyright is not about copying. It is less an exclusive right of reproduction than an exclusive right of presentation to another. Because the work is a communicative act, to reproduce the work is rather to recommunicate it. Copyright is a right to preclude another from repeating one's own speech. The mischief of copyright is a wrong to the author's autonomy as a speaking being. Copyright infringement is compelled speech.

Baker v. Selden

In *Baker*, the United States Supreme Court dealt with the copyrightability of accounting forms included in a book explaining the operation of a novel accounting system. The plaintiff complained that the defendant's unauthorized use of the system amounted to an infringement of his copyright in the book explaining the system. The Circuit Court found for the plaintiff.[3]

In reversing the Circuit Court's judgment, the Supreme Court notes that the "plausibility" of the plaintiff's claim arises from a "confusion of ideas" resulting from "the peculiar nature of the art described in the books which have been made the subject of copyright." The peculiarity in question turns out to be that the accounting forms copied by the defendant have twofold significance. On the one hand, as part of the plaintiff's book, the forms are part of the explanation of how the accounting system operates. That is, the forms are part of the plaintiff's communication, as an author, of his contribution to the art and science of accounting. On the other hand, in addition to being an aspect of the plaintiff's explanation of the accounting system, the forms are integral to the very operation of the system that, as an inventor, the plaintiff had devised. The forms are thus part and parcel of both book and system, of both work and invention.[4]

"In describing the art," the Court writes, "the illustrations and diagrams employed happen to correspond more closely than usual with the actual work performed by the operator who uses the art. Those illustrations and diagrams consist of ruled lines and headings of accounts; and it is similar ruled lines and headings of accounts which, in the application of the art, the book-keeper makes with his pen, or the stationer with his press; whilst in most other cases the diagrams and illustrations can only be represented in concrete forms of wood, metal, stone, or some other physical embodiment."[5] In "most other cases," explanation and function, words and tools, appear separated—naturally distinguished, as it were, because the tools to operate what the words describe are physically embodied as things. He who tells us about a mousetrap in words or diagrams does not use those words or diagrams to catch mice. The telling is patently different from the doing. As distinct from its description, no question arises as to the copyrightability of the mousetrap as such. The mousetrap is a tool, not a work.

By contrast, the peculiarity of the art of accounting, as the Supreme Court sees it in *Baker,* is that the very same or substantially similar "ruled lines and headings of account" that do the telling also do the doing. The forms both describe accounting and do accounting. The "confusion of ideas" that misleads the Circuit Court is this peculiar merger of work and invention, word and tool. The forms conceal the fundamental distinction between the plaintiff as author and the plaintiff as inventor—copyright and patent. The key to the case is seeing through this confusion.

In spite of the peculiar merger at stake, the Court notes, "the principle is the same."[6] The description of an accounting system is as susceptible to copyright as the description of a mousetrap. By the same token, an accounting tool is no more susceptible to copyright than a mousetrap: "The description of the art in a book, though entitled to the benefit of copyright, lays no foundation for an exclusive claim to the art itself. The object of the one is explanation; the object of the other is use. The former may be secured by copyright. The latter can only be secured, if it can be secured at all, by letters-patent."[7] The distinction between copyright and patent pierces through the peculiar confusion that sustains the plausibility of the plaintiff's claim. It dissolves its verisimilitude. "The copyright of a work on mathematical science," the Court explains, "cannot give to the author an exclusive right to the methods of operation which he propounds, or to the diagrams which he employs to explain them, so as to prevent an engineer from using them whenever occasion requires."[8] Thus, evidence presented by Selden that Baker used the novel accounting system explained and illustrated in Selden's book is entirely irrelevant to the copyright issue. Baker's operation of Selden's system can no more give rise to copyright liability than making a pie by following a recipe can be said to infringe the copyright in the text of the recipe. It is not as if proving that A made and ate a pie following B's recipe amounts to proving that A infringed B's copyright. A can eat his pie even though B taught him how to make it.[9]

The Court develops the twofold juridical significance of Selden's accounting forms through an example involving a book on perspective:

> The copyright of a book on perspective, no matter how many drawings and illustrations it may contain, gives no exclusive right to the modes of drawing described, though they may never have been known or used before. By publishing the book without getting a patent for the art, the latter is given to the public. The fact that the art described in the book by illustrations of lines and figures which are reproduced in practice in the application of the art *makes no difference.* Those illustrations are the mere language employed by the author to convey his ideas more clearly. Had he used words of description instead of diagrams (which merely stand in the place of words), there could not be the slightest doubt that others, applying the art to practical use, might lawfully draw the lines and diagrams which were in the author's mind, and which he thus described by words in his book.[10]

As it is with a pie and its recipe, so it is with the practice of the art of perspective and its description; and so it is, too, with the operation of

Selden's accounting system and its explanation: "The copyright of a book on bookkeeping cannot secure the exclusive right to make, sell, and use account books prepared upon the plan set forth in such book. Whether the art might or might not have been patented is a question which is not before us. It was not patented, and is open to the use of the public."[11] It is true, of course, that unlike the case of a pie and its recipe, the case of accounting, like that of perspective, exhibits the peculiar convergence of explanation and operation, description and function, that animates *Baker.* But, as the Court says of the case of perspective, this "makes no difference." It does not matter that, in operating Selden's accounting system, Baker reproduced the forms, the ruled lines and headings, which are also part and parcel of Selden's explanation of the accounting system. The fundamental distinction between copyright and patent persists regardless of the convergence, in the accounting forms, of explanation and operation. The empirical merger of work and invention does not obscure the juridical insight into the distinction between copyright and patent. It is not the bare act of copying ruled lines and headings but rather its purpose that is at issue: reproducing the forms for the purpose of explanation is just not the same thing as reproducing the forms for the purpose of operating the accounting system. The former is copyright infringement. The latter is—if a patent obtains—patent infringement.

Juridically, the twofold significance of the forms amounted to the finding that the forms were copyrightable as aspects of the book but not as aspects of the system. The defendant in *Baker* was free from liability because the use complained of by the plaintiff was a use of the accounting system, to which copyright law could not grant exclusivity. The plaintiff's claim as an author is untenable as a claim to the exclusive use of the system.

We must note very carefully that the point is not that there is no copyright, whether in the plaintiff's book or in the forms as substantial part of the plaintiff's book. On the contrary, the copyright is as operative and as ordinary as would a copyright in the text of a recipe or a work on mathematical science. The plaintiff did indeed author a work. The point is not that the plaintiff had no copyright but that the copyright in his work is not an exclusive right to the content expressed in that work. The proposition is exceedingly familiar: "there is a clear distinction between the book, as such, and the art which it is intended to illustrate. The mere statement of the proposition is so evident, that it requires hardly any argument to support it."[12]

Of course, this is true not only of the book but also of the forms themselves, conceived as substantial part of the book. The forms are necessary to the use of the accounting system. They are, as the Court puts it, "necessarily . . . incident" to the art described in the book: "And of course, in using the art, the ruled lines and headings of accounts must necessarily be used as incident to it."[13] Thus the forms are, like the system, given over to public use. But this is a far cry from saying that the forms attract no copyright protection. The forms are unlike the system in one crucial respect. They are also part of the description of the system; that is, of the plaintiff's copyright protected work. Liberation of use of the forms from copyright liability is liberation of use of the forms as accounting tools, but not as substantial part of the plaintiff's expression. The forms do indeed attract copyright protection. The distinction is not either copyright or no copyright. It is between communicative and technical use. Communicative use of the forms (i.e, use of the forms to explain rather than operate the accounting system) *would* give rise to copyright liability. While Baker could operate Selden's system free from copyright liability, he could not have reproduced the forms in another book explaining the plaintiff's system.

The Court could not be clearer: " . . . the teachings of science and the rules and methods of useful art have their final end in application and use; and this application and use are what the public derive from the publication of a book which teaches them. But as embodied and taught in a literary composition or book, their essence consists only in their statement. This alone is what is secured by the copyright. *The use by another of the same methods of statement, whether in words or illustrations, in a book published for teaching the art, would undoubtedly be an infringement of the copyright.*"[14] And again: "And where the art it teaches cannot be used without employing the methods and diagrams used to illustrate the book, or such as are similar to them, such methods and diagrams are to be considered as necessary incidents to the art, and given therewith to the public; *not given for the purpose of publication in other works explanatory of the art,* but for the purpose of practical application."[15] In *Baker,* then, the defendant's reproduction of the forms is free from liability, not because the forms attract no copyright, but because the defendant's use of the forms is not a use implicating their expressive significance. The defendant used the plaintiff's forms as aspects of a novel accounting system, not as aspects of an explanation of the accounting system. The use is technical rather than communicative. The defendant escaped copyright liability because he used the forms as *tools* and not as *works*. To be sure, there can be no doubt that the defendant copied the plaintiff's forms. But he copied the plaintiff's *invention,* not the plaintiff's *work*. This is why the plaintiff may have succeeded in a patent infringement action, had she been able to pursue one, but she could not succeed in a copyright infringement action.

The significance of this distinction between copyright and patent can be most clearly discerned when considering the principle of independent creation in copyright law; more precisely, when considering that while independent creation is a defense in copyright, there is no defense of independent invention in patent. Let us assume counterfactually that, without ever having heard of Selden's system or book, Baker had independently invented the accounting system and independently authored a substantially similar book which included, as part of its description of the accounting system, forms identical to Selden's and thus necessarily incidental to the operation of the system. Lingering for a moment on the copyright and patent implications will prove instructive.

The patent situation is simpler. Baker would not be liable for patent infringement because Selden had no patent. Assuming a patent, however, Baker would be liable for its infringement, or at least he would not escape liability on the grounds of independent invention. Independent invention is not a defense to patent infringement. An identity between the plaintiff's invention and the defendant's invention, regardless of the whether the identity results from copying, is enough to ground liability.

The copyright situation is slightly more complex. Baker would not be liable for copyright infringement, not because Selden had no copyright, but because independent creation is indeed a defense. Upon staring at the identity between the forms in Selden's books and the forms in Baker's book, we can declare that this identity is but a mere appearance. The identity is not a copy but a coincidence. Not only is there no liability, but—in accordance with the principle of independent creation—the seemingly identical forms in fact give rise to two independent copyrights, one Selden's, the other Baker's. As a copyright matter, the forms of each *look* like the other's, but juridically they are just *not* the same. They are, on the contrary, independent acts of authorship. Each speaks in his own words (or diagrams)—notwithstanding that the words (or diagrams) happen to be identical. The principle of independent creation teaches that a work cannot be equated with its physical embodiment. It is not a thing but rather a communicative act.

In the actual case, of course, there is no question of independent creation. The identity between the forms in Selden's book and the forms Baker used to operate the accounting system is no coincidence; not by any means. Baker did indeed copy the forms, and did so deliberately. Still, the Court finds no liability. What permits the Court to see through the mere appearance of identity is the distinction between the forms-as-work and the forms-as-invention, copyright and patent. To assume that the forms attract no copyright would be to weaken the force and depth of the distinction.

The distinction lays bare the "confusion of ideas" that animates the case. It reveals that the apparent identity between the plaintiff's invention (which the defendant copied and used without authorization) and the plaintiff's work (which the defendant neither copied nor used) is no more than an identity at the level of material form. It is a merely physical identity of patterns of ink on a page. The legal meaning of these patterns, and of their unauthorized use, varies in accordance with the juridical order from which they are interpreted. It cannot be at all surprising that as a copyright law matter a "copy" is not an empirical but a juridical phenomenon. In *Baker,* we learn that it is not as a pattern of ink on a page but only as a communicative act that a work falls within the purview of copyright law. The use of the very same pattern of ink for purposes other than communication—e.g., as an accounting tool—is not a use of copyright subject matter. This is because the copyright is not in the pattern of ink as such but in the communicative act that it embodies. *Baker* stands for the proposition that because a work subject to copyright is a communicative act, its infringement must arise as an unauthorized communicative use. Not any and all unauthorized copying of the material form of a work gives rise to copyright liability: actionable copying is copying of a work *as a work.*[16]

Thus *Baker* renders explicit an aspect of the principle of independent creation that remains implicit in the defense of independent creation (and also in the idea/expression dichotomy and unauthorized transformative use of an author's work in another's). The defense of independent creation teaches that two (or more) independent copyrights, and thus two (or more) distinct works, can subsist in respect of one and the same material form. The distinction between a work and its material form is thus necessarily present in the defense, yet embedded in the context of relations between authors, ensuring that an author's entitlement is consistent with the equal authorship of others. An author, that is, is always among others. Similarly, albeit in different senses, both the idea/expression dichotomy and lawful yet unauthorized transformative use also situate the author among others: copyright law authorizes these others to take up the invitation to speak necessarily implicit in the author's own speaking, and thus both permits and encourages the author's interlocutors to avail themselves freely of any aspects of the author's work reasonably necessary for their own authorial engagement. In these situations, the other always appears as another *author*.

Baker sharpens the distinction between a work and its material form. It permits us to see that, regardless of the user's authorship, not any and all uses of the work's material form are uses of the work. From the standpoint of the distinction between the work and its material form, the latter is but a vehicle of the communication of the former—it is, so to speak, the physical embodiment or carrier of the author's speech. Unauthorized use of the work's material form therefore is actionable only so long as this use is a use of the work and not merely of its material form. In *Baker*, the defendant's use was use of the material form but not of the work. There was no liability because the defendant copied the material form but not the work. He did not reproduce the author's speech. It is not that he took up the invitation to reply implicit in the work as speech. It is rather that he did not use the work at all. *Baker* thus deploys the insight inherent in the principle of independent creation (i.e., that the work is an act, not a thing) to encompass unauthorized yet lawful uses *in the absence of the defendant's authorship.*

To grasp the implications of this insight most deeply it will be helpful at this point to contrast *Baker* with idea/expression cases and with merger cases. The contrast shows that whereas idea/expression and merger cases are centered on the distinction between ideas and expression, *Baker* is centered on the distinction between expression and material form. The latter distinction thus arises more sharply through the contrast.

As formulated in *Nichols v. Universal Pictures Corporation,* the idea/expression dichotomy denies copyright to ideas on the grounds that ideas are too generalized an abstraction from the plaintiff's expression. Hand J.'s formulation is worth repeating: "Upon any work, and especially upon a play, a great number of patterns of increasing generality will fit equally well, as more and more of the incident is left out. The last may perhaps be no more than the most general statement of what the play is about, and at times might consist only of its title; but there is a point in this series of abstractions where they are no longer protected, since otherwise the playwright could prevent the use of his 'ideas,' to which, apart from their expression, his property is never extended."[17] The idea/expression dichotomy thus applies to cases in which copyright obtains, and the defendant raises the proposition that the plaintiff's right cannot extend as far up the pattern of abstractions as the plaintiff claims. We might say that the plaintiff fails not for want of subject matter but for want of scope. In *Nichols,* the plaintiff authored a play about feuding families. But the copyright in her play did not entitle her to every other play about feuding families. Even if drawing on the same idea, the defendant's expression was different from the plaintiff's.

That was not the case in *Baker.* It is true, of course, that Selden held a copyright in his book explaining his accounting system. It is also true that Baker copied the system, not the book. But neither of these observations is enough to assimilate *Baker* to *Nichols.* In *Nichols,* the defendant copied idea but not expression. The defendant's copying was too generalized an abstraction from the plaintiff's book to be actionable. In *Baker,* Baker copied both idea and its particularization. Baker copied at the purest level of specificity. He copied what was arguably the most concrete manifestation of Selden's idea, the very diagrams through and with which Selden both described and operated his system. *Nichols* tells us that the defendant can copy idea, where idea means general rather than particular, abstract rather than concrete. Thus in *Nichols* the defendant's play is different from the plaintiff's at the requisite level of particularity. *Baker* must explain something altogether different, which is when it is lawful for the defendant to take the particularization itself. It is not as if Baker escaped liability because his forms, like the defendant's play in *Nichols,* were sufficiently different from Selden's. The problem is precisely that they were the same forms. In *Baker,* the defendant escaped liability not because what he copied was general rather than particular, but because his use was technical rather than expressive. *Baker* is just not an idea/expression case.

It is tempting to argue that *Baker* is but a corollary of *Nichols*. That is, it is tempting to argue that to the extent that *Nichols* liberates ideas from copyright protection, it also liberates expression that is necessarily incidental to the ideas. Were things otherwise, a plaintiff would be permitted to monopolize ideas when granted a copyright over the necessary expression. Thus (so the argument would go), in *Baker* the defendant must be permitted to take the plaintiff's expression because the accounting forms used to explain the system are necessary to the operation of the system.

That line of thought, of course, is reminiscent of a venerable dimension of copyright law, known as the doctrine of "merger." As a corollary of the idea/expression dichotomy, merger focuses on a specific kind of relation between idea and expression. It provides that no copyright arises where the expression of an idea is but the only way (or one of a limited number of ways) of expressing the idea expressed.[18] Merger denies protection where protection would contradict the free availability of ideas in copyright law. As Pamela Samuelson notes, however, "the merger doctrine did not begin to emerge until the late 1950's and did not reach its apogee until 1983."[19] Thus, it would be anachronistic to raise a question about *Baker* as a merger case. Indeed, the issue is less about *Baker* as a merger case than about the formative influence *Baker* had in the emergence and consolidation of the merger doctrine.[20] The point I want to emphasize is that such influence should not mislead us into reading *Baker* as a merger or merger-like case.

Two related observations will help to bring the point into relief. First, *Baker* does not present as a merger case. A finding of merger is a finding that no copyright subsists. Merger denies copyright. In *Baker*, however, there is no denial that Selden's book and Selden's forms as aspects of the book are indeed subject to copyright. The Court is clear that reproduction of the forms for the purposes of a rival publication would indeed attract copyright liability. As Benjamin Kaplan remarks, "[a]nother book about bookkeeping tracking Selden's books would infringe them; but anyone was free to use the system disclosed, in the absence of a patent, and that immunity carried with it the forms, even in the case of one who sold them for use by others."[21] The question the Court poses in *Baker* is not whether copyright subsists, but whether the plaintiff can wield his copyright so as to preclude the defendant from operating the accounting system described. The finding that Selden's copyright cannot reach Selden's system is not derivative of an analysis of the number of ways in which Selden may have described his system in his book. The Court makes no finding as to (nor does it inquire into) the relation between idea and expression, system and explanation, in a merger sense. The Court's finding is far wider and deeper. Selden's copyright cannot reach Selden's system because authors cannot claim as inventors. *Baker* is about the distinction between copyright and patent, works and tools, not about the number of ways in which an idea can be expressed. Even if there were hundreds of ways in which Selden's system could be described, or for that matter even hundreds of ways in which Selden's system could be operated, Selden's copyright could still not reach Selden's system.

Second, there is no merger on the facts in *Baker*. Selden used his diagrams of ruled lines and headings (i.e., his accounting forms) to describe his system, *but he need not have*. The diagrams, as the Court says of its pivotal book on perspective example, "merely stand in the place of words."[22] Selden could have described his system in words. His use of the diagrams in his books is by no means necessary to the expression of his idea. Idea and expression are not inseparable. Indeed, so far is the *Baker* Court from a finding of merger that, on the contrary, the observation that there were alternative ways (i.e., verbal rather than graphic) to express Selden's idea is, once again via the book on perspective example, part and parcel of the Court's reasoning: "Had he used words of description instead of diagrams (which merely stand in the place of words), there could not be the slightest doubt that others, applying the art to practice use, might lawfully draw the lines and diagrams which were in the author's mind, and which he thus described by words in his book."[23] On the one hand, this hypothetical prevents and cures the confusion that the copyright in Selden's diagrams as forms of expression could ground an exclusive claim to the operation of the system described. On the other, it confirms that the *Baker* ruling is not in any sense mediated through the proposition that Selden's idea and Selden's expression are merged. Albeit anachronistically, we might say that, precisely because idea and expression are not merged, the Court sustains rather than denies the copyright in

Selden's expression: "Where the truths of a science or the methods of an art are the common property of the whole world, any author has the right to express the one, or explain and use the other, in his own way. *As an author, Selden explained the system in a particular way.* It may be conceded that Baker makes and uses account-books arranged on substantially the same system; but the proof fails to show that he has violated the copyright of Selden's book, regarding the latter merely as an explanatory work; or that he has infringed Selden's right in any way, unless the latter became entitled to an exclusive right in the system."[24] Once again, *Baker* is not about the idea/expression relation but about the copyright/patent distinction.

In idea/expression dichotomy cases, the defendant copies idea but not expression. In merger cases, the defendant copies (presumably otherwise copyrightable) expression that, because merged, is not subject to copyright. In *Baker,* the defendant copies expression clearly subject to copyright. *Baker* can nonetheless affirm the lawfulness of the defendant's act because it distinguishes between a work and its material form. Thus the key to the case is not the distinction between idea and expression but the distinction between expression and material form. Both the idea/expression dichotomy and merger deal, albeit in different ways, with the relation between idea and expression. Both preclude the plaintiff from reaching, so to speak, too far above her expression, into ideas over which she can claim no exclusivity as copyright subject matter. The distinction between a work and its material form operates in the opposite direction. It precludes the plaintiff from reaching, so to speak, too far below her expression, into the material form over which, once again, she can claim no exclusivity as copyright subject matter. The distinction between a work and its material form reminds us that an author can claim rights over her work as an act, not a thing. Use of the material form is actionable only where it is a prohibited communicative use.

There is indeed a kind of merger in *Baker,* but it is not a merger of idea and expression. It is a merger of work and invention. The distinction is worth explicating. The *Baker* Court does state that the accounting forms are "necessarily . . . incident" to the operation of the accounting system.[25] This means just what it says: that the forms are necessarily incidental to the *application* of Selden's idea—a novel accounting system. The forms are not, however, necessarily incidental to the *expression* of Selden's idea. That is why the Court suggests that Selden could have used words instead of diagrams to express his idea, to describe his system. In other words, Selden's accounting system appears in two distinct registers. As a copyright law matter, it is an occasion for explanation, for the communicative work of an author. As a patent law matter, it is an occasion for application, for the technical labor of an inventor. The peculiar merger (so-called) at issue in *Baker*—the "confusion of ideas" that animates the case as a whole—is of expression and application, invention and work. When the Court says that the forms are necessarily incidental to the operation of the system, the Court is not saying, along merger lines, that the forms are not subject to copyright. On the contrary, the Court is saying that the copyright subsisting in the forms as descriptions of the system does not protect use of the forms as tools. This is just not the logic of the doctrine of merger properly so-called, which denies copyright altogether.

The Court can sustain the copyright in the forms while liberating use of the forms as tools from that copyright by distinguishing the work from its material form. Use of the forms as tools is use of the material form but not of the work. Most deeply at stake is a use-driven definition of copyright protection. Because the work is an act but not a thing, its infringement is and must be prohibited communicative use. *Baker* is thus an authoritative assertion of the foundational principle of independent creation. It tells us not only what copyright is not but also what it is. It refuses to protect the material form of the work as merely dead, mute matter. A work is not a pattern of ink. Like the principle of independent creation, *Baker* protects the material form of the work only as a form of expression, as the work of an author.[26]

Fair Use and Nonuse

Baker affirms the lawfulness of unauthorized use of the material form of a work subject to copyright. The *Baker* doctrine is different from the idea/expression dichotomy and from the doctrine of merger because it affirms lawful unauthorized use while simultaneously affirming copyright. In that respect, the *Baker* doctrine resembles fair use or fair dealing. Yet in *Baker* the defendant escapes liability not because his use of the work is a fair use but because it is not a use of the work as such. *Baker* is about nonuse. *Kelly v. Arriba Soft Corp.*, a case involving "the application of copyright law to the vast world of the internet and internet search engines", is a good starting point to broach the significance of the distinction between nonuse and fair use.[27] The point I want to bring into relief is that because merely technical or noncommunicative uses are not uses of a work as a work, they are not subject to a fair use analysis.[28] As in *Baker*, such uses are not uses of copyright subject matter.[29]

In *Arriba Soft*, the plaintiff complains of the defendant's use of small sized reproductions of the plaintiff's photographs as thumbnails to facilitate the operation of the defendant's digital search engine. There is no doubt on the facts that (a) the plaintiff's photographs are works of authorship subject to copyright protection, (b) the plaintiff holds the copyright therein, and (c) the defendant copied the plaintiff's photographs. The defendant argues that his reproduction of the plaintiff's photographs as thumbnails for the purposes of digital searching is a fair use.[30]

The fair use factors in United States jurisprudence are the purpose and character of the use, the nature of the work, the amount and substantiality of the use, and the effect of the use on the potential market for or the value of the work. The Court's treatment in *Arriba Soft* of the purpose and character of the use factor is particularly instructive:

> Although Arriba made exact replications of Kelly's images, the thumbnails were much smaller, lower-resolution images that served an entirely different function than Kelly's original images. Kelly's images are artistic works intended to inform and to engage the viewer in an aesthetic experience. His images are used to portray scenes from the American West in an aesthetic manner. Arriba's use of Kelly's images in the thumbnails is unrelated to any aesthetic purpose. Arriba's search engine functions as a tool to help index and improve access to images on the internet and their related web sites. In fact, users are unlikely to enlarge the thumbnails and use them for artistic purposes because the thumbnails are of much lower-resolution than the originals; any enlargement results in a significant loss of clarity of the image, making them inappropriate as display material.[31]

The use in *Arriba Soft* is analogous to the use in *Baker*. Arriba's use is not of Kelly's work as a work (i.e., as a portrayal of "scenes from the American West in an aesthetic manner") but rather as an aspect of an investigative tool (i.e., a digital search engine). The fact that the small reproductions are unlikely to be enlarged by users is evidence that the use is not some kind of disguised use of the work as such. On the *Baker* analysis, the thumbnails are an instance of nonuse, no more an infringement of the copyright in Kelly's photographs than Baker's use of the accounting forms as accounting forms is an infringement of the copyright in Selden's book.

But once the *Baker* analysis is applied to determine that the use in *Arriba Soft* is an instance of nonuse, the subsequent application of the fair use factors is unnecessary. The determination that the work has not been used makes redundant a series of questions about the nature of the work, the amount and substantiality of the use, or the effect of the use on the potential market for or the value of the work. The plaintiff in *Arriba Soft* is no more entitled to value arising from nonuse of his work than the plaintiff in *Baker* is entitled, on the basis of his copyright, to value arising from the defendant's use of the accounting forms as inventions rather than works. Selden's copyright in his book is no more an entitlement in or to the operation of his accounting system than Kelly's copyright in his photographs is an entitlement in or to methods of searching for his photographs digitally.

The point is not that no market or potential market for Kelly's photographs as thumbnails in a digital search engine exists or can exist. After all, a thriving market for Selden's accounting forms as accounting forms more than certainly existed. That market was indeed the engine and prize of litigation. The point, rather, is that the fact that copyright law protects works of authorship does not mean that copyright law protects any and all uses of a work's material form from which value can be derived. In both *Baker* and *Arriba Soft,* the defendant's use of the work's material form is not a use of the work of authorship. The term "nonuse" captures situations of that kind. The defendant escapes liability not because her unauthorized use is fair but because it is not a use.

The impression that fair use is an appropriate category in cases of nonuse is rooted in the assumption that any and all uses of a work's material form are uses of the work. There can be no doubt, for example, that in *Arriba Soft* the defendant's thumbnails are "exact replications" of the plaintiff's photographs.[32] But this is but a bare physical fact, an identity at the level of material form. It is only on the assumption that a work and its material form are the same that this bare physical fact can give rise to the juridical proposition that the defendant's thumbnails are an actionable use of the plaintiff's work, triggering thereby application of the fair use defense. That assumption, however, is at odds with *Baker.* That a work has (or must have) material form does not mean that it *is* its material form. The action in *Arriba Soft* can proceed to a fair use analysis only on the basis of an equation of the work with its material form. This equation is not uncontroversial. On the contrary, it is inconsistent with the foundational principle of independent creation, which entails that multiple works can exist as the same material form and which is therefore premised on the distinction between a work and its material form.

Saint George and the Squirrel

The distinction between a work and its material form is operative in other instances of the conflicted relation between copyright law and digital technology. Consider the simple act of Internet browsing. The technology involved in displaying a webpage on a computer requires making temporary copies. To browse is to reproduce. Few would question that the practice is lawful, of course. Generally speaking, its legality is construed either as a statutory "exception" to copyright infringement, or under the rubric of "implied license."[33] In either case, however, browsing appears as *prima facie* unlawful, yet saved, as it were, through the imposition of a statutory exception to what would otherwise be unlawful, or through the implication of some sort of authorization from the person whose rights would otherwise be infringed. On the implied licensee approach, for example, the view is that browsing is lawful because, by posting the work online, the poster is granting an implied license to others to reproduce that work in order to view it. It is as if reading digitally incurs royalties that the copyright owner is deemed to forgive, or that the copyright owner is deprived of by virtue of the legislation.

The distinction between a work and its material form provides a framing of the issue that avoids the contorted mystery of postulating a right that is immediately denied. The temporary reproductions involved in browsing are copies of the material form of the work, not of the work as a work. They are but likenesses, semblances technically required for the completion of the poster's own act in respect of the work, not communicative dealings with the work *qua* work on the browser's part. There is no *novus actus* somehow transforming the browser into a wrongdoer. The browser is doing nothing more—and nothing less—than reading a work. She requires neither permissions nor exceptions.

Like browsing, "caching," too, is about likenesses technically involved in the operation of the Internet. In *Canadian Ass'n of Internet Providers v. Society of Composers, Authors, & Music Publishers of Canada,* the Supreme Court of Canada held that "'[c]aching' is dictated by the need to deliver faster and more economic service, and should not, when undertaken only for such technical reasons, attract copyright liability."[34] The Court reached this conclusion on the basis of the public interest in "the economy and cost-effectiveness of the Internet 'conduit.'"[35] But the appeal to the public interest is unnecessary. Like browsing, caching is about technically necessary reproductions of the material form of the work, not of the work *qua* work. It would truly be a melancholy state of affairs for copyright jurisprudence if something as utterly fundamental to the very operation of the Internet required the force of a public interest exception to sustain its lawfulness. One need not summon St. George to slay a squirrel.

The statutory exception, implied license and/or public interest approaches are understandable, yet less than successful efforts to cloak the rupture between digital technology and an unsustainable version of copyright law that deems any and all copying as *prima facie* unlawful. The traditional yet foundational principle of independent creation is far more helpful and straightforward. Because it construes the work as a communicative act, it can more readily identify and name nonuses of a work that, as such, cannot fall within the purview of the copyright therein. Browsing is no more an exception than reading is unlawful.

The encounter between copyright law and the digital environment is an encounter between a body of law apparently suspicious of copying and a revolutionary technology—of which the search engine in *Arriba Soft,* and the instances of browsing and caching, are but salient examples—that irremediably operates through copying. The possibilities of a rapprochement are, no doubt, many and manifold, but none can afford to overlook the crucial distinction between a work—conceived as a communicative act—and its material form. Copyright, to recall the definition provided in the Canadian *Copyright Act,* is the exclusive right to "reproduce the work . . . in any material form."[36] The crucial observation to bring into relief is that an exclusive right to reproduce the *work* in any material form is not an exclusive right to reproduce the *material form* of the work. Nonuse is nonactionable. It is reproduction not of the work but only of its material form. The challenge of the digital environment is not to impose juridical limits on the scope of the copyright holder's fetishized right over a work's material form. It is rather to pierce through the reification of the work as a thing. Written in 1879, *Baker v. Selden* remains the most far-reaching reflection available on the relation between copyright law and digital technology.

Beyond Reproduction

Baker's reach is certainly not confined to the digital context, of course. The logic of the decision can contribute to the resolution of copyright conundrums elsewhere. Consider, to give but one example, the issue of the copyrightability of patent specifications. Assume that a patentee has submitted to the Patent Office as part of her patent specification certain diagrams disclosing her invention. Also assume that these diagrams are copyrightable as artistic works, and that, because the invention disclosed is a reproduction of those diagrams "in any material form," the construction of the invention infringes the copyright in the diagrams.[37] Thus, *prima facie* it would seem that both during and after the expiration of the patent, the patentee has a cause of action in copyright against unauthorized construction of the invention disclosed in her drawings. If this option were pursued after the expiration of the patent, the copyright would have the effect of providing a "back-door" extension of the patentee's monopoly, even if it would not, of course, protect the patentee against independent creation.

Courts have handled this difficulty by appeal to a concept of deemed abandonment of the relevant copyrights in patent drawings.[38] The concept of deemed abandonment, however, seems less than accurate. The point is not so much that the patentee has a right—albeit deemed abandoned or licensed by implication—to rely on her copyright in the patent diagrams, but rather that her copyright does not from the very outset encompass noncommunicative uses of the diagrams; that is, nonuse of the work as a work. Thus, reproduction of the diagrams as posters (or perhaps even as three-dimensional models) would be actionable.[39] But reproduction of the diagrams as working inventions would fall outside the legitimate domain of the copyright, not because the patentee has abandoned or licensed the latter reproduction, but because it was not within the purview of her right to begin with.[40]

The issues involved in the copyrightability of patent specifications are analogous to those raised in the relation between the forms-as-work and the forms-as-invention in *Baker*. Thus, holding that reproduction of patent diagrams as working inventions does not infringe the copyright in the artistic works is the same as holding that the operation of the accounting system does not infringe the copyright in Selden's book. Similarly, holding that reproduction of the patent diagrams as artistic works does infringe the copyright therein is the same as holding that reproduction of the forms-as-work infringes the copyright in Selden's book. The nonuse of the diagrams as inventions triggers no further copyright issues. The use of the diagrams as works, however, need not be the end of the analysis. Use of the diagrams in an accounting journal to describe, explain, report, review, and criticize Selden's system, for example, would give rise to a fair use or fair dealing analysis. Once nonuse has been withdrawn from the purview of an author's entitlement, the operations of copyright remain intact, as capable as always to grapple with its own specific set of issues and problems, free from the confusion of ideas that mistakenly lends copyright significance to noncommunicative uses, and that therefore detracts from its coherence as a juridical order.

The convergence of those two analytical paths (nonuse and fair use) in respect of one and the same material form illustrates a more general observation: because it defines the work as a communicative act, the foundational principle of independent creation generates two broad kinds of limitations attendant on the right it grounds. First, there are limitations flowing from the proposition that, because it is a communicative act, a work cannot support entitlements in respect of noncommunicative uses. On the foregoing construal, noncommunicative use is nonuse. Precisely as a speaker, an author cannot claim rights inconsistent with the nature of his speech as speech. Second, there are limitations flowing from the proposition that, as a communicative act, a work of authorship invites and elicits responses from those to whom it is addressed. The lawfulness of unauthorized use reasonably necessary for these responses appears in paradigmatic instances of fair use involving transformative use of a work in another. Precisely as a speaker, an author cannot claim rights inconsistent with another's speech. Neither kind of limitation is imposed on the author, as it were externally. Rather, both flow immanently from the nature of the work as a communicative act.

Because they are but determinations of the nature of copyright subject matter, these limitations are best conceived not as exceptions but as user rights integral to the copyright system. They do not suspend or constrain the otherwise normal operation of an author's copyright. On the contrary, they guarantee that its operation remains consistent with its origin in the principle of independent creation. They arise from and affirm the same considerations that ground the right they limit. Rather than curtailments, they are constitutive aspects of the very definition of the right.

The idea of user rights as integral to the copyright system necessarily requires a dislodging of the centrality of the concept of reproduction in copyright law.[41] Consider transformative use. At first sight it may seem difficult to characterize it as anything other than an exception—as anything other than a suspension of the normal operations of copyright law. Normally, one might say, substantial reproduction of a work in the absence of authorization amounts to infringement of the copyright therein. Transformative use, however, specifies situations in which unauthorized substantial reproduction is not infringement. Transformative use says: "There is no infringement here, even though there is substantial reproduction." Thus, if the general rule is that substantial reproduction amounts to infringement, then transformative use is a special situation to which the rule does not apply, a situation left out or excluded from the rule. In short, transformative use is nothing other than an exception to the general rule. The point, of course, is that thinking through exceptions rather as user rights requires dislodging the assumption that reproduction is the mischief that copyright law targets. User rights mean that reproduction is not *per se* wrongful.

Transformative use and nonuse both accomplish the required dislodging of the concept of reproduction by affirming, albeit in different senses, the familiar proposition that not all copying is copyright infringement. Prohibited communicative use, not any and all unauthorized use, is wrongful. Copyright is not an exclusive right to reproduce the work, but an exclusive right to reproduce the work *as a work*. Transformative use appeals to the equality as authors of the parties to a copyright action. The defendant reproduces the plaintiff's work not as a work but as a reasonably necessary aspect of the defendant's own authorial engagement. Nonuse appeals to the distinction between a work and its material form. The defendant reproduces the material form of the work but not the work as such. Both limitations make clear that copyright law is not a *prima facie* prohibition on copying but rather an institutionalized distinction between permissible and impermissible copying. Their combined operation indicates that (1) lawful copying is as constitutive of the copyright system as wrongful copying; and that (2) the wrong in wrongful copying is the repetition of another's speech in the absence of authorization.

Consider, for example, the finding that it is not an infringement of copyright to reproduce a work of authorship substantially, provided that the reproduction is for the purpose of criticism and that the reproduction is reasonably necessary to achieve that permitted purpose. It is only natural to look at this as an indication of what a defendant in a copyright action can do without fear of liability, stipulating the conditions necessary to make unauthorized reproductions lawful. Yet it is equally natural to look at this as an indication of the contours of an author's rights to her work. This shift in focus from the defendant's act to the plaintiff's right suggests that the plaintiff has exclusive rights to her work for *some* but not *all* purposes. In this example, the plaintiff has no exclusive rights to her work in respect of the purpose of criticism. For the purpose of criticism, her work is, quite literally, public domain material.

To put it otherwise, the proposition that substantial reproduction for the purpose of criticism is lawful can be understood in two ways. On the one hand, it can be understood as an assertion that fair use or fair dealing is an exception to infringement, where infringement is defined as substantial reproduction. On the other hand, it can be understood as an assertion that copyright is not an absolute right of exclusive reproduction, but rather an exclusive right of reproduction only for certain purposes that do not include, *inter alia,* the purpose of criticism. To follow the latter characterization is to conceptualize the category of purpose as internal to the definition of an author's copyright. The point is not that certain purposes excuse the defendant from liability, but rather that the plaintiff has rights to the work only when used for certain purposes. Fair use or fair dealing is not about excused wrong but about the absence of wrong. Grasped from the vantage point of the work as a communicative act, the purpose-driven definition of the right means than an author has exclusive rights not to any and all uses of her work but only to specifically communicative uses.

A very brief comparison of copyright and trademark will once again prove instructive. Recall that a trademark owner holds his mark for a particular purpose. He has an exclusive right to use the mark as a signifier of source in the marketplace, but not an exclusive right to any and all uses of the mark. My reproduction of the word "Corona" here, for example, is not a trademark infringement because it is not a use of the word as an indicator of source in the marketplace. I am not selling you or trying to sell you beer. Thus my use of the word "Corona" is not a use of the trademark *as a trademark*. To capture this, we might say that the trademark *is* its use as a distinctive indicator of source. The right that the law of trademark confers is not an exclusive right over the mark as a thing. It is rather an exclusive right to perform a certain act in respect of the "thing"—that is, an exclusive right to use what we might call the material form of the trademark as a trademark. Thus, merely reproducing another's trademark in an academic discussion is no more trademark infringement than using another's work fairly for the purpose of criticism is copyright infringement.[42]

Holding a work is in one important respect similar to holding a trademark. If holding a trademark means having an exclusive right to use the mark *as a trademark*, i.e., using it for the particular purpose of distinguishing goods or services, then holding a work means having an exclusive right to use the work *as a work*, i.e., using it for the particular purpose of communicating it to another. To copy a work is neither to respond to it in one's own nor to reproduce it mechanically as a mere pattern of ink on a piece of paper. Rather, to copy it is to recommunicate it.

In short, the principle of independent creation entails that the paradigmatic wrong in copyright is not unauthorized reproduction but unauthorized publication. It is the act of recommunication, not of merely physical reproduction, that triggers the operations of copyright law. As we shall presently see in Chapter 4, copyright law protects an author's choice to speak or not to speak. The mischief it targets is compelled speech. The question is not whether the defendant's copy extracts value from the plaintiff's labor but whether the impugned copy impinges on the plaintiff's autonomy as a speaking being. This is the mischief that elevates the infringement inquiry from the physics of mere copying to the jurisprudence of copyright.

4

Infringement as Compelled Speech

The principle of independent creation posits that the subject matter of copyright law is a communicative act. It insists that copyright is about expression, not patterns of ink; words, not things. At stake is a right not over the material form of a work but only over its specifically communicative use. The right attendant on speaking in one's own words is thus a right to preclude others from repeating one's speech.

What is it, then, about the act of speaking in one's own words that entitles the speaker to prevent others from repeating it? What plausible justification could such an entitlement invoke?

The dominant justification, certainly in North America but more than likely globally, is incentive-based. The right to preclude others from repeating one's speech is designed to provide incentives for the speaking itself. The public interest in the production of works of authorship would no doubt remain unsatisfied were copyright not to step in to protect the required investments from piracy. By the same token, the limits imposed on the rights granted are but the manifestation of the public interest in the dissemination of works of authorship. Were the rights granted not balanced against the imperatives of further creativity and of access to its products, their very *raison d'être* would be undermined. The dominant paradigm has thus been aptly referred to as the "incentive-access paradigm."[1]

The trouble with it is that, notwithstanding its popularity, it is singularly unpersuasive. Empirically, it is by no means clear that copyright law facilitates rather than hinders creativity. Even its most ardent proponents tell us as much quite candidly.[2] Conceptually, as I argued in Chapter 1, the paradigm cannot account for basic copyright distinctions. Nothing immediately apparent in the concept of the public interest, for example, requires that the investments involved in collecting factual information should never enjoy copyright protection, and that those involved in the creation of poetry should always do so. The doctrine of originality, however, does just that, and not accidentally but—to use the language of *Feist Publications Inc. v. Rural Telephone Service Co. Inc.*—as a matter of "bedrock principle" and "constitutional requirement."[3] The doctrine of originality consistently and unabashedly discriminates in favor of bad poetry and against great information, as if being badly informed and badly entertained were indeed both a requirement of the United States Constitution and a copyright goal. That the doctrine of originality produces that result is not an argument against it. It is rather an indication that, from the very outset, the incentive-access paradigm has difficulty grappling with basic copyright distinctions. Justification of the central copyright entitlement to preclude others from repeating one's speech must be sought—or at the very least explored—elsewhere.

In a brief 1785 essay entitled "On the Wrongfulness of Unauthorized Publication of Books," Immanuel Kant formulated the insight that, considered as the work of an author, a book is not a thing but a "speech to the public."[4] Elsewhere Kant defines a book as "a writing . . . which represents a discourse that someone delivers to the public by visible linguistic signs."[5] Adopting Kant's insight, the argument I want to present in this chapter is that because a work subject to copyright is the "*speech* of a person," infringement of the right attendant on the work is best grasped as a disposing of another's speech in the absence of her authorization.[6] As Kant puts it, "[t]his right of the author is . . . not a right to the thing, namely to the copy (for the owner can burn it before the author's eyes), but an innate right in his own person, namely, to prevent another from having him speak to the public without his consent. . . ."[7]

Kant's insight into copyright subject matter as a speech to the public thus gives rise to an understanding of copyright infringement as compelled speech. Copyright infringement is ventriloquism practiced on an unwilling subject. The infringer speaks not from his mouth but from his belly, making it seem that it is another who speaks. This seeming is the wrong to this other, whose mouth is being moved, so to speak, behind her back. The depth of the wrongfulness of copyright infringement is nothing other than this unauthorized use of another's speech to deny her the very autonomy manifested in and through her speech. It is as if the infringer were using another's speech to prove that this other is not worthy of the respect she is owed as a speaking being. An author's right to preclude the repetition of her own speech is justified as an affirmation of the author's autonomy as a speaking being.

While Kantian, the argument I offer is not Kant's. In other words, I am less concerned with an exegesis of a philosophical text than I am with an account of copyright law.[8] Accordingly, I have set forth in Chapters 1 through 3 the proposition that a work is a communicative act not by appeal to Kant's text but through exegeses of well-settled copyright doctrines. Analyses of originality, the idea/expression dichotomy, merger, transformative use and nonuse (as I have called the *Baker* doctrine) reveal, elucidate, and confirm a view of the work subject to copyright as a speaking in one's own words. Copyright doctrine is on this view nothing more than a systematic elaboration of the principle of independent creation.

The insight that a work is a speaking in one's own words grounds the proposition that copyright infringement is compelled speech. The argument in this chapter takes off from the intuition that an infringement of the right of first publication is an instance of compelled speech—that is, the defendant publishes the plaintiff's unpublished work without the plaintiff's authorization.[9] I canvass several explanations of what the intuition brings into relief. The upshot is that the wrong to which the intuition reacts is not that the defendant's unauthorized publication breaches the plaintiff's privacy; misrepresents the plaintiff's work; fails to attribute the plaintiff's work; or converts the plaintiff's property conceived either as property in the physical manuscript or as property in the work construed as a metaphysical chattel. Rather, the intuition goes to the fact that the defendant's publication is unauthorized. From a copyright perspective, the fact that the publication is also of unpublished work is of secondary significance.

The chapter first finds that the privacy, misrepresentation and misattribution options all fail to capture the copyright-specific significance of the wrong involved in unauthorized publication of unpublished work for the same reason. They each focus, albeit in different senses, on the content of the unauthorized publication rather than the fact of unauthorized publication. Privacy inquires into the content of the unauthorized publication with an eye to assessing whether the information conveyed is personal, and on that basis subject to protection. Misrepresentation takes up the accuracy or lack thereof of the content of the unauthorized publication. And misattribution targets the unauthorized publication as content to which the name of the author is (or not) attached. From a copyright-specific perspective, however, an entirely impersonal, accurate and duly attributed publication is wrongful if unauthorized. The wrong goes to the very fact of publication, not its content. It goes to the author's prerogative whether to publish, not to the published content.

The property option, too, is misguided due to a focus on content. The issue here is the assumption that a work of authorship can be regarded as an object of ownership, as owned content. The author's choice whether to publish or not, however, is not an object but a prerogative. Its specificity cannot be adequately captured under the rubric of ownership. Thus the property option is misplaced because, as the principle of independent creation teaches, the copyright-relevant factor is the form of expression as such, neither its content nor itself as content.

With the distinction between form and content in the foreground, the chapter returns to the privacy option in order to take issue with the celebrated article by Warren and Brandeis, "The Right to Privacy."[10] In "The Right to Privacy," Warren and Brandeis seek in existing law a foundation for a privacy action. They find it in the law of unpublished works. Thus they postulate that (a) the jurisdiction of copyright law properly so-called is restricted to published works, and that (b) the law of unpublished works is rather privacy law masquerading under another name. Privacy comes to occupy exclusively, as it were imperialistically, the field of unpublished works. Copyright begins only where privacy ends, upon publication of the work. While noting that when "The Right to Privacy" was written the US copyright statute did not apply to unpublished works, I nevertheless show that, conceptually, its privacy-imperialism in respect of unpublished works stands in the way of the development of a unified theory of copyright, focused not on the bifurcation of the unpublished or published status of the content of a work, but rather on the author's irreducible prerogative whether to publish. What is required is not a bifurcation of the unpublished and the published but rather a distinction between the meaning of publication in copyright and the meaning of publication in privacy. It is only when examined through a privacy optic that the act of voluntary publication amounts to a deprivation of protected subject matter—a kind of disclosure that deprives the subject matter of its privacy. From a copyright perspective, publication neither can nor does deprive a work of its originality. An author does not deprive herself of the prerogative to publish by virtue of exercising it. The intuition of the wrongfulness of unauthorized publication of unpublished work is thus applicable to unauthorized publication *simpliciter*.

In short, the thread I develop in this chapter is that no meaningful normative distinction can be drawn on a copyright basis between unauthorized publication of unpublished work and unauthorized (re) publication of (already) published work. What matters in either instance is that, in the absence of authorization, the defendant disposes of the plaintiff's speech. *Author*ization is the author's paradigmatic prerogative. Infringement of the right of first publication is not qualitatively distinct from copyright infringement generally. A unified theory of copyright formulates the wrongfulness of pre- and postpublication infringement from a single point of view: whether of unpublished or published work, unauthorized publication is compelled speech.

Privacy, Misrepresentation, Misattribution

As I just noted, the view that copyright infringement is compelled speech is intuitively available in the case of unauthorized publication of *unpublished* work. Unauthorized publication of unpublished work is publication outside the conditions of the author's consent or voluntariness. Because the author did not consent to the publication, the publication is a forcing her to speak. Unauthorized publication can thus be characterized as a wrong to a right to remain silent. Because the right of first publication is a clearly recognized aspect of an author's copyright, this characterization supports the view that, at least in one of its determinations, copyright infringement impinges on the author's autonomy as a speaker.

It is more difficult, however, to characterize the unauthorized republication of *published* work as a matter of compelled speech. If an author has already spoken, and has done so voluntarily, in what way can it be said that her autonomy is impinged because another reprints her work without her consent? To wrench unpublished work from an author's hands, so to speak, and to thrust it upon the public in the absence of her authorization, does seem to involve a violation of her autonomy. But it seems more far-fetched to characterize an unauthorized repetition of her published work as an autonomy violation. The repetition of published speech seems less a matter of compelled speech than of disseminating voluntary speech.

It goes without saying that this distinction between pre- and post-publication situations is extremely important. If copyright is anything at all, then it must be a postpublication right. Any and all versions of copyright law must account for an author's claim in respect of *published* work. Thus, the intuition that unauthorized publication is wrongful because it amounts to compelled speech can be helpful in an account of copyright infringement only to the extent that it is applicable also to the postpublication situation. In what way, then, can the intuition that unauthorized publication of unpublished work is wrongful help to account for the wrongfulness of unauthorized publication of published work?

I want to posit a continuity between pre- and postpublication situations. My point is that the wrongfulness of unauthorized publication of unpublished work has nothing to do with the work's unpublished status. The wrong is in the *unauthorized* nature of the publication, not in the fact that it is a publication of unpublished work. Thus an intuition into the wrongfulness of unauthorized publication of unpublished work is also an intuition into the wrongfulness of unauthorized publication of published work. At stake is unauthorized publication, whether of unpublished or published work. Analyzing the intuition further, so as to grasp more precisely what it is, and what it is not, will yield that conclusion.

To begin with, it is clear that, from a copyright standpoint, the wrong in unauthorized publication of unpublished work is not that the publication amounts to a violation of privacy. Unauthorized publication amounts to copyright infringement even where the publication reveals nothing previously unavailable to the public. Consider, for example, a celebrity's autobiography containing only material already made public in an earlier biography. The attraction of the autobiography is not that it reveals new material but that it presents the old material in the celebrity's own words. Unauthorized publication of the autobiography is still copyright infringement. That is, unauthorized publication infringes copyright even in the absence of any breach of privacy. This is because the infringed right is not a right to privacy but a right of first publication. The author's complaint is not that his privacy has been violated but that his autonomy as a speaker—his right to speak or not to speak—has been ignored.

Of course, breach of privacy need not be narrowly confined to situations involving unauthorized disclosure of previously undisclosed personal information. Privacy may be conceived as involving not only previously undisclosed personal information, but also the very transmission or use of personal information—regardless of previous disclosure—in varying contexts.[11] In this vein, use of personal information for a purpose other than that for which it was previously disclosed may amount to a breach of privacy. Unauthorized publication of a celebrity's autobiography can thus be characterized as a breach of privacy even if the autobiography contains no previously undisclosed personal information. From that point of view, the unauthorized publication of the unpublished autobiography could involve both breach of privacy and copyright infringement. Still, whereas the privacy analysis would target the defendant's unauthorized dealings with personal information, the copyright analysis would target the defendant's unauthorized dealings with a work of authorship. Interference with the plaintiff's privacy is not the same as interference with her choice to speak or not to speak.

While privacy and copyright could each come to bear on the fact of unauthorized publication of unpublished work, the distinction between "personal information" and "work of authorship" would ensure that each regime would construe that fact from its own distinct juridical standpoint. Just as privacy law does not require that the personal information in issue be "original" in the copyright sense, so does copyright law not require that a work of authorship be "personal" in the privacy sense. Unauthorized disclosure or use of personal information in an unpublished autobiography would amount to a breach of privacy even if no part of the actual text of the manuscript were published. This is breach of privacy in the absence of copyright infringement. Similarly, unauthorized publication of substantial parts of the actual text of the manuscript would amount to copyright infringement even if the published parts involved no personal information. This is copyright infringement in the absence of breach of privacy. That privacy and copyright may overlap over identical facts, especially in the case of unpublished works of authorship, need not obscure the fundamental distinction between the causes of action.

Thus, for example, unauthorized publication by a third party of an unauthorized biography containing undisclosed personal information amounts to an infringement of the *author's* copyright and to a breach of the *subject's* privacy. Where A writes a book containing undisclosed personal information about B, C's publication of the work without authorization from either A or B amounts both to an infringement of A's copyright and to a breach of B's privacy. The distinction between the two causes of action would in that instance arise also as a distinction between plaintiffs. Privacy and copyright are distinct juridical regimes addressing categorically distinct interests. This is why the intuition that there is something wrong with unauthorized publication of unpublished work cannot be fully captured as a privacy matter. The intuition persists even where no breach of privacy obtains.

The special difficulty with the privacy aspect of the issue is that the intuition in respect of the wrongfulness of unauthorized publication of an unpublished work is over-determined. It simultaneously includes breach of privacy and copyright infringement aspects. This makes it possible to suspect that if we were to remove the breach of privacy aspect, the force of the intuition as to the wrongfulness of the act would in fact dissolve with it. Any remaining sense of wrong is perhaps but a residue of privacy intuitions. What could possibly be wrong, after all, with disseminating information made public by the author herself?

One can readily imagine a defendant charged with unauthorized publication of an unpublished work containing nothing but previously available information addressing the plaintiff as follows: "I am not sure what bothers you so. Nothing in the manuscript reveals anything about you that was not known before. Every single detail has either been already told by others or, indeed, discussed by you yourself in previous publications. It is not as if I have in any way impinged upon your privacy."

The plaintiff's rejoinder is as readily available: "I am not worried about my privacy. You know me better than that. I am annoyed that you have disposed of my work as though it were some kind of thing you found on the street. You disposed of my words as if I were your puppet, devoid of choice as to when it says what it says. I really cannot understand what makes you feel entitled to move my mouth for me. There is a time to speak and a time to remain silent. Your act has deprived me of my choice."

The intuition as to the wrongfulness of unauthorized publication stands, perhaps even more forcefully, when privacy concerns are removed. Our plaintiff's point is that speaking in one's own words means that the words must be spoken at a time of one's own choice. Otherwise they are not one's own, for in that case it is another who speaks.

Nor is the wrong in unauthorized publication of unpublished work a matter of misrepresentation. Unauthorized publication is wrongful even if entirely faithful to the original. Accurate yet unauthorized publication of our celebrity's unpublished autobiography is still copyright infringement. This is because the infringed right is not a right to accurate representation but a right of first publication. Once again, the problem is not that the author has been misrepresented but that his autonomy as a speaker has been ignored. Our plaintiff's complaint is not that the puppeteer has made him say what he wouldn't have said but, simply, that he has been made to speak at all—that his choice whether to speak has been removed.

In fact, the wrong involved in unauthorized publication of unpublished work is the very opposite of whatever wrong is involved in misrepresentation. The greater the misrepresentation, the less plausible would the plaintiff's claim be that the defendant has published his work. Where the defendant attaches the plaintiff's name to another's work, the wrong is not in misuse of the plaintiff's work but in misuse of the plaintiff's name.

This is just not the wrong of unauthorized publication of unpublished work. We are concerned here with the author as author, not with the author's name as trademark. In contrast to the wrong of misrepresentation, the wrong of unauthorized publication presupposes an accurate representation of the plaintiff's work. The wrong is not that the defendant has made the plaintiff's speak someone else's words, but precisely that the defendant has made him speak his own words. We might say the problem is not that you are making me salute the flag before others against my convictions but that, precisely as a patriot, I salute the flag each and every time, whether before others or not, as my own choice to do so.[12]

Finally, one might be tempted to suggest that the wrong in unauthorized publication of unpublished work has something to do with lack of attribution, as when I publish someone else's work under the pretense that it is mine (what we commonly call plagiarism), or when I publish someone else's work and credit no one or someone other than the author. But that is clearly not the wrong at issue. The author's right of first publication is infringed even if the author is duly acknowledged. Proper acknowledgement is no defense because the complaint is not lack of attribution but rather infringement of the author's autonomy as a speaker, of her choice to speak or not to speak.

It may even be suggested that, paradoxically, it is the very lack of attribution that would provide the defense. In what sense is an author compelled to speak when she who publishes his work without authorization fails to attach his name to the work? The suggestion is intriguing but unconvincing. The problem is that the defendant has treated the plaintiff as a puppet, not that others know about this. The wrong is not mediated through another's knowledge of it. It is no less a wrong if secret. The problem is that you are making me salute the flag, not that you are making me salute the flag before others. That I am wearing a mask while doing so, or that onlookers believe me to be someone else, does not undo the wrong.

Property

It is even harder to argue that the wrong in unauthorized publication of unpublished work is somehow a wrong against the author's property. This view could take one of two forms, one focusing on the author's property in the unpublished manuscript conceived as a chattel, and the other focusing on the author's work conceived as a kind of metaphysical chattel. Neither view can account for the wrong in unauthorized publication of unpublished work.

The wrong at stake is certainly not the wrong in using the author's manuscript, in the sense of pages with patterns of ink imprinted on them, without his consent. Copyright infringement is not conversion. If I borrow your pen to write a short story in your notebook, your ownership of ink and pages does not deprive me of my copyright. You can no more publish the poem without infringing my copyright than I can rip the pages out of your notebook without infringing your property right. Similarly, if the author of the work and the owner of the ink and pages happen to be the same person, as in the usual case where I write a short story in my notebook with my pen, the distinction between the copyright claim and the proprietary claim nonetheless remains valid. Unauthorized publication of my unpublished short story is wrongful in its own right, so to speak, and not because it may have also involved, as a proprietary matter, conversion of my manuscript. From a copyright perspective, the right infringed is a right of first publication, not a property right in a chattel.

Nor can the wrong in unauthorized publication of unpublished work be captured as a conversion of, or trespass on, the work conceived as a metaphysical chattel. If the work were conceived as a metaphysical chattel, such that any and all uses of the work could be regarded as *prima facie* infringing, then the act of reading the work, for example, would presumptively count as infringement. Of course, there is no known formulation of copyright law that construes reading as infringing, whether presumptively or otherwise.

More importantly, as I argued in Chapter 2, the principle of independent creation entails that a work is not a thing but a communicative act, not an object of ownership but the speech of a subject. To say it once more, if a work were an object of ownership, copyright infringement would amount to a conversion of, or trespass on, the owned object, and independent creation could no more be constitutive of an independent copyright than finding a lost chattel would grant the finder property rights against the true owner. The propertization of copyright subject matter is inconsistent with the fundamental principle of independent creation. Copyright involves relations not between a person and her possessions but between a person, her speech and the public to which it is addressed. Yet the view of copyright as some kind of proprietary entitlement is so pervasive, and its gravitational force so powerful, that I want at this point to return to the issue to deepen the observations made in Chapter 2.

What I want to do is compare and contrast originality in copyright and first possession in property. Because it specifies the mode of acquisition in copyright law, the originality requirement is analogous to the requirement of first possession or occupation in property law. Just as originality describes what a person must do in order to constitute herself as an author for copyright law purposes, so does first possession describe what a person must do in order to constitute herself as an owner for property law purposes.

Analysis of this homology will reveal a truly striking correspondence between two parallel distinctions: (a) the distinction between the intention to possess and the fact of possession—*animus possidendi* and *factum possidendi*—in property law, and (b) the distinction between idea and expression in copyright law. I develop the correspondence through a juxtaposition of a classic first possession case, *Pierson v. Post,* and a classic idea/expression case, *Nichols v. Universal Pictures Corporation.*[13] So striking is the correspondence that it indeed suggests that no distinction can be drawn between property and copyright on the grounds of the tangibility or lack thereof of the subject matter in each body of law. Thus the point of developing the homology at length is to show that emphasis on the intangibility of a work of authorship is in fact radically insufficient to bring into relief its specificity vis-à-vis an object of ownership.

We must seek that specificity elsewhere. I find it on the very surface of *Feist.* Albeit intangible, facts are not subject to copyright. Copyright subject matter is what it is not because it is intangible but because it is communicative. What the juxtaposition of originality and first possession brings more deeply into relief is that the nature of the exclusionary act involved in speech is far more elusive than it is in first possession, as in the classic example of capture of a wild animal. The hunter ensnares his prey, draws boundaries around it to tell the world to keep out. Property law makes available to the hunter the coercive apparatus of the state to ensure that those who do not listen must at least behave as if they do.

The speaker, by contrast, cannot help but share. As a matter of copyright law, she invites responses (fair use) and contributes ideas (idea/expression dichotomy) at the very moment at which she claims exclusivity in respect of her expression (originality). She cannot do otherwise. Thus fair use, for example, is not some legislatively institutionalized "taking" of her objects of ownership or the value thereof. It is a necessary incident of the very act of authorship whereby her copyright arises. Fair use literally drops out of the author's mouth as she speaks. This is because the subject matter of her ownership is not a thing—whether intangible or otherwise—but a communicative act. Thus, the wrong in copyright cannot be adequately captured in proprietary terms. To wrong someone in respect of her authorship is not to trespass on her ownership but to compel her to speak.

In *Pierson,* plaintiff Post was pursuing a fox. Just as he was about to capture the fox, defendant Pierson caught, killed, and ran off with the fox, and so prevented Post from getting at his intended prey. Post is the frustrated pursuer. Pierson is the "saucy intruder."[14] It is common ground between the litigants that first possession, or occupation, constitutes a property right to a previously unowned object. The question before the court is whether, by virtue of his pursuit, Post had already constituted a right to the fox such that he could sustain an action against the saucy intruder.

The Court answers the question in the negative. Nothing short of mortal wounding by one not abandoning pursuit is sufficient to constitute possession.[15] Mere pursuit, even if such pursuit has reached a reasonable prospect of capture, is not enough.[16] Thus the saucy intruder gets the fox: "However uncourteous or unkind the conduct of Pierson towards Post, in this instance, may have been, yet this act was productive of no injury or damage for which a legal remedy can be applied."[17]

Let me start by saying a word or two about the figure whom I take to be the silent and ignored, yet in my view, indisputable protagonist of the case: the fox. I want to start by talking about the silence of the fox. Imagine the following scenario. Imagine that it is not Pierson who intrudes to kill and take away the fox that was about to become Post's. Imagine, rather, that another fox appears on the scene. Call it Fox 2. So now we have Post about to capture Fox 1, and instead of Pierson, we have Fox 2. Assume now that just as Post is about to capture Fox 1, Fox 2 intrudes at the last moment, kills Fox 1 by biting its neck, and carries it off. You will agree with me that it does not occur to us (or at least it does not occur to property law as we know it) to ask whether Post could sustain a cause of action against Fox 2 in respect of Fox 1, which he was about to capture. On the contrary, if immediately after Fox 2 intrudes on the scene to bite Fox 1, Post smiles gleefully and ensnares either or both foxes, it is clear that Post has indeed constituted a property right to either or both foxes by virtue of the operation of the rule of first possession.

The silence of the fox, then, signifies its exclusion from the community of entities whose voice is recognized as a voice that counts, whose acts are worthy of respect. When the fox screams because a hunter mortally wounds it, we do not ask it to tell us its story. On the contrary, we kill it to silence it. But when a hunter screams because another hunter snaps up a prey about to be captured, then we find ourselves before a very difficult question about the origins of ownership, and we in fact ask both hunters to tell us their stories. The point is simply that persons, not animals, have standing as owners, as entities capable of claiming entitlements through their acts, as beings whose stories get a hearing. An entirely different set of concerns would have arisen, for example, had Pierson ensnared and killed Post rather than the fox. The lesson we learn by listening to the silence of the fox is that *Pierson,* a classic first possession case, proceeds on the twofold assumption that (1) there is a categorical difference between persons and nonpersons (i.e., foxes, or things in general), and that (2) Pierson and Post are each of them a person. Thus, the case is a dispute between persons about who gets to keep a thing.

There is a third proposition that we can now state. If a distinction between persons and things is at the heart of the case, as indeed it is, then the case must be resolved in a manner that respects that distinction. Neither of the parties can be treated as a mere fox. Neither of the parties can be silenced—or treated as if it were nothing more than a means to the satisfaction of the other party's desire. That is what the fox is, and that is why it is dead: silent or silenced. As far as the law of property is concerned, the fox is a mere object of desire, a mere thing whose claim to be a part of the legal story is only that two persons want it simultaneously. We bother about the fox not because we care about the fox *per se,* but because the parties or persons involved have something to say about the fox. The fox has no independent status or meaning here. Only the parties do. And because each and both of them do, we cannot resolve the dispute by denying either of them that status. We must arrive at the decision of who is legitimately entitled to the fox in a manner that is respectful not only of the winner's but also of the loser's status as a person. That is, we must decide the conflict between persons by being respectful of the principle of personality that, according to the case's own presuppositions, each of them equally embodies. On this view, the case is not only about the difference between persons and things, but also about the litigants' equality as persons. In fact, to speak about the equality of the litigants as persons is but another way of saying that there is a difference between persons and things.

Yet, the mere assertion that the two parties are persons does not help us decide the case. We need to fill this out a bit more, so as to enable us to decide the case. So far we can hear Pierson saying: "Hey, I am a person." But we can also hear Post saying: "Hey, I am a person." We cannot disagree with either of them on that score, yet given the structure of the legal action we must find a way to give one of them, and not the other, the fox.

What, then, does it mean to be a person, and how does the principle of personality help us decide the case?

There is no need to ask anyone but the Court, or rather the law of property, to answer this question. Here is what the Court says: "That is to say, that actual bodily seizure is not indispensable to acquire right to, or possession of, wild beasts; but that, on the contrary, the mortal wounding of such beasts, by one not abandoning his pursuit, may, with the utmost propriety, be deemed possession of him; since, thereby, the pursuer manifests an unequivocal intention of appropriating the animal to his individual use, has deprived him of his natural liberty, and brought him within his certain control."[18] When the Court thinks about the difference between persons and foxes, it thinks about the formation of a specific kind of intent—*animus possidendi*—in respect of the world. To be a person is to be capable of intending to appropriate objects in the world in a manner that, so far as the rule of first possession is concerned, foxes cannot intend.

Of course, in the Court's eyes, intent alone is not sufficient to make out a claim of first possession. It is not enough for Post to say that he thought about the fox first, that he saw the fox first, or even that he was the first to form an intent to appropriate in respect of the fox. If the night before the hunt he dreamed that he caught the fox, that is just not enough. These merely internal or subjective musings are insufficient.

We can go even further here, if we are to follow the logic of the case. We know that not even hot pursuit of the fox is enough. That is, not even manifesting one's intent in the world, such that the intent is obvious to others, is enough. Post's intent was perfectly clear to Pierson at the time that Pierson caught the fox for himself. Pierson knew very well of Post's intent to capture the fox, and the court is careful to point out to us that Pierson's saucy act lacked courtesy. But even so, the point is that intent by itself will not do. The intent must not only be unequivocally communicated to the world, so as to be outside the claimant's head. The intent must also be materialized or embodied in the world, so as to have left its mark on the object claimed. In this case, the required mark is said to be a mortal wound on the body of the fox. Not pursuit alone, nor pursuit known by another, but nothing short of mortal wounding by one not abandoning pursuit is the requirement.

The mortal wound on the body of the fox is not just a sign. It is a privileged sign. It is *the* sign that gives rise to normative relations in the eyes of the law of property. What this sign signifies is the reality not of a prospect but of an accomplishment, not of a purpose but of an achievement. I do not merely wish or desire the fox to be mine. I have made it mine by subjecting it to my control, by depriving it of its liberty, by demonstrating, as it were, that it has no significance independently of what I give it. This is why the wound must be mortal, undoing any prospect of healing. I not only intend to dominate a thing; I have actually done so. My intention to appropriate is not just a wish, but a deed, not a project but an act.

The law of first possession enshrines that deed when it says that where a person exercises control over a previously unowned thing, the person now has a proprietary claim over the thing. On that basis, the Court in *Pierson* decides in favor of the saucy intruder. The point is that the saucy intruder's capture of the fox is worthy of respect because such capture is a person's act—where an "act," as distinct from a mere intention, is nothing other than the convergence of intent and fact, *animus possidendi* and *factum possidendi.*

But in what sense is this requirement of embodiment not only consistent with, but in fact required by, the equality of the litigants as persons?

Simply put, the point is that the principle of personality requires respect for deeds but not for projects, for actions, not for intentions. My wish to capture the fox is not sufficient to restrict you from pursuing the fox yourself because pursuit of *my* purposes is in no way entitled to more respect than pursuit of *your* purposes. I cannot legitimately claim that you be restricted from pursuing the fox just because I have it in my line of sight any more than I can ask you to stop pursuing your own purposes just because they conflict with mine. To force you to give up your projects for the sake of mine would be in fact to subject you to my desire, to treat you like a fox. But by the same token, you cannot legitimately ignore the mark I have placed on the body of the fox as I subject it to my control. To disregard my completed act, my deed, as distinct from my mere project, is to disregard the fundamental proposition that, because I am a person, my acts are worthy of respect. It would be to treat me like a fox. Thus, my project to capture the fox cannot be constitutive of your obligation to forgo pursuing the fox anymore than you can ignore the wound through which I have marked the fox as mine. Respect for the equal personality of each requires that a completed act, not a mere project, be necessary for first possession.

It is true, of course, that the difference between a wish and a deed, a project and an act, an intention and an action, in any given case may not be altogether clear. The facts leading to a finding of possession—and hence of first possession—can be ambiguous.[19] Nonetheless, it is clear that mere thought is insufficient, and that actual manucaption (i.e., bodily seizure) is unnecessary. Between thinking and touching, *animus* and *factum,* there is an expanse of possible moments, a spectrum of possible points at which a court may decide that possession obtains. My point here is not that this point can be determined *a priori.* My point is that the question of where an intention has become an action, or a project a deed, is a question inseparable from a particular conception of the equality of the litigants as persons. The point is that possession is a normative, not a physical phenomenon.[20] Thus, whether possession obtains in any given set of facts is a question not only about the possessor's relation to the thing possessed, but also about her relation to other persons: it is a question about whether her claim to have constituted a special relation to the object is consistent with another's personality.

In *Pierson,* the plaintiff-pursuer had placed himself in a special relation to the contested fox. He was within a reasonable prospect of capture.

Yet the Court held that such relation is devoid of legal significance. The holding is intelligible from the standpoint of equality. The law of first possession governs the appropriation of previously unowned things. It defines the circumstances that must obtain for a person to impose upon all others an obligation they would not otherwise have. This is the obligation to abstain from use of the appropriated thing without that person's authorization. The law of first possession requires that she who claims a previously unowned thing must demonstrate control over the thing claimed. This is because ownership arising from anything short of a completed act, as evidenced by that control, would subject parties other than the claimant to the claimant's mere desire. But such subjection is incompatible with equality. The requirement that the claimant demonstrate a publicly accessible deed—and not only a mere prospect or wish—is thus rooted in the very concept of property as an interpersonal relation between equals with respect to things. It is because of equality that possession is—and must be—always already something that has been done, not something that is about to take place. One's *deed* is one's official proof of ownership.

This distinction between intention and action, wish and deed, appears also in copyright law as a distinction between idea and expression, an author's project and an author's completed work—the *animus* of his idea, we might say, and the *factum* of his expression. I argued in Chapter 2 that the exclusion of ideas from the purview of copyright structures the relation between the parties to a copyright action as a relation between equals. The affirmation of expression, and not idea, as the subject matter of copyright is a normative exercise conducted under the rubric of equality between persons. Copyrighting ideas expressed in a plaintiff's work would be inconsistent with the defendant's equal authorship. Like "possession" in property, "expression" in copyright is a normative category through and through traversed by and constructed as a relation between equals. We can pursue this homology further.

The well-known "series of abstractions" test formulated by Learned Hand in *Nichols* sets up a spectrum from generality to particularity in terms of which copyright law is said to demarcate the scope of the author's right, the level of specificity and/or generality at which expression ends and idea begins.[21] This spectrum from generality to particularity, from idea to expression, parallels the spectrum from intention to act, wish to deed, that informs the law of first possession. In copyright law, "expression" is somewhere between literal text and mere idea. Were expression restricted to the literal text, the copycat would escape through immaterial variations. But at the same time, were expression to extend beyond a certain level of generality, the author would be permitted to assert her entitlement in a manner inconsistent with another's authorship. Similarly, in the law of first possession, "possession" is somewhere between actual manucaption and the mere intent to capture. Were possession to require actual manucaption, the saucy intruder would get away with the fox even after it had been mortally wounded by one not abandoning pursuit. But at the same time, were the law of first possession to accept anything less than certain control of the claimed object as evidence of possession, the pursuer would be permitted to impose his mere projects or wishes on another in a manner inconsistent with her personality. In short, just as one's *deed* is one's official proof of *ownership,* so is one's *expression* one's official proof of *authorship.*

The plaintiffs in *Pierson* and *Nichols* are in homologous positions. In *Pierson,* the plaintiff-pursuer has not completed his act. He can claim the fox only on the basis of his mere pursuit, his mere project. The fact that this claim fails is but a way of saying that pursuit *per se* cannot give rise to property. The parallel point in copyright law is that ideas *per se* do not give rise to copyright. They represent mere projects, as yet incomplete acts, dreams, so to speak, that cannot as such be constitutive of another's obligation. To be sure, the plaintiff in *Nichols* has completed her copyrightable work. Nonetheless, the plaintiff in *Nichols* must still fail because her claim against the defendant could stand only at a level of generality inconsistent with the defendant's own authorship. As Learned Hand puts it, that they are free for the taking is "the penalty an author must bear for marking them [i.e., his characters] too indistinctly."[22]

Ideas, one might say, are like wild foxes, as yet to be ensnared in the web of one's own expression. What holds these two cases—*Pierson* and *Nichols*—together is the concept of equality that, homologically, structures them both and that renders each of their holdings intelligible. In both cases—the case of mere pursuit and the case of mere idea—granting protection would amount to a violation of the principle of equal personality. The familiar metaphor that one can never capture ideas expresses that parallel.

The homology between first possession and original expression indicates that the distinction between tangible and intangible is insufficient as a starting-point for an account of the specificity of copyright. The exclusive right of use to which first possession gives rise follows from the fact that such possession is an agent's whose deeds are worthy of respect. Thus, in *Pierson,* Pierson keeps the fox not because the fox cannot be used simultaneously by someone else (i.e., not because the fox is rivalrous in consumption), or because he has excluded others from it (i.e., the fox can be physically sequestered), but because his exclusionary act is the act of a person. Fox 2 in my example above consumes and excludes but does not thereby appropriate in any legally cognizable sense. Similarly, the copyright to which original expression gives rise follows from the fact that such expression is an author's whose works are worthy of respect. An author has a copyright in her work not because the work can be used by someone else without her being deprived of it (i.e., the work is nonrivalrous in consumption), or because she would have difficulty excluding others from enjoying her work once she releases it (i.e., the work is nonexclusive), but because she authored it. In both cases, the exclusivity in question is a normative phenomenon about the principle of personality, not an empirical phenomenon about the nature of the objects claimed. From the standpoint of the homology between first possession and original expression, there is no specific normative (i.e., justificatory) significance to be attributed to the tangibility or lack thereof of the subject matter protected under either body of law. In distinct spheres, the principle of first possession and the principle of independent creation each assert the juridical principle of personality and of equality between persons.

My point is not that no normatively significant distinction between property and copyright can be drawn but—quite the contrary—that the distinction needs to be configured along an axis different from that of the tangible/intangible distinction. The dominant theoretical approach to copyright takes the intangibility of copyright subject matter as its starting-point. More precisely, it takes the "public goods" nature of works of authorship as its starting-point. Because works are nonrivalrous (i.e., can be enjoyed by more than one person at once) and nonexclusive (i.e., cannot be physically sequestered from others), it is difficult to obtain payment for them once released in the marketplace. The "public goods" nature of works of authorship thus generates the market failure that copyright law is designed to cure.[23] Copyright law intervenes to generate the missing features of rivalrousness and exclusivity. It propertizes. It grants rights of exclusion in order to construct and to demarcate metaphysical chattels, juridically imagined objects of ownership. It encourages the author's productivity by turning her words into things.

Paradoxically, the account acknowledges the specificity of copyright vis-à-vis property by seeking to dissolve it. Copyright law is a mechanism to transform public goods into private ones. But the account cannot succeed. We learn from *Feist* that facts are categorically not subject to copyright protection. Yet, like works of authorship, facts are public goods. In other words, the concept of public goods cannot explain why copyright law focuses on works rather than facts.[24] Integrating *Feist* into the foregoing juxtaposition of *Pierson* and *Nichols* will help to bring this observation more sharply into relief, and thus to ascertain more precisely the specificity of copyright vis-à-vis property.

In *Feist,* the plaintiff, Rural Telephone Service Co., fails on the grounds that a white pages phone directory, while clearly the product of effort, is not sufficiently creative: "Rural expended sufficient effort to make the white pages directory useful, but insufficient creativity to make it original." "This decision should not be construed as demeaning Rural's efforts in compiling its directory, but rather as making clear that copyright rewards originality, not effort."[25] At first sight, the Court's distinction between mere effort and creativity in *Feist* may seem to suggest that, like *Nichols, Feist* also maps onto the structure of *Pierson.* In *Pierson,* the plaintiff fails to recover because the Court refuses to find an entitlement arising out of mere pursuit. Similarly, in *Nichols,* the plaintiff fails to recover because the Court refuses to extend copyright protection to mere ideas. In this context, it seems but a short step to the observation that, in *Feist,* the plaintiff fails to recover because the Court refuses to extend copyright protection to raw facts on the basis of the compiler's mere effort. Thus, one may be tempted to suggest that the compiler's mere effort *(Feist)* is as insufficient to give rise to legal protection as are a hunter's mere pursuit *(Pierson)* and an author's mere project or idea *(Nichols).*

The analogy between the hunter's mere pursuit and the compiler's mere effort, however, breaks down almost as soon as it is asserted.

Chasing a fox can be reasonably described as an incomplete act. So can an author's mere idea for a work. Both are projects envisioning future completion. But having compiled information and assembled it in the shape of a phone directory cannot be so described. There is nothing incomplete about a phone directory; nothing, in any case, that would permit an analogy to a pursuer who has not quite captured her prey. The pursuer is attempting to get something done. The compiler who holds the directory in his hands has completed his task of compilation. Hers is not a project but a deed. She cannot be refused copyright protection for her phone directory on the basis that her act is incomplete. She has certainly moved well beyond mere pursuit. She has caught her prey. Her problem is by no means analogous to that of the mere pursuer in *Pierson.* Her problem is that, while she has caught her prey, she has not caught the kind of prey that copyright will recognize.

Operative in *Feist,* in other words, is not a distinction between wish and deed, intention and action, but rather between different modes of action. The plaintiff in *Feist* does not fail because she has failed to complete her act. Rather, she fails because what she has accomplished is not an original work of authorship. She has produced a phone directory. She has not authored a work.

Doctrinally, the distinction could not be clearer. An author, *Feist* tells us, is "he to whom anything owes its origin: originator; maker."[26] Facts are not subject to copyright because "facts do not owe their origin to an act of authorship."[27] In the result, the raw data collected by Rural does not "owe its origin" to Rural. Rather, the Court adds, "these bits of information are uncopyrightable facts; they existed before Rural reported them and would have continued to exist if Rural had never published a telephone directory."[28] Whereas the compiler gathers preexisting material, the author originates her work.

From this point of view, the compiler is a great deal closer to the hunter than to the author. In respect of things and information, it is possible to separate act (e.g., capture, collection) and subject matter (e.g., wild foxes, facts). Possession or collection is possession or collection of preexisting material. But in respect of works of authorship, it is impossible to describe the act (i.e., expression) without also describing the subject matter (i.e., expression) to which the act gives rise. The act is, quite literally, the origination of its subject matter. There can be no doubt that works, like facts, are public goods. Yet from the standpoint of originality doctrine, facts are more like foxes than they are like works. Authorship neither captures nor gathers but originates that which it claims. Copyright law frames its subject matter not through the distinction between public and private goods but through the distinction between the preexisting and the original. This is why the public goods prism can warn us, it is true, that works of authorship can generate market failure, but it cannot tell us why they are specifically copyrightable. The specificity of copyright is rather in the identity of act and subject matter characteristic of originality.

To broach this identity of act and subject matter we need to do no more than recall the combined operation of the doctrines of originality and the idea/expression dichotomy. Copyright subject matter is "original expression." This is neither the capture nor the collection of an externally preexisting object—whether intangible or otherwise—but the conveyance of meaning to another, the movement from the generality of idea to the particularity of expression. The identity of act and subject matter is that of an act of communication: the work of an author is both her act of expression and the form of expression in and through which she conveys her meaning.

The identity of act and subject matter in fact runs deeper than it at first appears. It is not quite enough to say that an act of authorship originates that which it claims, as if copyright law were to regard a work as a finally externalized, self-subsisting object subject to its author's ownership. If that were the case, it would be impossible to say, as does *Feist,* that when "two poets, each ignorant of the other, compose identical poems . . . [n]either work is novel, yet both are original and, hence, copyrightable."[29] There are indeed two poems, albeit identical, and two copyrights, because neither is a thing; each is instead the emblem of its author's own speaking. Once a work is properly conceived as a speaking in one's own words, in abstraction from the content of one's speech, then the infringement of the right attendant on the work must also be conceived as impinging on the speaking itself rather than its content. It is not in the unauthorized taking of another's possessions—whether intangible or otherwise—but in the unauthorized repetition of another's speech. Copyright is not about one's things. It is about one's words.

While it is tempting to suppose that a construal of the work as a metaphysical chattel would provide an explanation of sorts of unauthorized publication of unpublished work as some kind of conversion, this so-called explanation would tell us little about the specificity of copyright law. It would subsume copyright as a sub-category of property, bypass the need to account for copyright as such, and leave us in the end unable to elucidate the fundamentals of copyright doctrine. The basic point is that wronging an author is not the same as wronging an owner. Insisting that a work is a metaphysical chattel, and that copyright infringement is a variety of conversion, does little to further the analysis, and a great deal to obfuscate it.

Beyond Warren and Brandeis

Thus the categories of privacy, misrepresentation, attribution and property cannot account for the intuition as to the wrongfulness of unauthorized publication of unpublished work. Each of those categories, albeit in its own way, focuses on the content of the work rather than on the work as a communicative act. Privacy focuses on the content of the work from the standpoint of its previous public availability or personal import, and hence on the entitlements that may or may not obtain in respect of rendering that content publicly available or in respect of the use of personal information. Copyright infringement, however, has nothing to do with whether unauthorized use of the content of a work is actionable as breach of privacy. Misrepresentation goes to the accuracy or lack thereof of the content of the unauthorized publication, whereas copyright infringement goes to the very fact of the unauthorized publication, even if faithful to the original content. Attribution targets the author's entitlement to attach (or refuse to attach) her name to her work, treating the work as an external content to which an author chooses (or not) to attach her name. But, once again, copyright infringement goes to the very fact of the unauthorized publication, even if attributed correctly. Finally, the wrong involved in copyright infringement cannot be characterized as a conversion of the work because the copyright holder does not hold her work as owned content or as an object of ownership. The work is not an intangible object but an instance of speech. From a copyright standpoint, it is true not only that an author has no exclusive rights in respect of the content of her work, but also that she does not hold her work as owned content.

Perhaps the category of privacy comes closest to capturing the intuition that unauthorized publication of unpublished work is wrongful. For that reason, I want now to return to it. My interest in doing so is to bring into relief the observation that privacy and copyright operate with different conceptions of publication. It is not until we grasp this clearly that we can ascertain the specificity of copyright vis-à-vis privacy, and thus the reach of the intuition that unauthorized publication of unpublished work is wrongful.

To recapitulate, then, we noted that privacy must fail as an account of the wrongfulness of unauthorized publication of unpublished work because it targets the status of the work as unpublished or as container of personal information. What is at stake from a copyright standpoint, however, is the unauthorized nature of the publication, neither the unpublished status nor the personal content of the work. The copyright-specific wrong has nothing to do with whether or not the unauthorized publication is or is not a first publication, or with whether or not the unauthorized publication amounts to unauthorized use of personal information. The author complains neither because what she had to say was personal nor because, whether by her or by others, it had never been said before. She complains because she had not chosen to say it. She has been deprived of her choice whether to speak.

We can broach the implications of this view by juxtaposing it with Warren and Brandeis's classic deployment, in "The Right to Privacy," of the copyright law of unpublished works as evidence for the proposition that a recognized legal interest in privacy exists.[30] It may well be true that legal concern over unpublished works evidences legal concern over privacy interests. But this is a far cry from the quite different proposition that privacy interests animate the copyright law of unpublished works. Copyright infringement does not require infringement of privacy interests. Nor does infringement of privacy interests require copyright infringement. The copyright law of unpublished works is not an understudy for poorly developed privacy law. It is not there to fill gaps left untreated by privacy law. To deploy the copyright law of unpublished works as evidence of legal concern over privacy interests is problematic to the extent that it (1) misunderstands the distinction between the two legal interests, and (2) in so doing, deprives copyright law of the opportunity to formulate its own view of the wrongfulness of unauthorized publication of unpublished works. The reduction of the law of unpublished works to privacy interests in effect precludes the possibility of grasping the legal issues pertinent to unpublished *and* published works from a single, copyright-specific, point of view. It precludes, that is, the possibility of grasping the core of the legal issues involved as a matter pertinent to works of authorship, rather than as a matter pertinent to their unpublished or published status.[31]

A brief excursus into "The Right to Privacy"—and specifically into the critical role that the article accords to the law of unpublished manuscripts—will bring the idea of a single, copyright-specific point of view more sharply into relief. At stake is nothing less than the place and meaning of the unpublished work in copyright law.

"The Right to Privacy" starts with a description of the common law as anchored in the "principle" that "the individual shall have full protection in person and in property."[32] Political, social and economic changes require "the recognition of new rights": the "common law, in its eternal youth, grows to meet the new demands of society."[33] It is not so much that the common law is an instrument of social change, but that in light of social change the common law ensures and enriches the protection of individuality.

Whereas early conceptions of the protection of life and property targeted only "physical interference," later ones involve "recognition of man's spiritual nature, of his feelings and his intellect."[34] Battery gives rise to assault and defamation as legal injuries. Property comes to include incorporeal rights "in the products and processes of the mind."[35] This spiritualization of the common law, if we may put it thus, "was inevitable."[36] The "advance of civilization" brings an intensification of "intellectual and emotional life" and a "heightening of sensations."[37] To be civilized is to have depth. It is to realize that "physical things" comprise "only a part of the pain, pleasure, and profit of life."[38] Thus, with civilization, "[t]houghts, emotions, and sensations demanded legal recognition, and the beautiful capacity for growth that characterizes the common law enabled judges to afford the requisite protection, *without the interposition of the legislature*."[39]

This vignette on the relation between history and the common law has a twofold function in the structure of the argument in "The Right to Privacy." On the one hand, the vignette provides the occasion for Warren and Brandeis to assert that a "next step" must be taken in "the protection of the person."[40] The complexity of civilized life has rendered "some retreat from the world" necessary for the individual.[41] At the same time, "modern device[s]" make the invasion of this effort to retreat more and more effective and threatening.[42] "Solitude and privacy," and hence their protection, have become "more essential to the individual."[43] The purpose of "The Right to Privacy" is to examine this required next step in the development of the common law.

On the other hand, the vignette permits Warren and Brandeis to announce that the purpose of "The Right to Privacy" is not merely to carve out the emerging terrain of solitude and privacy but "to consider whether the *existing law* affords a principle which can properly be invoked to protect the privacy of the individual."[44] The eternal youth of the common law thrives through finding the seeds of the new in the womb of the old. "The Right to Privacy" announces itself as a catalyst in that movement: it seeks to find the law of privacy not in the interpositions of the legislature but in the interstices of existing (common) law. The proposition that the legal recognition of privacy requires not the invention of new categories but coordination of already existing practices and intuitions is thus fundamental to the argument. The common law proceeds through analogy.

Warren and Brandeis begin by dismissing defamation as the analogical soil from which to cultivate invasion of privacy concerns. Privacy bears no more than a "superficial resemblance" to the integrity of a person's reputation.[45] The law of defamation deals with an injury to the individual "in his external relations to the community."[46] Invasions of privacy involve "mental pain and distress" arising from breach of the individual's vital effort to retreat from the community.[47] The "class of effects" covered by the "principle on which the law of defamation rests" are thus "radically different" from the privacy concerns "for which attention is now asked."[48]

Yet defamation turns out to be not only unsuitable but also unnecessary to find in the existing common law a "principle applicable to cases of invasion of privacy": "for the legal doctrines relating to infractions of what is ordinarily termed the common law right to intellectual and artistic property are, it is believed, but instances and applications of a general right of privacy, which properly understood afford a remedy for the evils under consideration."[49] "The Right to Privacy" is thus pitched as nothing less than a thoroughgoing reduction of an author's common law right to prevent publication of her unpublished work to privacy interests. Its fundamental thesis is that "no basis is discerned upon which the right to restrain publication and reproduction of such so-called literary and artistic works can be rested, except the right to privacy, as a part of the more general right to immunity of the person,—the right to one's personality."[50]

The point is worth repeating. It is not that we may learn about privacy from the law of unpublished manuscripts. Nor is it that we must disentangle privacy interests from copyright interests embedded in the law of unpublished manuscripts. Far from it: the point is that common law copyright is *nothing but* privacy law masquerading as copyright. In respect of the terrain of unpublished manuscripts, authorship interests must give way to the imperialism of privacy. It is as if, in their effort to midwife the birth of privacy from existing law, Warren and Brandeis do violence to the womb of authorship.

The argument presented has three related strands. The first is that an author's common law right to prevent publication of her unpublished manuscript is "entirely independent of the copyright laws."[51] Whereas common law copyright is a prepublication right, statutory copyright is a postpublication right. Common law copyright enables an author "to control absolutely *the act of publication*, and in the exercise of his own discretion, to decide whether there shall be any publication at all."[52] Statutory copyright aims to secure to the author "the entire profits arising *from* publication."[53] Thus, "[t]he statutory right is of no value, *unless* there is a publication; the common-law right is lost *as soon as* there is publication."[54] This chronology of loss (of the prepublication common law right) and gain (of the postpublication statutory right) captures the conceptual dichotomy between the law of unpublished manuscripts and copyright law. The prepublication world is just not the domain of statutory copyright. Copyright begins when—and as soon as—privacy stops.

Historically speaking, the point is correct: unpublished works did not come under the jurisdiction of the United States *Copyright Act* until

1976.[55] But Warren and Brandeis are well aware that to point out that statutory copyright does not cover unpublished manuscripts is not quite to demonstrate that the law of unpublished manuscripts is, conceptually speaking, "entirely independent" of the law of copyright. It may well be the case, and it was indeed routinely understood to be the case, that the difference between common law copyright and statutory copyright is less about the nature than the duration of protection, with statutory copyright lasting only for limited times and common law copyright lasting in perpetuity.[56] Casting the distinction as a matter of duration, however, would vitiate the strategy to banish copyright law altogether from the prepublication world.

Accordingly, Warren and Brandeis must now argue, in the second strand of their reduction of common law copyright to privacy, that the nature of common law protection of unpublished work is qualitatively distinct from copyright law. The relevant passage is worth quoting at length:

> If the letters or the contents of the diary were protected as literary compositions, the scope of the protection afforded should be the same secured to a published writing under the copyright law. But the copyright law would not prevent an enumeration of the letters, or the publication of some of the facts contained therein. The copyright of a series of paintings or etchings would prevent a reproduction of the paintings as pictures; but it would not prevent a publication of list or even a description of them. Yet in the famous case of *Prince Albert v. Strange*, the court held that the common-law rule prohibited not merely the reproduction of the etchings which the plaintiff and Queen Victoria had made for their own pleasure, but also "the publishing (at least by printing or writing), though not by copy or resemblance, a description of them, whether more or less limited or summary, whether in the form of a catalogue or otherwise."[57]

The merits (or, rather, lack thereof) of this reading of *Prince Albert v. Strange* aside, its function in the unfolding argument of "The Right to Privacy" is clear.[58] Once the law of unpublished works has nothing to do with works of authorship as such (i.e., a diary is not protected "as a literary composition"), it is but a small step, if a step at all, to the observation that "this protection cannot rest upon the right to literary or artistic property in any exact sense."[59] Nor is it now difficult to draw "the conclusion that the protection afforded to thought, sentiments, and emotions, expressed through the medium of writing or of the arts, so far as it consists in preventing publication, is merely an instance of the enforcement of the more general right of the individual to be let alone."[60] The law of unpublished manuscripts is entirely independent of copyright law because the former is far wider in scope than the latter.

The third strand of the argument ensures that the analytical work accomplished in differentiating the law of unpublished works from the law of "literary or artistic property" does indeed thrust privacy onto center-stage. So-called literary property, that is, is rather privacy. "The principle which protects personal writings and all other personal productions, not against theft and physical appropriation, but against publication in any form, is in reality not the principle of private property, but that of inviolate personality."[61] It is this, Warren and Brandeis conclude, that grounds the sought-after assertion that "the existing law affords a principle which may be invoked to protect the privacy of the individual from invasion."[62] Because the protection existing law grants is not confined to works of authorship, we must see it rather as indicative of a "general right to privacy" inclusive of "thoughts, emotions, and sensations . . . whether expressed in writing, or in conduct, in conversation, in attitudes, or in facial expression."[63] The irony could hardly be greater: Warren and Brandeis emancipate the unpublished work from property to bury it under the yoke of privacy.

The iconic stature of "The Right to Privacy" is unchallenged. It can be regarded not only as a contribution to the study of privacy but also as the very creation of the discipline.[64] In his thoughtful review of the piece on the occasion of its hundredth anniversary, Robert Post remarks that its "central thrust" is to "disentangle privacy from property," and that its "subsequent influence rests in great measure upon its success in that effort."[65] "The Right to Privacy" is thus about the emergence of privacy from property. Still, it is not quite clear why the birth of privacy had to take place at the expense of the role and the place of the unpublished work in copyright theory and practice. Post notes that Warren and Brandeis sought to find privacy in existing law, so as to avoid the charge of judicial activism.[66] That is no doubt correct, but it seems hardly sufficient to explain why Warren and Brandeis could not make the appropriate distinctions between privacy and copyright. For example, the holding in *Strange*—even taking the Warren and Brandeis reading at face value—clearly strayed from what could have been held as a matter of copyright law. But while that permits the inference that the judgment evidences privacy concerns, it does not follow that copyright concerns are absent. Warren and Brandeis approached the teasing out of privacy concerns from the existing law of unpublished works with an imperialist animus, so to speak, seeking to conquer a terrain rather than to share it. They excised the unpublished work from copyright law.

Consider, however, that an unpublished work can give rise simultaneously to both privacy and copyright concerns. Awareness of this simultaneity generates an attitude less hostile to the place and meaning of the unpublished work in copyright law. One might say that a more federalist mind-set toward concurrent and overlapping jurisdictions would prove more fruitful. Historical questions of copyright duration aside, the nature and scope of copyright protection does not at all vary significantly in accordance to whether a given work is published or unpublished. The law of copyright does not itself place the distinction between the published and the unpublished at center-stage. A work of authorship is a form of expression, not the content expressed. Neither facts nor ideas are within the purview of copyright law. Thus, as Warren and Brandeis note, it is emphatically true that evidence of concern over undisclosed facts, ideas, thoughts, emotions, sensation, feelings, or information generally is *ultra vires* copyright law. But this is not because the copyright law has nothing to do with unpublished works. It is because the status of a work as unpublished is not fundamental or even relevant to its status as copyright subject matter. Copyright protects works of authorship, whether published or not. There is a sense, then, in which Warren and Brandeis were ironically and indisputably correct to have excised the unpublished work from copyright law. They were profoundly mistaken, however, not to have realized that excising it *as unpublished* is just not the same as excising it *as a work*.

Strictly speaking, there is no such thing as an unpublished work in copyright law. The set of unpublished works is empty. Works are subject to copyright not as unpublished but as works, as forms of expression. The locution "unpublished work" is as extraneous to copyright law as the phrase "novel work." Recalling the copyright/patent distinction will be helpful here. The principle of independent creation teaches that, unlike novelty in patent law, originality in copyright law has absolutely nothing to do with novelty or lack thereof, whether of idea expressed or of expression itself. The phrase "novel work" thus connotes a categorical error. What matters is not whether what an author has to say (or her form of expression) was or was not, to use the language of the patent law, "previously available to the public." What matters is whether the author speaks in her own words. Of course, a work may indeed be novel, in the sense, for example, that neither the idea it expresses nor the form of its expression, are previously available. But this novelty is not determinative from the copyright standpoint. Works are original, not novel.

The distinction between privacy and copyright has a similar structure. The principle of independent creation teaches that, unlike privacy in privacy law, originality in copyright law has nothing to do with privacy or lack thereof, whether of idea expressed or of expression itself. The phrase "unpublished (or private) work" is thus a categorical error. What matters is not whether what an author has to say (or her form of expression) has been made public before. What matters, once again, is whether the author speaks in her own words. Of course, a work may be unpublished, in the sense, for example, that neither the idea it expresses nor the form of its expression, are previously available. But this unpublished status is not determinative from a copyright standpoint. Works are original, not unpublished.

My point is not to equate patent and privacy, of course, but to point out that "publication" has a meaning in patent and privacy entirely different from its meaning in copyright. In patent law, a patentee takes to the patent office not only his invention but also the fact that it is not previously available to the public. More precisely, an invention *is* a previously unavailable way of achieving a result. Its previous unavailability is thus part and parcel of its identity. The patentee deprives himself of his invention when he publishes it. To publish it is to divest it of its novelty. This is why, on the bargain theory of patent law, the patentee makes his invention public (patent to the public) only in exchange for the period of exclusivity during which he will hold a legal monopoly over the invention. He has in effect exchanged the novelty of the invention for the exclusive rights in respect of its use. The invention is rather old news as soon as it is made public. It is indeed described, and hence available to all, in the patent specification that the patentee hands to the patent office. It is no accident that a patent specification is, technically, a "disclosure." Publication is about deprivation.

Publication has a similar significance in privacy law. In the simplest case, information is private where it is unavailable to the public. My unlisted phone number is private, in the sense that publication deprives it of its private nature. To publish is to divest oneself of privacy. To be sure, if I give my torts Professor my unlisted phone number for the express purpose that he contact me for matters related to my schooling, and he calls me instead to ask me to make a financial contribution to a political party, we may say that his use of the information, albeit previously available to him through my own agency, amounts to an invasion of my privacy. This is to say that my disclosure of the information in issue (i.e., my phone number) for a particular purpose could not or should not be construed as a disclosure for any purpose. Still, my unlisted phone number is no longer unlisted for the specific purpose of being legitimately available to my Professor to contact me regarding matters related to my schooling. Even a conditional disclosure amounts to a loss of privacy in respect of the restricted purpose for which the disclosure takes place. As in patent law, publication is about deprivation.

An invention can lose its novelty through publication. Private information can lose its privacy through publication. A work of authorship, however, is forever original. Originality has nothing to do with previous public availability (whether in the novelty or in the privacy sense). Publication has nothing to do with its persistence or its demise. Publication does not deprive a work of its originality. Were things otherwise, we could not make sense at all of the paradigmatic mischief in copyright law: the wrongfulness of the pirate edition. A pirate edition is an unauthorized publication. It is not less wrongful because it arises on the heels of the authorized edition, and thus repeats (i.e., copies) what is already publicly available. Its wrongfulness is not predicated on its timing.

The operative distinction in copyright law, that is, is not between unpublished and published but between unauthorized and authorized. Once again, copyright is not about the content of what is said, whether private or novel, but about the speaking itself. To author is not to reveal secrets. Nor is it to hunt foxes. To author is to speak in one's own words.

To wrong someone in respect of her authorship is to compel her to do so. The pirate appropriates the author's voice.

Thus, grasped from a copyright-specific standpoint, the intuition that unauthorized publication of unpublished works is wrongful is equally applicable to the unauthorized publication of *published* works. What is wrong with each and both is that they amount to forcing another to speak. Unauthorized publication is compelled speech. The fact than an author has already spoken does not mean that we are thereby entitled to force him to speak again. A ventriloquist is not any less a ventriloquist because he compels me to say what I have already said. That his belly happens to speak through my mouth exactly what I have already spoken—or what I would have spoken—does not make me any less of a puppet. On the contrary, the injury is even greater where he uses my very own speech to treat me like one. In short, an author does not relinquish his right to speak or not to speak merely because he has already spoken. By no means: the view that an author somehow loses something as a result of publication seems at best in tension with, if not radically inconsistent with, the essence of copyright as a right involving enforceable claims over published works of authorship.

5

The Public Domain as Dialogue

Generally speaking, copyright theory and practice can be characterized as divided into two broad copyright cultures. On the one hand, in common law jurisdictions, copyright is regarded as a policy instrument designed to serve the public interest in the production and dissemination of works of authorship. Not the author's right, but the public interest that both generates and justifies that right is the central animating concern of copyright law. On the other hand, in civil law jurisdictions, authorial entitlement is conceived not instrumentally but as a juridical recognition of rights inherent in the act of authorship as such. Not the public interest, but the inherent dignity of authorship is the axis around which copyright revolves. Terminologically speaking, these distinctions recall for us that what the common law world regards as *copyright* is rather known as *author's right* (*droit d'auteur, derecho de autor, diritto de autore, Urheberrecht,* for example) in the civil law world.[1]

In the common law world, and in the United States in particular, the idea that the purpose of copyright law is to provide incentives for creativity is less an occasion for debate than the very terrain within which debate can take place at all. To be sure, copyright discourse is highly conflicted and contested. But the so-called "copyright wars" between maximalists and minimalists—advocates of high copyright protection and advocates of low copyright protection—do little to obscure the latent agreement that frames them. Few would question the bedrock proposition that copyright law is about providing incentives for creativity.[2] In the United States, the proposition has, or is widely said to have, nothing less than entrenched constitutional pedigree.[3] For all their manifest vigor, the "copyright wars" are not a truly disruptive struggle threatening foundations. They are rather a series of skirmishes on a basically shared playing field. The unifying pervasiveness of the hold that instrumentalism has over the United States copyright imagination is paralleled only by the ease with which that imagination summarily rejects or dismisses rights-based accounts of copyright law—accounts rooted in a vision of the inherent dignity of authorship. For good or ill, the United States is likely the only place in the global village where the vexing parochialism of American copyright discourse remains proudly unnoticed.

One of the nodal points of the copyright wars is the ongoing discussion about the expansion of copyright scope and copyright subject matter since the enactment of the Statute of Anne, the world's first copyright statute, in early 18th-century England.[4] Predictably, whereas copyright minimalists object strenuously to this expansion, copyright maximalists support it. In North America, equally unsurprisingly, both maximalists and minimalists formulate their position from the shared standpoint of instrumentalist copyright theory.

From an instrumentalist perspective, the perceived difficulty of formulating copyright fundamentals as a matter of voluntary speech, and of the correlative proposition that copyright infringement is compelled speech, is that the derivation of the right from voluntariness seems to preclude the limitation of the right. It is as if the author, enshrined in the sanctity of her voluntariness, were now in a position to make all kinds of plausible demands in the name of her autonomy as a speaking being.

Portrayed as a voluntary speaker, she may now seek to determine unilaterally the scope of her entitlement, alleging that any limitations imposed by law would amount to nothing less than compelled speech—that is, any and all unauthorized uses of a work would on this basis amount to actionable involuntary speech. The status of the public domain as a necessary, integral, and irreducible aspect of copyright law thus threatens to dissolve in the solvent of the author's autonomy. This perception that a rights-based account of copyright cannot provide adequate foundations for the public domain is part and parcel of the widespread view that the instrumentalist view of copyright is theoretically superior.[5]

I want in this chapter to broach the theme of the public domain from a twofold perspective. On the one hand, I want to show that, contrary to widely held presuppositions, the instrumentalist account of copyright law provides, if at all, a highly unstable ground for the public domain. On the other, I want to set forth the dynamic whereby an affirmation of authorial right can provide solid and clear grounding for the public domain. A rights-based account rooted in the author's autonomy as a speaking being offers a markedly superior grasp of the necessary, integral and irreducible status of the public domain.

My purpose is to offer minimalists some words of both caution and comfort. The cautionary aspect is that minimalism ought to be far more suspicious than it actually is about the instrumentalist hegemony in copyright discourse. Instrumentalist discourse is, in my view, part and parcel of the very expansion that minimalism seeks to counter. Copyright protection has consistently expanded since the landmark decision of the House of Lords in *Donaldson v. Beckett* affirmed (a) the supremacy of the Statute of Anne over common law copyright, and (b) the still prevailing view that copyright law is not a juridical recognition of rights inherent in the act of authorship but rather a policy instrument designed to promote the public interest in creativity.[6] Thus, historically speaking, copyright expansion has taken place and continues to take place under the supremacy of instrumentalism. To be sure, this historical correlation is not by itself sufficient to persuade us that instrumentalism is necessarily complicit in the constriction of the public domain. It does strike me as sufficient, however, to generate significant unease about any uncritical adoption of the instrumentalist paradigm in the name of the expansion of the public domain.

The comfort I seek to offer is that there are, of course, alternative accounts of copyright law. These accounts are none other than the rights-based accounts that, in its habitual endorsement of instrumentalism, minimalism dismisses far too summarily. As I just noted, one of the major complaints that minimalism levels against rights-based discourse is that, once enshrined as a matter of inherent dignity, the rights of authors under copyright law cannot be easily constrained. With this complaint in mind, I want to emphasize that, on the contrary, rights-based discourse envisions not only the claims of authorship but also, and therefore, those of the public domain as a matter of the reciprocity inherent in right. The rights-based account of authorship is also a rights-based account of the public domain. My purpose is, in short, to generate minimalist unease about instrumentalism and to evoke the as yet largely unexplored potential of a rights-based minimalism. At the very least, I seek to undo the widespread apprehension that rights-based accounts are necessarily maximalist accounts, and to voice the parallel apprehension—insufficiently heeded—that instrumentalism has deep maximalist affinities at its core.

The chapter begins with a brief sketch of the shared terrain on which the copyright wars take place. This sketch prepares the ground for an analysis of minimalism as a critical stance seeking to vindicate a particular normative conception of copyright law against the realities of copyright expansion. The analysis finds that, pitched within instrumentalist terrain, the minimalist stance is involved in a striking reversal whereby it becomes complicit in the very expansion it seeks to counter. Exploring the historical roots of the conceptual structure informing that predicament, the chapter then examines the conditions for the possibility of reversing the reversal itself. In this vein, the chapter offers rereadings of the judgments of Lord Mansfield and Yates J. in *Millar v. Taylor*, finding in Lord Mansfield's judgment unexpected indications of a communicative rather than proprietary construal of a work of authorship.[7] The examination concludes that the vitality of the minimalist project is best sustained in and through a rights-based account of authors as speakers, works as communicative acts, and of the public domain as the site of ongoing dialogue. The chapter confirms that conclusion by demonstrating that—grasped from a rights-based perspective—the idea/expression dichotomy entails the lawfulness of any and all unauthorized copying for personal use.

A Shared Terrain

Because they unfold under the unifying aegis of instrumentalism, the so-called copyright wars are far less disruptive than they at first appear. They are not foundational struggles about the very purpose and meaning of copyright. Rather, they resemble civil wars in which the combatants are equally faithful to the common nation each feels the other betrays. By creating the appearance of controversy, the struggle between maximalists and minimalists sustains the underlying hegemony of the instrumentalist paradigm. As much as maximalists, minimalists deploy the concept of copyright as a way of providing incentives for creativity. The debate is not about the appropriateness of that concept but about the way in which it should be operationalized.

Generally speaking, the minimalist view is not that copyright is about something other than incentives but that, while central, incentives to produce works of authorship are not the whole of the copyright story. The role of incentives must be grasped within the larger context of a view of copyright law as a balance between incentives and dissemination, creator-interests and user-interests.[8] An overemphasis of the incentive-function of copyright protection can sabotage the equally constitutive dissemination-function of copyright law. In a word, to recall Jessica Litman's felicitous formulation, copyright is as much about reading and listening as it is about writing and composing works of authorship.[9]

Of course, maximalism is by no means indifferent to the dissemination-function of copyright law. The maximalist point is that, as distinct from production, dissemination of works of authorship itself requires incentives, and that therefore the dissemination-function of copyright law is best supported not by limiting copyright protection but, on the contrary, by strengthening it further so as to render it serviceable from the standpoint not only of production but also of dissemination.[10] Not only authors but also publishers and distributors need incentives to fulfill their role in the copyright system. According to the maximalist account, it is short sighted to believe that liberating use (or aspects thereof) from protection would be in and of itself sufficient to catalyze modes of dissemination consistent with the incentive-function of copyright protection.

The minimalist challenge to the maximalist construal arises from a different assessment of the effects that certain levels of copyright protection (and hence certain corresponding levels of user rights or privileges within the copyright system) do or do not have (and would or would not have) on the public interest in the production and dissemination of works of authorship. In this vein, the minimalist complaint against copyright expansion is not a complaint against that expansion *per se*. It is rather about the *effects* of that expansion. If copyright expansion were shown to be conducive to the public interest in production and dissemination, then there would be nothing wrong with it, at least from a copyright perspective. The dispute between maximalists and minimalists is in this respect largely empirical and proceeds from common assumptions shared by the two camps.[11] It seems that the extent to which one feels uncomfortable with copyright in general, or with copyright expansion in particular, is related to the degree to which one believes that copyright does in fact promote the production and dissemination of works of authorship. But the bedrock proposition that copyright is an instrument designed to foster and disseminate creativity is common to maximalists and minimalists alike. It is the common terrain that the copyright wars leave uncontested.

Empirical and Normative

To the extent that this common terrain remains uncontested, minimalist opposition to copyright expansion is likely to remain not only largely ineffective but also self-defeating. The "loyal" nature of its opposition to the maximalist project constrains minimalism to an impoverished vision of the public domain as nothing more than freely accessible value, and thus weakens the force of its critical stance toward copyright expansion. The affirmation of the public domain requires challenging not merely the maximalist construal of the instrumental copyright calculus, but also, and more fundamentally, the very premise that copyright is an instrumental calculus to begin with.

In instrumentalist terms, the minimalist stance toward copyright expansion is that expansive copyright is at odds with copyright's own purpose of promoting creativity. Formulated in that way, the stance is particularly interesting because, faced with evidence it accepts that copyright has as a matter of fact expanded to such an extent that, systemically speaking, it stifles rather than promotes creativity, the minimalist stance nonetheless insists on the view that copyright is about promoting creativity. This ambiguity is, of course, easily resolvable. When faced with the empirical reality of copyright expansion, the minimalist stance distinguishes copyright as an empirical reality from copyright as a juridical order. That is to say, the solution to the ambiguity is to reformulate the idea that copyright is about promoting creativity as a normative rather than an empirical proposition. The absence of empirical evidence to substantiate the minimalist thesis is therefore not immediately relevant to its validity. It is perfectly possible to say (a) existing copyright law does not promote creativity; (b) copyright law ought to promote creativity; (c) we should therefore alter existing copyright law so as to make it live up to its own creativity-promoting purpose.

In this way, the idea that copyright is (i.e., normatively speaking) about promoting creativity may be sustained even if copyright is not in fact (i.e., empirically speaking) promoting creativity. Copyright both is (normatively) and is not (empirically) about promoting creativity. This seems plausible enough. But we must note that the proposition that copyright is about promoting creativity now arises, at least in one of its determinations, as what we might call an autonomously normative proposition. It is a proposition about what copyright ought to be rather than about what copyright is. Thus, whether that proposition is correct or not is not a question that can be answered empirically. The basic thrust of the proposition is to insist that, regardless of the empirical reality of copyright expansion, copyright ought to be different. From this point of view, to seek to evaluate or validate the proposition empirically is but to have misunderstood its very nature. There is nothing surprising about that. The critical bent that the minimalist stance adopts is an admission that, if it were determinative, the empirical evidence would disprove the proposition that copyright is about promoting creativity. The minimalist point is actually that copyright has failed to become what it truly is.

The obvious advantage of the distinction between empirical and normative from the standpoint of the minimalist stance is that the stance need not be abandoned in the wake of copyright expansion. The expansion of copyright protection as an empirical matter of fact need not invalidate the normative claim that copyright is about promoting creativity. On the contrary, the divergence between fact and norm, between history and juridical order, has the ironic yet welcome effect of strengthening the stance, casting it not as a merely descriptive account, but rather as a critical theory seeking to push the actual beyond its limits.

At the same time, however, the distinction between empirical and normative also entails that if by some magic we were to find ourselves in an alternate universe in which copyright protection would have contracted and, correlatively, the public domain would have expanded, this contraction and this corresponding expansion would still not validate the normative claim that copyright is about promoting creativity. That is, we could not in such a universe happily say to ourselves: "Oh, well, isn't that wonderful! Copyright truly is about promoting creativity." The reason we could not do that is straightforward: just as the divergence between copyright theory and copyright practice cannot normatively *disprove* the theory, so the convergence of theory and practice cannot *prove* the theory. The minimalist stance cannot very well refuse to find itself normatively invalidated by the empirical expansion of copyright, yet seek to see itself normatively validated in an empirical contraction of copyright. It cannot just pick whatever facts it wants in order to feel self-satisfied. All that could be said in an alternate universe where copyright protection has contracted is that the minimalist stance has moved from being descriptively inaccurate to being descriptively accurate. But its normative validation would still remain an open question. Just as the actual success of the maximalist expansionist project is no reason to accept it, so would the implementation of the minimalist project not amount to proof of the normative validity of the minimalist theory. In short, the very structure of the minimalist stance as a stance critical of existing reality entails that it cannot seek to find its normative aspirations empirically validated.

Of course, especially in the United States, the proposition that copyright is about promoting creativity is, quite obviously, a constitutional imperative about the "Progress of Science and useful Arts," not some sort of empirical hypothesis to be empirically validated in practice.[12] But that is precisely the point. If that observation were taken seriously, one would expect that the copyright wars would look less like a largely empirical debate about the requirements of progress, and more like a deeply juridical debate about, *inter alia,* the meaning of authorship, the meaning of progress, the nature of their interrelationship, and the sense in which legal protection of authorship can be meaningfully understood as a mere means to progress. Questions about the nature of authorship are plainly prior to questions about how to promote it. One would need to know what progress is in order to provide incentives for its production.

These observations are relatively simple. Yet they are worth making explicit because they reveal that to the extent that the copyright wars are but largely empirical debates about how to provide incentives for authorship, the copyright wars either (a) treat the constitutional imperative as a "mere" empirical hypothesis to be validated in practice, or (b) assume that the meaning of authorship in particular or of the constitutional imperative in general is so plain and self-evident that it does not require elaborate discussion. In neither case does the bare invocation of the constitutional imperative as such resolve the predicament in which the minimalist stance must find itself as long as it persists in framing the problem of copyright as a merely (or largely) empirical matter. The problem is not so much that we do not have enough social science evidence to assess the effects of copyright protection. Nor is it that social science evidence about such effects is hard to collect. That may well be true. But the problem is deeper. It is that copyright justification, precisely as such, is not an empirical matter to be resolved through social science evidence collection. More to the point, to the extent that justificatory problems are drowned in oceans of social science evidence, it becomes more and more difficult to raise the question whether instrumentalism itself, rather than its specifically maximalist construal, directs the relentless march of copyright expansion. If that were the case, minimalism would become, as if by virtue of some kind of ironic reversal, an integral participant in the very expansion it seeks to counter.

A Striking Reversal

Matters are not helped by the persistent prejudice, widespread in North America, that noninstrumentalist accounts of copyright law are irremediably unfriendly to the public domain. Indeed, it is by no means difficult to detect the presence of that view as early as the foundational "literary property debate," the great "battle of the booksellers," that took place in 18th century-England in the wake of the enactment of the Statute of Anne. We will have occasion to return to this more or less well known story.[13] Suffice it to say at this point that the great battle of the booksellers opposed statutory copyright to common law copyright, giving rise thereby to the still prevailing sense that whereas instrumentalist accounts construe copyright as a statutory scheme designed to provide incentives for innovation in the name of the public interest, rights-based accounts of copyright protection favor authorial interest at the expense of the public interest.

Mark Rose frames his classic account of the period as a chronicle of the overturning of *Millar v. Taylor* in *Donaldson v. Beckett.* If *Millar* affirmed copyright in published works as a perpetual common law right, *Donaldson* held, to the contrary, that the Statute of Anne occupied the field of published works, such that copyright duration was to be limited as provided by the Statute. This is, of course, a familiar story. The London booksellers (who had argued for perpetual copyright) lost the great literary property debate. The Statute of Anne, a statute ostensibly premised on the public interest in the "encouragement of learning," prevailed victorious over their common law claims to perpetual copyright.[14]

Less familiar but equally true is that the story Mark Rose tells us is actually less about the victory of *Donaldson* over *Millar* than it is about the very opposite—about the victory of *Millar* over *Donaldson.* The story of the literary property debate is not the story of the triumph of statutory copyright over common law copyright. In Rose's hands, it is rather the story of the emergence of the author as "proprietor," of the work subject to copyright as an instance of commodified value, and of copyright law itself as a mechanism designed to distribute or to balance the products of authorial labor between authors and users, creators and public. "Let us note a striking reversal," Rose writes. "*Donaldson v. Becket* is conventionally regarded as having established the statutory basis of copyright, and of course it did. But given the way *Donaldson* came to be understood, perhaps it should be simultaneously regarded as confirming the notion of the author's common-law right put forward by Mansfield and Blackstone."[15] While the London booksellers failed to secure perpetual copyright, their representations of the author as a proprietor and of the literary work as an object of property were widely and successfully disseminated. These representations are, of course, still with us today in one form or another. They continue to provide rhetorical and juridical tools that enable and facilitate the propertization of the "learning" that the Stature of Anne was ostensibly intended to encourage. The *manifest* story about the triumph of public interest concerns turns out to be a *latent* story about the commodification of knowledge.

The structure of this "striking reversal" is by no means some merely historical curiosity. It is with us today. One example will suffice. We considered in Chapter 1 the more or less recent transition in North American copyright law from a "sweat of the brow" standard of originality to a "creativity" or—as we now put it in Canada—a "skill and judgment" standard of originality.[16] Here, too, there is a manifest story and a latent story. Manifestly, the move away from the sweat of the brow standard appears as a heightening of the copyright threshold and therefore as a victory of the public domain. The classic case of *Feist* puts this eloquently. The Court notes that the move toward a creativity standard entails that "much of the fruit of the compiler's labor may be used by others without compensation." "This result," the Court adds, "is neither unfair nor unfortunate. It is the means by which copyright advances the progress of science and art."[17] The Canadian version of the public's victory over the sweat of the author's brow is similar.[18]

The latent story of this movement from sweat of the brow to creativity is of course far less cheerful. Permit me to put it as follows. As we noted in Chapter 1, we are accustomed to thinking of the sweat of the brow standard as a standard providing that an author is entitled to the products of her labor—to the value she originates through her labor. Under sweat of the brow jurisprudence, curing misappropriations of that value is perhaps the very purpose of copyright law.[19] But the sweat of the brow standard is in fact composed of two related aspects. One is that the author is entitled—or at least *prima facie* entitled—to the value she originates. The other, implicit in the first, is that the author is an originator of value. These two aspects are separable. That is, it is possible to dislodge the first aspect (that the author is entitled to the value she originates) while retaining the second (that the author is an originator of value). In fact, that is precisely what happens when the shift from the sweat of the brow standard to the creativity standard is conducted under the rubric of balance: while the victory of the creativity standard affirms and sets the stage for what we might call a redistribution of value from author to public, the very concept of the author as value-originator remains unchallenged, perhaps strengthened for having persisted through the mutation. The image of the author as an originator of commodified value emerges triumphant, even as the distribution of that value is no longer *prima facie* weighted in her favor.

This redistribution is by no means undesirable. But I would not take it at face value. Celebrating it uncritically is as misguided as taking for granted the so-called victory of *Donaldson* over *Millar*. The difficulty is that the distributive image of copyright law, the image of copyright law as a balance, carries with it an understanding of the work as an instance of commodified value, and, no less importantly, of the expansion of the public domain as a decrease in the price that the public must pay for the production of works of authorship. Even when deployed in support of a vigorous public domain, that is, the image of copyright law as a balance cannot help but generate an impoverished vision of the public domain as nothing other than a lower or lowered price.

Unsurprisingly, it is at best difficult to insist upon the stakes of the public domain in a language that reduces those stakes to some sort of entitlement to values for which no payment is in order. Publicity is very hard to establish in a discursive context that would construe publicity as bargain prices for otherwise valuable commodities. The public domain as "freebie" obtained at the author's expense is far from providing an image capable of anchoring a critical theory of existing copyright. The upshot is that the public domain contracts through the operation of the very framework that was ostensibly designed to further it. Thus, for example, the claim to perpetual copyright that *Donaldson* did indeed debunk is no longer as implausible today as it appeared to be then, unless of course one cares to distinguish ever so subtly between life plus seventy, on the one hand, and perpetuity, on the other.[20] Similarly, the author's *prima facie* entitlement to the full value of her labor, as provided in sweat of the brow jurisprudence, is not all that distant from current and ongoing, pervasive and successful, claims that technical protection measures can and should lock up that value to make sure it is not unfairly misappropriated.[21]

In both instances, albeit in different senses, the failure to develop the integral role of the public domain is inseparable from a failure to challenge the representation of the author as proprietor—that is, a failure to formulate radically nonproprietary conceptions of the author-work relation. Even efforts to formulate the fundamentals of copyright law as a distributive balance are in the end insufficient. They are part and parcel of the same problem. So long as copyright balancing is conceived as a balancing or distribution of commodified values (even if these values are regarded as so-called temporary monopolies rather than as objects of property) chances are that we will encounter ever-recurrent repetitions of the striking reversal whereby *Millar* asserts its claims not against but precisely *through Donaldson.* Copyright expansion has in large part taken place and continues to take place under the dominance of a conception of copyright law as a statutory instrument of learning or progress.

The Inherent Dignity of the Public Domain

The problem is that instrumentalism can offer no concept of the necessary role of the public domain in copyright law. To understand this, it suffices to note that instrumentalism posits not only the author's right but also the public domain as an instrument of the public interest in the production and dissemination of works of authorship. The entirety of copyright law, and thus the public domain as an aspect of copyright law, is conceived instrumentally. Thus, for example, both originality and fair use are doctrinal means whereby the public interest is served. Precisely as an instrument of the public interest, the public domain has a role in copyright law only to the extent that it is deemed necessary to the implementation of the public interest. The public domain's role in the structure of copyright law is contingent upon the performance of a function. Where this function can be more efficiently performed by other means, the public domain can and ought to be minimized or eliminated in the name of the public interest. The point to grasp is that the instrumentalist commitment to the *public interest* is not a commitment to the *public domain.*

Consider, for example, the view that a public domain is necessary to the extent that transaction costs involved in licensing the use of works of authorship would operate contrary to the public interest in the efficient use of those works. By eliminating the need for a license, the public domain inserts itself, as it were, where the market fails to produce the efficient outcome. The role of the public domain is thus contingent on more or less empirically driven assessments of the degree to which certain transactions would or would not take place in the absence of the free availability of the works in question. Once the public domain is instrumentalized in this way, as a kind of safety net designed to protect us from market failure, then its role in copyright law is negotiable, derivative of more or less empirical assessments of the likelihood or lack thereof of particular behavioral patterns. Thus, where technological developments make it possible to overcome transaction costs in the way of licensing, it becomes more and more difficult to postulate the need for a public domain. One-click licensing can liberate us from the public domain. If fair use is market failure, the degree to which technology can help the market cure itself, so to speak, is the degree to which the public domain is but the obsolete manifestation of a now-overcome failure.[22] Once we have agreed that the public domain is what it is too expensive to charge for, we can just get rid of it as soon as we come up with more and more frictionless ways of charging for it.[23]

The basic problem is that instrumentalist theory is not a theory of the necessary role of the public domain in copyright law. It is a theory of the public interest in the production and dissemination of information commodities known as works of authorship. Thus, within instrumentalist discourse, the question of the public domain, like that of the author's right, is a question about the requirements of the public interest. To be sure, nothing about the concept of the public interest requires a constricted public domain. But nor does anything in that concept necessitate a vigorous public domain. The important point is that, even under the rubric of minimalist aspirations, the dominance of instrumentalist discourse means that it is the public interest, and not the public domain, that is of primary and fundamental importance.

Of course, minimalism does and will insist that the public interest requires a vigorous rather than a constricted public domain. To the extent that it takes shape in instrumentalist terms, however, this very insistence arises from and responds to a context in which the contingency and hence negotiability of the role of the public domain in copyright law is both presupposed and unchallenged. Waged empirically, the copyright wars have already been lost: they unfold on the assumption that the public domain is disposable.

Minimalism would be well advised to heed the observation that the market failure theory of the author's right carries in its wake a market failure theory of the public domain. The rights-based account, by contrast, is not merely an account of the author but also of the public domain as a matter of inherent dignity. It is an account of the radical nonnegotiability of the constitutive role of the public domain in copyright law.

Reversing the Reversal

The basic outline of the striking reversal Rose identifies at the core of the foundational literary property debate is worth elaborating further. "The principle in question," Rose writes of *Donaldson*, "was whether literary property was a statutory right, a limited creation of the state, or a common-law right and therefore absolute and perpetual. Did the Statute of Anne (1709), the long-standing copyright law under which the term of copyright was strictly limited, determine the whole extent of protection, or did the statute merely supplement the common-law right?"[24] The London booksellers sought to assert perpetual common law copyright in order to forestall the operation of the Statute of Anne against their otherwise perpetual monopoly over book printing. They presented the theory that the Statue supplemented but did not eliminate the perpetuity of an author's copyright at common law. The role of the Statute was to provide specific remedies available to an author for limited times commencing with publication. But because copyright existed and subsisted at common law independently of the Statute, the expiration of the statutory period did not entail the expiration of the copyright as such. The Statute hovers temporarily, as it were, over the untrammeled perpetuity of the common law. It was this position that, scarcely five years before *Donaldson,* Lord Mansfield had affirmed over Yates J.'s dissent in *Millar* (1769).

Donaldson is regarded as an overturning of *Millar* because it decided that the expiration of the statutory period amounted to the expiration of the copyright as such. It asserted the radically limited duration of copyright over published works. Post-*Donaldson,* the expiration of the statutory period marks the work's irrevocable ascension to the public domain. *Donaldson* is in this respect a victory of a statutorily enshrined public domain over perpetual copyright.

As we noted, the reversal Rose has in mind is that, while the booksellers failed in their attempt to have copyright declared perpetual, their vision of the author as proprietor, and of the work as a commodity, became the grammar through which the Statute came thenceforth to be interpreted. What emerges from the literary property debate is not only a limitation of the copyright term. What emerges is also an interpretation of the Statute as an affirmation of the very image of the author as proprietor purportedly elaborated by Lord Mansfield in *Millar.* The so-called overturning of *Millar* is thus reduced to a temporal limitation, a quantitative burdening, so to speak, of the author's entitlement as defined at common law, not a redefinition of its very nature.

As Rose puts it, "The opponents of perpetual copyright were unable to produce an effective representation of authorship with which to counter the Lockean representation developed by the defenders of the author's right. . . . Thus although the struggle concluded with a rejection of the London booksellers' claim that copyright was perpetual, it by no means concluded with a rejection of the powerful representation of authorship on which that claim was based—and this affected the way in which the Lords' decision [i.e., *Donaldson*] came to be understood."[25] This absence of an alternative representation of authorship results in an entrenchment of a reading of *Donaldson*—and hence of the Statute—as a lasting affirmation of the author as proprietor. Like some kind of statutory Trojan Horse, the limitation of the copyright term is the vehicle through which the author's common law property right is granted statutory recognition. The upshot of the literary property debate is thus much less the opposition than the deep continuity of *Millar* and *Donaldson* as moments in the formation of the legal status of authorship as ownership.

Even Yates J.'s forceful dissent in *Millar* had a role to play in this continuity. As framed by Yates J., *Millar* examined the question "whether, after a voluntary and general publication of an author's works by himself, or by his authority, the author has a sole and perpetual property in that work; so as to give him a right to confine every subsequent publication to himself and his assigns for ever."[26] Does the author's common law exclusive right to publish his unpublished work survive the act of publication? Yates J.'s reply is unequivocal. It is true that no one can lawfully "compel him [i.e., the author] to publish against his will."[27] But "the act of publication, when voluntarily done by the author himself, is, virtually and necessarily, a gift to the public."[28] In Yates J.'s view, there is no such thing as common law literary property in respect of published works: "when the author makes a general publication of his work, he throws it open to all mankind."[29] The common law did indeed protect unpublished manuscripts. But it did not protect published works.

For Yates J., copyright over published work is nothing more than a statutory scheme intended to regulate book publishing. There is no such thing as copyright outside the terms of the statute. In 1979, the Supreme Court of Canada echoes this by no means unfamiliar view: " . . . copyright law is neither tort law nor property law in classification, but is statutory law. It neither cuts across existing rights in property or conduct nor falls in between rights and obligations heretofore existing in the common law. Copyright legislation simply creates rights and obligations upon the terms and in the circumstances set out in the statute. This creature of statute has been known to the law of England at least since the days of Queen Anne when the first copyright statute was passed. It does not assist the interpretative analysis to import tort concepts. The legislation speaks for itself and the actions of the appellant must be measured according to the terms of the statute."[30] Like a patent, Yates J. proposes in *Millar*, postpublication copyright is but a "temporary privilege."[31] It is not in any sense a species of "property" properly so-called.[32] As we will presently see in more detail, Yates J.'s dissent in *Millar* thus amounts to a thoroughgoing refusal of the conditions for the possibility of authorship as ownership. Accordingly, as a statutory privilege, copyright duration can amount to no more than the limited times specified in the statute.

It would be only natural to suppose that, considered as an overturning of Lord Mansfield's affirmation of perpetual common law copyright in *Millar*, the holding in *Donaldson* represented a vindication of Yates J.'s dissent in *Millar*. But that is not how *Donaldson* was read. As Rose's image of a "striking reversal" suggests, subsequent interpretation found in *Donaldson* confirmation of a so-called common law right over published work (albeit of limited duration) that in fact had no previous existence. *Donaldson* thus created the very right that Yates J. found nonexistent. Whereas Yates J. had understood the Statute as having *created* a temporary privilege, *Donaldson* was read as if the Statute *limited* a preexisting right. "That the House of Lords in *Donaldson* rejected the existence of any common law copyright," Ronan Deazley writes, "is not of course how their decision is popularly portrayed or understood." On the contrary, he adds, "[t]he ontology developed at that time, in support of the common law right, has since come to inform our understanding of copyright, as *Donaldson* was mistakenly taken to validate the existence of that common law right."[33]

It would be equally natural to suppose that precluding the reversal would have required an insistence on Yates J.'s view that copyright is nothing more than a statutory creation. Speculating as to what the history of copyright may have been, had the opponents of literary property fared better in the literary property debate, is not necessarily a fruitless exercise, of course. But it seems fair to assume that an insistence on Yates J.'s dissent would have been as fruitless as we are told it actually was. The problem at the core of the "striking reversal" of *Donaldson* was precisely that neither Yates J.'s dissent, nor the opponents of literary property generally, developed an effective alternative representation of authorship. To insist again on Yates J.'s opinion is to reiterate that absence. It is to reproduce the role that the Yates J.'s dissent had in crafting the striking continuity between *Donaldson* and Lord Mansfield's judgment in *Millar.*

The narrative of a "striking reversal" is a lament for the loss or betrayal of the public interest purpose of copyright law. Evoking C. B. MacPherson's classic analysis of Hobbes and Locke, Rose's image of reversal is intended to capture the infiltration of "possessive individualism" into copyright law—perhaps even the very origin of copyright law as possessive individualist to its core.[34] The narrative requires, first, an interpretation of Lord Mansfield's judgment in *Millar* as possessive individualist, and, second, a tracing of the pathways through which the possessive individualist image of authorship comes to preside—through the reversal of *Donaldson*—over the interpretation of the Statute of Anne. The result is a pervasive sense that the villains of the story, the greedy Stationers supported by no less a legal luminary than Lord Mansfield, suppressed and obscured the public interest promise of *Donaldson.* "The centrality of the public interest," as Ronan Deazley puts it, "identifiably there, is once again concealed."[35]

But it does not follow that the antidote to this reversal is an assertion of the public interest over and against the interests of authorship. On the contrary, the binary opposition of author and public is itself part and parcel of the possessive individualist story. It is the possessive individualist author, we might say, that generates a view of the public as its own opposite, just as the unbridled freedom of the atomized Hobbesian individual generates an absolutely sovereign State required to subjugate it. What is required, instead, is a redefinition of authorship, neither its denial nor its limitation in the name of the public interest. The story that needs to be told is the story of the immanent public content of authorship—a juridical representation of authorship as constitutively open toward the public domain. The antidote to the author as proprietor is the retrieval of the author as speaker.

Indeed, it is difficult to read the prevailing accounts of the literary property debate without wondering why the opponents of literary property did not develop an alternative image of authorship. After all, if the proponents of literary property triumphed by presenting an interpretation of a public interest statute from a possessive individualist standpoint, would the response not have been one of articulating an interpretation of the author's common law right as immanently oriented toward the public domain? Perhaps part of the explanation is that opponents of literary property were too busy formulating not the limits but rather the intolerably expansive features of common law copyright. As Benjamin Kaplan put it, "[p]roponents would be intent to show that the perpetual right was narrow enough to be tolerable, while opponents would try to show its inordinate potential breadth as a reason for denying its existence in the first place."[36] Thus, it is in the efforts of the proponents of literary property to minimize the scope of the common law right, rather than in those of the opponents to maximize that scope, that one may expect to find the seeds of an image of authorship open toward the public domain. Lord Mansfield, not Yates J., holds the key to reversing the reversal.

Lord Mansfield's "Copy"

Lord Mansfield frames his judgment in *Millar* as a response to the objections presented in Yates J.'s dissent. Noting that "[t]his is the first instance of a final difference of opinion in this Court, since I sat here," Lord Mansfield observes that the fact of disagreement is but yet another guarantee that the opinions delivered were "formed upon the fullest examination."[37]

Immediately following his introductory remarks, Lord Mansfield announces that his judgment will unfold, from premises shared by Yates J. himself, a response to the objections raised against common law copyright: "From premises either expressly admitted, or which cannot and therefore never have been denied, conclusions follow, in my apprehension, decisive upon all the objections raised to the property of an author, in the copy of his own work, by the common law."[38] Yet before stating the "expressly admitted" common premises he will deploy, Lord Mansfield is careful to define the key term at issue: "I use the word 'copy,' in the technical sense in which that name or term has been used for ages, to signify an incorporeal right to the sole printing and publishing of somewhat intellectual, communicated by letters."[39] We are now told the shared premises Lord Mansfield has in mind: "It has all along been expressly admitted, that, by the common law, an author is intitled to the copy of his own work until it has been once printed and published by his authority . . . "[40] Moreover, this prepublication "property in the copy" "is equally an incorporeal right to print a set of intellectual ideas or modes of thinking, communicated in a set of words and sentences and modes of expression. It is equally detached from the manuscript, or any other physical existence whatsoever."[41] Lord Mansfield's opening claim, then, is that he can respond to Yates J.'s dissent by broaching three related propositions: namely, that (1) there is a common law right of first publication; that (2) this right is "incorporeal" in the sense of "detached from the manuscript, or any other physical existence whatsoever;" and that (3) this right is an exclusive right to printing and publishing an author's work. This is the right he calls a "copy." In short, his point is that to grant the right of first publication in this way is to concede the case. Once an exclusive right of publication is granted in respect of unpublished work, nothing in the act of publication can be regarded as an abandonment of that right. The exclusive right of publication therefore subsists through publication and thus applies to published work as well. A "copy" is a "copy," whether in respect of unpublished or published work.

We can get at Lord Mansfield's argument through a couple of examples. Assume that an author hands an unpublished manuscript—or a copy thereof—to a friend for comments and review. Assume also that the friend prints and publishes the work without authorization. We would have no difficulty finding that, in spite of his being lawfully in possession of a copy of the manuscript, the friend infringes the author's right of first publication. The transfer by the author of a copy of the manuscript to the friend is not a transfer of the right to print and publish the work.

The transfer of a physical copy is not a transfer of the "copy." Similarly, if an author—or his authorized publisher—sells several thousand copies of the manuscript, the transfer of these copies is not a transfer of the "copy." "Does a transfer of paper upon which it [a book] is *printed* necessarily transfer the copy, more than the transfer of paper upon which the book is *written*?"[42] An author does not give up his sole right to print and publish the work when he publishes the work any more than when he hands a copy of his manuscript to a friend. The common law right of (so-called) *first* publication is in truth a sole right of publication *simpliciter*. "[T]he same reasons hold," Lord Mansfield writes, "*after* the author has published."[43]

In Lord Mansfield's view, the author's common law copyright subsists through publication because it is not a property right in respect of the manuscript. Its being "detached" from the manuscript or from any given copy is absolutely essential to its remaining unaffected by the act of publication—the act of making copies available to the public.[44] Because the author's "copy" at common law is "incorporeal," nothing in the act of publication can be deemed (to recall Yates J.'s words) a "gift to the public," a throwing of the author's work "open to all mankind."

Lord Mansfield's answer to Yates J., then, is that to posit the author's prepublication right is thus necessarily to posit the author's postpublication right. But the ground on which Lord Mansfield builds his argument is by no means as shared as he appears to believe. It is true that both Lord Mansfield and Yates J. assume a common law right of first publication. But their respective understandings of the nature of this right could not be further apart. For Lord Mansfield, the right subsists and must subsist independently of the manuscript. For Yates J., the right is radically mediated through the manuscript. It is in fact a property right in respect of the manuscript, a right to the sole use of the manuscript conceived as a chattel. Thus, Yates J. observes that while it is "most certainly true" that "a literary composition is certainly in the sole dominion of the author, till he thinks proper to publish it," it is also true that "this holds good no longer than *while it is in manuscript*."[45] Yates J. adds that, on the facts in *Millar*, "the defendant has not meddled with the author's manuscript. The work was published forty years ago. The defendant has printed a sett of his own. He has not meddled with any property of the author's; unless the very style and sentiments in the work were his."[46] Yates J.'s point is that because the author's right of first publication is an incident of the author's property right in the manuscript, the prepublication right cannot possibly survive publication. Once copies are made available to the public, anyone can print the work without "meddling" with the subject matter of the author's right—the manuscript itself. For Yates J., infringement of the right of first publication is a mode of conversion of the manuscript.

For Yates J., property must be property of corporeal objects: "And it is a well-known and established maxim, (which I apprehend holds as true now, as it did 2000 years ago,) 'that nothing can be an object of property, which has not corporeal substance.'"[47] Thus, as a property right, the prepublication right cannot be other than a right in respect of the physical manuscript. It follows that, once released through publication from its shackles in the brute physicality of the manuscript, an author's work is "free as the air to common use."[48] Nothing in the author's ownership of his physical copy can prevent someone else from copying her lawfully acquired copy. When the author sells the physical book, he parts with the work. He cannot, as property lawyers like to say, suck and blow at the same time.

Lord Mansfield agrees. He knows very well that to posit publication as something one does with a manuscript, as some sort of dealing with a chattel, is to posit the impossibility of a postpublication right in respect of the work. There is absolutely nothing entailed in the ownership of ink and pages that can entitle the owner to prevent others, once the patterns of ink on those pages are lawfully available to the public, from reproducing those patterns on another set of pages. As Yates J. correctly puts it, "the defendant has printed a sett of his own."[49] If we were to think through these concepts aurally rather than visually, we might say that there is nothing in an author's ownership of the phonograph he uses to amplify his voice that precludes another person from parroting his words or songs using her own phonograph. Lord Mansfield neither can nor does disagree. That is precisely why he repeatedly insists that the right in issue is "incorporeal." He is well aware that the prepublication right can subsist through publication only if conceived as "detached" from the manuscript. Thus, for Lord Mansfield, publication is and must be not a use of the manuscript but a use of the work. It is something one does not with *a* copy but with *the* "copy."

Yet we must be very careful here. This does not mean that Lord Mansfield propertized the work, framing it as a metaphysical chattel. Even if we were to adopt it, nothing in the idea of an intangible object of ownership would resolve the difficulty Yates J. presents. Assume for a moment that the author's object of ownership is not the physical manuscript but the intangible work. It is true that this shift from manuscript to work permits us to say that when the author sells the physical book he does not part with the work. But it is not any easier to see what in the author's ownership of the intangible work prevents a buyer of the book from copying her own lawfully acquired copy. Nothing she can do with the physical book, including copying it, would as a matter of property law amount to a conversion of the intangible work. Conversion requires depriving the owner of the object of ownership, but once the work is posited as intangible, the author cannot be deprived of the work. There is irony here: the work cannot be converted precisely because it is posited as intangible.[50]

The idea that the work is intangible cannot without more ado account for the subsistence through publication of the exclusive right of first publication. At most, what that idea does is translocate the problem. If, following Yates J., we posit the prepublication right as a property right in the physical manuscript, we are left with the mystery of trying to think through how a book buyer's use of her own lawfully acquired chattel (i.e., the physical book) can be a conversion of an author's chattel (i.e., a manuscript). If, alternatively, we decide to posit the prepublication right as a property right in the intangible work, we are left with the no less challenging mystery of trying to think through how a book buyer's use of her own lawfully acquired chattel (i.e., the physical book) can be a conversion of an author's work that, precisely as intangible, cannot be converted. The options are equally unpromising. An author cannot suck the physical book back in once he has sold it. Nor can he blow away the intangible work once it is posited as intangible. In neither case can the concept of an object of ownership—whether tangible or otherwise—account for the subsistence through publication of an author's prepublication right in respect of his work.

We might wish to say at this point that the copycat's actions deprive the author of the profits he would have otherwise had. This is what we mean when we say that unauthorized use of a work deprives its author of profits expected from his investment in the creation of the work. That may well be correct. But even if correct, that assessment as to the consequences of the copycat's actions in respect of the author's expectations is not a proprietary claim. There is no doubt that, like anyone else, an author is entitled to profits derived from unauthorized use of his property. But this is a far cry from saying that the fact of investment, whether in a work of authorship or in anything else, generates ownership of expected profits. Nothing in labor or value *per se* necessitates property. That I have pursued a fox at great expense, even if I am within a reasonable prospect of capture, does not mean I have captured it. That I have invested in the creation of a work of authorship does not entitle me as a matter of property law to preclude you from copying it, at least not unless we have previously established independently that the work is the object of my ownership. Nor can we say that ownership of the paper on which it is written, or of the work itself conceived as a metaphysical chattel, can without more ado ground a cause of action in conversion against anyone for doing as one wishes, including copying it, with one's own lawfully acquired physical book.

That a jurist of Lord Mansfield's stature was unaware of these rather elementary points about property law is entirely unbelievable, even if Yates J.'s dissent had not formulated them as eloquently as it did, and even if Lord Mansfield had not prefaced his own judgment by emphasizing that the judges had "tried to convince, or be convinced: but, in vain."[51] Unsurprisingly, Lord Mansfield did not think through the continuity of an author's right through publication by appealing to the concept of ownership of an intangible object. Lord Mansfield does not say that the author owns his work. What Lord Mansfield says, as we noted, is that there is such a thing as "the property of an author, in the *copy* of his own work," and that by "copy" he means "an incorporeal right to the sole printing and publishing of somewhat intellectual, communicated by letters." The difference is worth pursuing.

As soon as he defines "copy" as a term of art, Lord Mansfield elaborates its eccentricity as a proprietary claim. This is a "property in notion" that, having "no corporeal tangible substance," cannot sustain an "action of detinue, trover, or trespass *quare vi et armis*." It is a "property" that, because "incorporeal," is "incapable of being violated by crime indictable"; a so-called property, in other words, incapable of being stolen.

It can be violated, Lord Mansfield tells us, only "by another's printing without the author's consent." Thus this property is not a thing of which the owner can be deprived. Nor is it a right to exclude others from the use of a thing, whether tangible or otherwise. The "copy" is rather an exclusive right in respect of an act that, therefore, only its holder is entitled to perform. The exclusivity of this performance *is* the "property" Lord Mansfield describes.[52]

Lord Mansfield's differentiation of an author's "copy" from "property" properly so-called is no accident. It is only because he frames the subject matter of the right not as a thing but as act that Lord Mansfield can think through the subsistence of the right through publication. Precisely as an act, the subject mater of the author's "copy" is not a thing that an author can transfer to another, nor a thing of which an author can be deprived. Only the author's authorization can entitle another to perform the act that the author has the sole right to perform: "No disposition, no transfer of paper upon which the composition is written, marked, or impressed, (though it gives the power to print and publish) can be construed a conveyance of the copy, without the author's express consent 'to print and publish;' much less against his will."[53] Because publication is not authorization, the author retains through publication the sole right to print and publish the work. Making copies available to the public gives others the "power" but not the authority to print and publish. Infringing the author's "copy" is not about converting either manuscript or work, but about doing in respect of the work what only the author has the right to do.[54] Not the intangibility of the subject matter of an author's "copy," but rather its nature as an act, permits Lord Mansfield to grasp the continuity between the unpublished and the published as a matter of copyright law.

Nor is the specific nature of the act—i.e., printing and publishing—a function of the intangibility of the work. That a work is intangible may well be sufficient to establish that it cannot be the subject of theft, detinue, trover, or trespass. But there is nothing in intangibility as such requiring that the author's right over the work be conceived narrowly as a right of printing and publishing. Thus, it can come as no surprise that Lord Mansfield says more than that the work is "incorporeal." He says that the work is "somewhat intellectual, *communicated by letters*."[55] His narrow construal of the author's right tracks the concept of the work as something the essence of which is to be communicated: "a set of intellectual ideas or modes of thinking, communicated in a set of words and sentences and modes of expression."[56] Lord Mansfield conceives the author's "copy" as a right to print and publish the work because he conceives the work as itself communicative. The author's "copy" is the author's prerogative to perform his act of authorship—to produce or reproduce the work.

Lord Mansfield's description of the author's "copy" precludes any classification of it as proprietary in any self-evident sense. His justification of the right, moreover, has the same effect. In a famous and frequently quoted passage, Lord Mansfield asks: "From what source, then, is the common law drawn, which is admitted to be so clear, in respect of the copy before publication?" And he replies: "From this argument—because it is just, that an author should reap the pecuniary profits of his own ingenuity and labor. It is just, that, another should not use his name, without his consent. It is fit that he should judge when to publish, or whether he will ever publish. It is fit he should not only choose the time but the manner of publication; how many; what volume; what print. It is fit, he should choose to whose care he will trust the accuracy and correctness of the impression; in whose honesty he will confide, not to foist additions: with other reasonings of the same effect."[57] It is hard to see this list of concerns as proprietary. Lord Mansfield's reasoning does not evoke the integrity of a person's entitlement to dispose of an object. His reasoning quite unequivocally singles out the integrity of an author's choices in respect of publication: the choice whether or not to publish, the choice of timing and manner of publication, and the choice of publisher. To be sure, in addition to the "fitness" regarding the integrity of the author's publication choices, Lord Mansfield also lists the "justice" of the author's entitlement to control use of his own name in relation to his work and to profit from his own ingenuity and labor. But neither the entitlement to control use of one's name, whether in relation to a work or more generally, nor the entitlement to reap profits from one's own labor, are necessarily or even *prima facie* proprietary in nature. What Lord Mansfield has in mind is not the author's work as a commodity but the author's autonomy in respect of publication. His judgment turns not on the author as proprietor but on the author as speaker. The author's "copy" is a prerogative in respect of a communicative act.

Yates J.'s Natural Law

Returning to Yates J.'s dissent will help us bring the depth of Lord Mansfield judgment more sharply into relief. We noted that, for Yates J., property is necessarily corporeal. As incorporeal, the work *per se* is unsuitable as proprietary subject matter. An author's prepublication right is thus mediated through the author's property in the physical manuscript. Once publication of the work makes copies lawfully available to the public, the author can no longer invoke ownership of his manuscript to prevent others from doing what they like with their own lawfully acquired copies. Publication is therefore abandonment of the author's physically mediated exclusivity in respect of the work.

The centrality of the concept of intangibility in Yates J.'s dissent has been, for good reason, frequently emphasized.[58] This is unsurprising. Yates J. prefigures discussion of the implications of the "public goods" nature of works of authorship for our conception of copyright law as a public policy instrument designed to wrestle with market failures hindering the efficient production and dissemination of works of authorship. He presents a theory of the necessarily statutory basis of copyright protection of published works, foreshadowing the now familiar mantra that copyright is not a natural right but a state-granted monopoly.[59]

It is equally unsurprising, of course, that Yates J. himself did not deploy intangibility as a "public goods" puzzle to be legislatively resolved. For Yates J., the intangibility of a work of authorship is a moment in a reflection about the inherent features and limits of property. At stake is not "market failure" but "natural law," the "general principles of property": "[H]owever peculiar the laws of this and every other country may be, with respect to territorial property, I will take it upon me to say, that the law of England, with respect to all personal property, had *its grand foundation in natural law.*"[60] Yates J. reasons from the standpoint of fundamental principles transcending any and all jurisdictions. He dissents not as a public interest instrumentalist, but as a natural law thinker affirming, against the proprietary pretensions of authorship, the "natural rights" of "all the rest of mankind."[61] He denies that copyright is a natural right on natural law grounds. For Yates J., the public domain is about fundamental natural law principles.

In this vein, intangibility is not merely a physical phenomenon. On the contrary, it has determinative normative significance. Yates J. elaborates this significance along two related axes. The first is about the impossibility of demarcating an intangible as a proprietary object. In the absence of demarcation, those subject to an obligation in respect of the intangible would lack notice thereof: "the obligation [to respect another's property] could only take place where the property was distinguishable; and every body knew that it was not open to another. Mankind must have a knowledge of what is their duty, in order to observe it by abstaining from every violation of it . . ."[62] Intangibility would render the imposition of proprietary obligation inconsistent with the rights of those subjected to it. The limits of the proprietary paradigm are the obverse of inviolable preexisting entitlements held by all as persons.

But while notice is necessary, it is not sufficient to render proprietary claims consistent with the rights of others. Regardless of notice issues, Yates J. identifies inconsistencies besetting the very concept of private appropriation of works of authorship. Yates J.'s passage is worth quoting at length. We will hardly fail to see that he lays hold of the problem of independent creation as an insurmountable normative obstacle to propertizing copyright:

> An author is fully possessed of his ideas, when they arise in his mind: and therefore from the time these ideas occur to him; or from the time he writes them down, they are his property. Then if another man has the same ideas as an author, he must not presume to publish them: he may be told these ideas were preoccupied, and thereby became private property.
>
> It would be strange indeed, if the very act of publication can be deemed the commencement of private property. Even after publication, many thousands may never set their eyes upon the book: yet would not these have a right to choose the same subject? and may they not have the same ideas upon it?
>
> The improbability of their hitting upon those ideas is not to the point. If they should occur to the author; he has a right to publish them. Of this, I think, there can hardly be a doubt. Yet property, says Pufendorf, is a right by which the very substance

> of a thing belongs to one person, so that it cannot, in the whole, nor after the same manner, become another's. And the digests speak to the like effect. Sentiments are free and open to all; and many people may have the same ideas upon the same subject. In that case, every one of these persons to whom they independently occur, is equally possessed and equally master of all these ideas; and has an equal right to them as his own. Is it possible then that any one individual can have sole and exclusive property in these?[63]

The issue this passage identifies is not that, because intangible, ideas cannot be readily ascertained. Nor is the issue that, because nonexcludable, ideas present peculiar difficulties in respect of efficient production and distribution. The issue, rather, is that, even if clearly ascertained and securely protected, the propertization of ideas remains inconsistent with the rights of others. Owning ideas is tantamount to owning another's thoughts. Thought is free not because it is impossible to capture but because, regardless of its source or origin, each and all have an equal right to it as one's own.

Propertizing ideas would deprive those other than the putative owner of the right to think through freely their own spontaneously and independently occurring thoughts. It would place a nonowner under the scandalous obligation to pay a royalty each and every time a thought that another had already thought or published would pass through his own mind. This would remain absurdly true even in the case of ideas that, rather than spontaneously and independently occurring to the nonowner, had been accessed in and through the owner's work. Subjecting that situation to proprietary analysis would render he who learns from an author into a bizarre kind of licensee, able lawfully to think what the author teaches only by becoming forever enslaved to the author's permission, perhaps as some kind of impossible bailee, radically unable to perform the duty to return the bailed object when demanded by its owner. Of course, this is the stuff of science fiction comedy, tragedy, or dystopia, but not of property law. Yates J.'s point is that, construed as proprietary subject matter, an idea would lodge itself, like an encysted foreign body, in another's mind. Learning cannot be a mode of trespass any more than breathing. Publication is and must be a "gift to the public" because retention of any postpublication rights in respect of ideas is contrary to natural law.

Invoking the idea/expression dichotomy here is not sufficient to address the fundamental problem that Yates J. identifies. A proprietary claim is a *prima facie* claim to any and all uses of the subject matter at issue. From this point of view, the possibility of independent creation, regardless of its likelihood, operates as an *indicium* that property law cannot provide the set of concepts required to grasp the author's entitlement in a manner consistent with the equal claims of others. The nexus between author and audience cannot be propertized. In respect of knowledge and its transmission, the concepts that property law provides are literally deficient, inconsistent with the rights of persons as independent thinkers. This is why Yates J. says that "improbability [of independent creation] . . . is not to the point."[64] Once a work of authorship is propertized, not only independent creation, but even the simple act of reading threatens to appear as a use of proprietary subject matter—as if the lawfulness of reading, otherwise an ordinary and necessary incident of publication, would require the formulation of exceptions to the author's *prima facie* claim of exclusivity. Like ideas, expressions, too, if construed as proprietary subject matter, become the cyst of another's presence in one's own mind. Yates J.'s insight is that, even descriptively, the language and categories of property are woefully inadequate to grasp relations between authors and public. For Yates J., this means that copyright as property is and must be inconsistent with natural law.

Yates J.'s challenge is as profound as its failure was predictable. There is no such thing as common law copyright, he tells us, because there is no such thing as property in intangibles. His judgment thus rests on an assumption that if there were such a thing as copyright at common law, it would be proprietary in nature. Where there is copyright, there must be property. In the end, it was this assumption that prevailed.

Of course, Yates J. formulated his denial of common law copyright as an assertion that the source of copyright law is solely statutory. Thus copyright is not property but a "temporary privilege," a statutory monopoly. Yet this terminological shift is simply not sufficient to generate an alternative representation of authorship capable of informing a nonproprietary interpretation of the statutorily granted privilege. On the contrary, the emphasis on the intangibility of copyright subject matter is at the root of the problem. It suggests a construal of the task of copyright as a problem about propertizing the intangible, domesticating the wild, erecting metaphysical fences to demarcate the nonexcludable.[65] As Yates J. has it, the common law right of first publication can subsist through publication only as the "property in the thing to be published" persists.[66] That Yates J. categorically denied that persistence is to no avail. What matters is that he defined it along proprietary lines. Ironically, it was the definition that persisted.

In this vein, the statute appears as a resolution to the problem of intangibility not solved at common law, a policy instrument designed to fill the common law void. Yates J.'s reading of the registration requirement imposed through the Statute of Anne is a good example. He understands registration as a solution to the absence of "distinguishing marks," and hence of notice, that the intangibility of works of authorship brings in its wake. "The Legislature had plainly this objection in view, when they penned the Statute of Queen Ann., . . . And from that register-book any person may see whether the author intended to make a property of his work; and they may see the duration of such property: for the property is to commence from the publication of the work, provided it be so regularly entered as the Act requires."[67] The statutory regime thus provides the lacking "property." It sutures the juridical emptiness. It grants legal corporeity to the intangible subject matter at issue. By framing the absence of common law copyright as the absence of property in intangibles, Yates J. in effect defined copyright as property. The subsequent vindication of the statutorily limited term in *Donaldson* confirmed this victory of the proprietary frame. Perhaps this was less a matter of a striking reversal than of the unfolding of a shared ill-fated logic. There is deep continuity between Yates and *Donaldson.* It is the continuity of a shared problem.

That is not all. There is only a short distance to travel from the assumption that the copyright problem is a problem about propertizing the intangible to the proposition that copyright is a solution to a "public goods" problem; that is, that copyright law is a policy instrument designed to create the conditions for the possibility of the efficient production and distribution of works of authorship. Just as, for Yates J., the Statute of Anne cures the absence of property in intangibles at common law, so does, for contemporary instrumentalist theory, copyright law cure the failure of the market in respect of public goods. Common law failure, so to speak, becomes transmuted into market failure. This transmutation is not devoid of very serious implications.

Yates J. premised his reflection about common law copyright on natural law grounds. Because in his view the common law has its foundation in natural law, his denial of common law copyright is a denial that copyright could find its justification in natural law. His argument is not merely that common law copyright did not exist, but also that common law copyright would have been inconsistent with natural law. The absence of common law copyright is not (only) an historical fact. It is also a normative insight.

This normative insight informs the interpretation of the statute. This is yet another angle from which to appreciate Yates J.'s observation that the statute deals with the problem of notice by requiring registration. Even as he asserted the radically and exclusively statutory source of copyright law, he interpreted (at least in part) the statute from the standpoint of normative constraints he regarded as natural. The interpretive stance thus makes it at the very least unlikely that the statute would grant rights inconsistent with the normative imperatives that render common law copyright inappropriate. The same natural law that precludes copyright at common law serves as a kind of unwritten constitution, as it were, that both informs the interpretation of the statute and limits thereby the temporary privileges it grants.

There is, in Yates J.'s worldview, what we might call a latent natural law constitution affirming the rights of each and all to think their own thoughts and publish their own works. From this point of view, there is and must be a public domain because monopoly over one's own work conceived as an object of ownership is monopoly over another's thought. Strictly speaking, we should say not that there must be a public domain but rather that (as Yates J. correctly and profoundly saw) copyright as property is normatively untenable, and radically so. Because it must be freely available to others as thinkers and authors, an author cannot exclude others absolutely—whether *prima facie* or otherwise—from the subject matter over which he would purport to claim an exclusive proprietary right. Rather, he must present himself juridically as a thinker among thinkers, and an author among authors. What Yates J. saw most clearly is that property law cannot formulate that alternative representation of the author. In his view, property necessarily construes the thought and authorship of others as incorporeal hereditaments, so to speak, burdening the territory of the author's work.

The thesis of the natural law impossibility of copyright as property contained and oriented Yates J.'s reading of the statute. Divorced from these natural law moorings, the deployment of the exclusively statutory source of copyright law within instrumentalist discourse, however, is devoid of any such normative constraints or guidelines. The denial of common law copyright arises for instrumentalism rather as a denial of natural law as such, even the natural law that Yates J. insisted must assert itself against copyright. The resulting interpretive stance is one in which the statute emerges triumphant, as it were, devoid of any nature against which it must be critically juxtaposed, freed from any normative limits that must orient and inform it. The public domain now arises not as the inviolable forum of the rights of each and all to independence of thought, but rather as the contingent manifestation of imperatives to reduce transaction costs in the name of efficiency. The problem is not so much that we cannot own each other's thoughts. The problem is only that it would be too difficult, too complicated, and too costly to charge each other for them. Instrumentalism thus constitutes itself as a shared terrain on which maximalists and minimalists endlessly evaluate and dispute the relative weights of high and low copyright protection, equally certain that nothing but efficiency can function as a limiting principle. By celebrating the victory against natural law, minimalism cheats itself out of the set of principles that, above and beyond empirical calculations, could justify its efforts to oppose copyright expansion. It forgets that, once it grants the proposition that copyright is a solution to a "public goods" problem, it is already on maximalist terrain.

A Gift to the Public

Approaching copyright from the standpoint of the tangible/intangible distinction induces an assumption that the task of copyright is to propertize intangibles. This assumption thus precludes and obscures discussion of alternative, nonproprietary conceptions. The interpretive force of the proprietarian frame is difficult to overestimate. Even Lord Mansfield's judgment in *Millar,* textually unsustainable as a judgment premised on ordinary proprietary concepts, nonetheless appears as an assertion of common law copyright as proprietary. Perhaps the deepest of ironies is that grasping Lord Mansfield as having posited copyright as property is grasping Lord Mansfield not in his own terms but from Yates J.'s point of view.

There can be no doubt, of course, that in the course of his discussion Lord Mansfield repeatedly referred to an author's "copy" as a mode of property. But nor can there be any doubt that Lord Mansfield's substantive description of the juridical interest renders the classification of copyright as proprietary radically unstable. Lord Mansfield does not anchor his judgment on the tangible/intangible distinction. He knows all too well that the characterization of a work of authorship as a thing, even if an intangible one, could not generate the proposition that an author's prepublication interest subsists through publication. In place of the distinction between tangible and intangible Lord Mansfield offers the distinction between thing and act, object and performance. He thus formulates the subject matter of an author's right not as a thing but as an act. The "copy," as we noted, is an authorial prerogative to perform a particular act in respect of the work. This act is the act of printing and publishing the work, of addressing the public in and through the work.

The implications of this move are monumental.[68] First, the construal of the work as a communicative act pierces through the Gordian knot of understanding the act of publication as the transfer of a thing—whether of the tangible book or of the intangible work—from author to public. Rather, to publish one's work is to communicate it—to speak in one's own words. Publication is not the use of a thing. It is an instance of speech.

Second, the construal of the work as a communicative act indicates that the wrong involved in copyright infringement is not some kind of conversion, whether of the tangible book or of the intangible work. Rather, copyright infringement is the exercise without authorization of the author's prerogative to speak his own words. It is compelling another to speak. Precisely because publication is an affirmation of an author's autonomy as a speaker, publication is not an abandonment of the prerogative to speak or not to speak. Thus, whether of unpublished or published work, copyright infringement is compelled speech. The concept of the "copy" as a right in respect of the performance of the act of publication thus provides a unitary account of infringement in respect of works of authorship as such, whether unpublished or published.

Third, the construal of the work as a communicative act tailors the scope of the right in accordance with its communicative subject matter. Thus, noncommunicative uses of the work, as in merely technical (non) uses of the work, are not actionable. By the same token, nor are transformative uses involving a defendant's own authorship actionable, because the plaintiff's entitlement as a speaker cannot preclude the valid exercise of another's speech. User rights thus appear neither as exceptions to or burdens on a would-be proprietary holding, nor as "balanced" compromises involving opposing or externally imposed interests or values. Rather, user rights flow immanently from within the communicative nature of the subject matter of the author's "copy."

Because it refuses to posit the work as an object of ownership, the communicative hermeneutic, as distinct from the proprietary one, provides a response to Yates J.'s normative concerns pertinent to the encysting of an author's propertized expression in another's mind. Construed as communicative acts, rather than owned content, works of authorship invite responses rather than encyst themselves in another's mind as fenced metaphysical terrain requiring permission to be explored. The concept of the work as communicative is thus consistent with and required by the equal autonomy of each and all as independent thinkers and authors. In short, Yates J.'s objections to the propertization of copyright subject matter are invitations to set forth a theory of copyright from the standpoint of the foundational principle of independent creation. The incoherence of the representation of the author as proprietor is but the starting point of the emergence of the author as speaker.

Once copyright is grasped in this way, emancipated from the second-order concern about domesticating or propertizing the intangible, the entirety of copyright doctrine is intelligible as juridical protection and cultivation of the integrity of speech as speech. Moreover, it is the integrity of speech as speech that reveals that the author's standing as autonomous speaker itself restricts and defines his ability to choose unilaterally the conditions under which he speaks. The author cannot impose conditions on his speech that deny its character as speech. Because the doctrine of originality grants the author rights for speaking in his own words, the author cannot derogate from his speech in the very same breath in which he claims standing as a speaker. He cannot, that is, ask copyright law to grant him rights inconsistent with the grounds upon which copyright law recognizes him as an author. Thus, his irreducible choice to speak or not to speak cannot as a copyright law matter translate into an unencumbered autonomy to restrict unilaterally the conditions under which his work is publicly available. The question is not about what the author wants but about what his autonomy as an author permits him to claim.

Consider, for example, an author alleging that he speaks on condition that others do not discuss or adopt without his consent the ideas expressed in his work. Use of those ideas would thus amount to an infringement of the author's copyright. Of course, it is uncontroversial that an allegation of that sort is inconsistent with the idea/expression dichotomy. This does not mean, however, that we must grasp the idea/expression dichotomy as some kind of doctrinal 'taking,' as it were, of aspects of the author's work without his consent. It is not as if copyright doctrine deprives the author of anything that is otherwise rightfully his. On the contrary, as we noted in Chapter 2, precisely as a communicative act, an author's work is an invitation to talk about the ideas it conveys. It is an invitation to dialogue. By asserting his copyright, the author seeks to be treated as a person, and not a mere puppet, and so insists that he not be compelled to speak. By the same token, his work is, as copyright subject matter, addressed to persons, and not mere puppets, and so contemplates the responses of its audience. By framing ideas as radically available, the idea/expression dichotomy protects and affirms the conditions for the possibility of those responses. It is but the doctrinal manifestation of the ongoing conversation from which an author's work arises and to which it must necessarily address itself. Far from 'taking' from the author, the idea/expression dichotomy affirms the nature of copyright subject matter as speech and of the author as a speaker engaged in dialogue with others. The same dialogical set of considerations underlies transformative fair use and, albeit in a different sense, nonuse. The author's autonomy as a speaker does not dissolve the conditions for the possibility of the public domain. Rather, it grounds them immanently within and through itself.

The point is that the determination made through the originality doctrine that a work is subject to copyright is not a once-and-for-all determination entitling the author to make exclusive claims of right to any and all uses of copyright subject matter. It is not as if a finding of originality were tantamount to a finding of owned content. Originality is not first possession. On the contrary, copyright doctrine as a whole is but an insistence that copyright subject matter be treated not as owned content but as speech and as nothing but speech. Following the principle of independent creation, the originality requirement, the defense of independent creation, the idea/expression dichotomy, the doctrine of merger, along with the concept of nonuse and the defense of fair dealing or fair use, ensure that the scope of the author's right correctly tracks the nature of copyright subject matter. It is as speech and only as speech that the work is subject to copyright protection. Copyright doctrine precludes the reification of copyright subject matter as a thing. It preserves the work as a communicative act. Thus, copyright protection neither permits the author to extend the scope of his entitlement in a manner that precludes another's speech responding to his, nor encompasses uses of the work as something other than speech. Viewed in this light, grounding the author's right in his autonomy as a speaking being is already a way of defining and limiting the scope of her entitlement. Not any and all unauthorized uses of a work or of a work's material form can be regarded as compelled speech.

The central and overarching difference between the speech model and the proprietary model is in the way in which each formulates the nature of the exclusion at stake in copyright law. Copyright excludes. It grants an author the exclusive right to summon the power of the state to preclude others from engaging in certain acts in respect of his work. In the proprietary model, this exclusion is an ejection. It keeps others out of the terrain of the author's work. Little changes if this exclusion is understood not formally as rooted in property concepts but functionally, and perhaps more flexibly, as the outcome of a balanced compromise between author and users mediated in and through the public interest in efficiency. In both instances, whether formally or functionally, the author's right is a right to exclude. Others arise in the system either as exceptions or as countervailing weights. Users burden the author's interests, and *vice versa,* as each and both dispute the distributive scope of their respective entitlements over works of authorship.

In the speech model, by contrast, the exclusion is of a qualitatively distinct kind. The right to exclude from the inviolable autonomy of one's choice to speak or not to speak is also, and necessarily, a mode of inclusion. An author chooses whether to speak or not to speak, but he cannot choose to speak *and* not to speak. Speech necessarily includes because it addresses others. Speakers contemplate audiences and interlocutors. Whereas proprietorship fears trespass, authorship seeks engagement. This seeking means that an author shares and must share precisely as he claims exclusivity in respect of his speaking. His insistence to be respected as an autonomous speaker thus constitutes itself as a gift to the public.

Yates J. was entirely correct to have understood that authorship is a gift to the public. But he was mistaken to have seen this gift as irremediably inconsistent with the author's "copy." On the contrary, it is precisely because the "copy" is a prerogative in respect of one's own speech that it necessarily and simultaneously constitutes itself as gift. Inclusion is a condition for the possibility of the author's exclusive right in respect of her work.

The focus on the author's autonomy as a speaking being thus opens up, rather than forecloses, the public domain in copyright law. It brings into relief the correlative autonomy of the members of the author's audience not as consumers of value but as speaking beings. By avoiding the deployment of the author's right along proprietary lines, the image of the author as speaker premises copyright law on the mutually constitutive reciprocity of speakers and interlocutors. Copyright law arises not as a distributive balance of intangible commodities but as a juridical order addressing aspects of the interaction between speaking beings. In so doing, it defines and confines the scope of an author's copyright in light of her place in the ongoing conversation of which she is but a participant. The public domain thus emerges far more forcefully, not as a depository of value for which no payment is extracted, but as a radically nonnegotiable set of conditions for dialogue flowing from the very nature of copyright subject matter as communication.

Personal Use

Finally, the communicative construal of the work brings into relief the lawfulness not only of nonuse and of transformative use but also of personal use. Because a work is a communicative act, to reproduce it is to recommunicate it. Not unauthorized reproduction but unauthorized publication is the paradigmatic mischief at the heart of copyright law. Personal use, precisely as such, involves no publication. It is therefore by definition outside the purview of an author's "copy." Setting forth the similarities and differences between personal use and both nonuse and transformative use will help deepen the portrayal of the public domain as dialogue. It will reveal that, as in nonuse and transformative use, the lawfulness of personal use flows from the principle of independent creation.

Paradigmatic instances of nonuse involve use of a work's material form not as a work but as a tool, not communicatively but technically. Thus, for example, neither the accounting forms in *Baker* nor the thumbnail images in *Arriba Soft* attract liability. This does not mean, however, that technical use is a requirement of nonuse.[69] Rather, the technical aspect functions as evidence that the use in question is noncommunicative. What matters is that, because the use is noncommunicative, it cannot be said to compel the author to speak.

Transformative use involves use in the context of the defendant's own authorship. Fair use for the purpose of criticism is thus a paradigmatic instance of transformative use. The defendant recommunicates the plaintiff's work in the absence of authorization. There can be no doubt that transformative use is unauthorized use above and beyond use of the material form of the plaintiff's work. This is not mere nonuse. At the same time, however, transformative use is use of the plaintiff's work only as a reasonable aspect of the defendant's own work. There is thus no use of the plaintiff's work as a communicative act in its own right. The defendant's authorship evidences that he does not appropriate the plaintiff's form of expressions as such. He does not compel the plaintiff to speak. Rather, he engages the plaintiff's work as an aspect of the subject matter of his own work. It is the defendant who speaks. Thus his use is neither nonuse nor actionable communicative use. In a word, it is transformative use.

Personal use is copying the material form of a work for the purpose of enjoying the work, as when I copy an article for purposes of private study. It is noncommunicative in the sense that it does not involve recommunication (i.e., publication) of the work. Strictly speaking, the lawfulness of the act, even when unauthorized, follows inexorably from the understanding of copyright as an exclusive right to publish the work: reproduction of the material form of the work in the absence of publication is lawful. Personal use thus resembles nonuse in that, as noncommunicative, it is not actionable. At the same time, however, the lawfulness of personal use is more complex than that of nonuse. Personal use involves enjoyment of the work as an instance of speech, as the work of an author. This is not mere nonuse. As in transformative use, there is unauthorized use above and beyond use of the material form of the plaintiff's work. Unlike transformative use, however, the lawfulness of personal use cannot be predicated on the defendant's authorship.

What, then, grounds the lawfulness of personal use?

The distinction between personal use and transformative use itself contains the answer. *Prima facie,* the distinction is twofold. First, personal use is noncommunicative, whereas transformative use involves recommunicating the work. Second, personal use involves the enjoyment of the work, whereas transformative use involves the defendant's authorship. Upon closer inspection, however, the second aspect of the distinction already entails the first: transformative use involves recommunicating the work precisely because it involves the defendant's authorship. The transformativeness of the use, we might say, arises as an issue upon the defendant's publication of, for example, his review or criticism of the plaintiff's work. The distinction between personal use and transformative use thus resolves into the distinction between the defendant's enjoyment of the work in the former and the defendant's authorship in the latter. In short, personal use invokes the defendant's enjoyment in place of the defendant's authorship.

But this distinction between personal use and transformative use, enjoyment, and authorship, should not obscure their shared aspect. As much as in transformative use, in personal use the defendant takes up the plaintiff's work as the subject matter of his own activity. Enjoyment of a work is not merely passive. There is a difference between copying and reading. To copy is to act as a conduit. It is to repeat passively, in the absence, so to speak, of any presence of one's own. But to read is to comprehend, to compare and contrast. It is to juxtapose in the context of previous understandings. Reading is thinking, as are viewing and listening. To enjoy a work is not to publish it but to orient oneself toward it as a medium in and through which one learns of and from the ideas expressed therein. It is not use of the form of expression as such but as a drawing of or a reaching toward its content. This is precisely what it means to say (in the case of literary works) that personal use is about reading, not recommunicating the work. It is about the enjoyment, not the exploitation of the work.[70]

The difference between a personal use and a pirate edition is not merely quantitative. It is not as if a personal use is the same kind of act, albeit on a *de minimis* scale, as a pirate edition. Personal use is not small-time piracy. The pirate's unauthorized publication is an exploitation of the work. The pirate is a conduit, a mouthpiece. He moves the work through himself to another, in the absence of anything of his own, as if the work were but a thing, an object that can pass through one's hands, as it were impersonally. He appropriates the work not as the subject matter of his own learning but indeed as nothing other than its form as such. He does not read but handles the work. In a word, he commodifies it. Of course, it would be a mistake to conclude that the wrongfulness of his act is that he deprives the author of a commodity. On the contrary, it is precisely the act of treating the work as a commodity that contains the wrong! The wrongfulness consists in treating the author's form of expression, her speech, as subject to the unconstrained will of another, to the pirate's whim. He presents or represents the author's work to the public, placing himself between author and public, yet without the author's knowledge or consent. By his act of unauthorized publication, that is, he appoints himself unilaterally as the author's agent without the author's request or authority. He speaks for the author, and thus robs her of her agency. His commodification of the work compels the author to speak.

Nothing in personal use amounts to an exploitation of the work. Nothing in personal use amounts to an appropriation of the form of expressions as such. Indeed, the lawfulness of personal use is perhaps the most pristine of implications flowing from the principle of independent creation and the idea/expression dichotomy. Form but not content, expression but not idea, is subject to copyright protection. This means not only that copyright law categorically excludes the content of a work of authorship from protection. Ideas are not subject to copyright protection. It also means that copyright law categorically excludes the use of the work *as content* from protection. It bears endless emphasis that the form of expression is subject to protection *as form,* as an act of authorship, not as owned content. Personal use is lawful because it uses the work as the content of its own activity and draws from the work nothing but content. He who uses the work personally does not appropriate but rather listens to the author's voice. This is why personal use is not about exploitation but about enjoyment of the work. It is not a repetition of the work as form but rather a learning from the work as content.[71]

From this point of view, the lawfulness of personal use is, paradoxically, even less problematic than the well-settled lawfulness of transformative use. Unlike personal use, transformative use does recommunicate the work. It incorporates aspects of the form of another work in its own. It thus draws from that work not only content but also form. Accordingly, the lawfulness of transformative use requires the defendant's authorship as a showing that his drawing of form from the plaintiff's work is a use of form not as such but as the content of his own activity. The function of the defendant's authorship is none other than to show that the use of the plaintiff's form is not an appropriation of the plaintiff's voice. In other words, it is rather the defendant who speaks in his own voice. Transformative use is thus brought within the protected ambit of the principle that the plaintiff cannot claim in a manner inconsistent with another's authorship. Personal use, however, is less encumbered. Because it involves no use of form, in the sense that it involves no publication of the work, it imposes no authorship requirement. It flows pristinely from the idea/expression dichotomy because it uses the work only as and only for content. It uses the work not as expression but solely as idea—as the subject matter of its own thinking.[72]

Personal use thus brings into relief the observation that the work of authorship presupposes the work of thinking. Just as an author cannot claim in manner inconsistent with another's authorship, nor can an author claim in a manner inconsistent with another's thinking. The lawfulness of personal use is but an indication that one's own thinking cannot require authorization from those who nurture and inspire it any more than does one's own authorship. Its freedom is not premised on its culmination as authorship. Nothing in personal use infringes the author's "copy." On the contrary, unencumbered personal use fulfills the destiny of the work as an instance in the dialogically shared universe of thought.

6

Copyright and the System of Rights

In *Théberge v. Galerie d'Art du Petit Champlain inc.*,[1] Justice Binnie of the Supreme Court of Canada formulated the purpose of copyright law as a balance between authors and users of copyright subject matter. "The *Copyright Act*," Justice Binnie wrote, "is usually presented as a balance between promoting the public interest in the encouragement and dissemination of works of the arts and intellect and obtaining a just reward for the creator . . ."[2] The concept of "balance" brings in its wake an unambiguous affirmation of the integral and ineradicable status of the many and varied limitations that copyright law imposes on authorial entitlement. Thus, Justice Binnie immediately added that "[t]he proper balance among these and other public policy objectives lies not only in recognizing the creator's rights but in giving due weight to their limited nature."[3] If copyright is a balance between authors and users, then the limitations imposed on authors in the name of balance are part and parcel of the core, as distinct from the periphery, of copyright.

Once the concept of "balance" is explicitly invoked and affirmed, the very term "copyright" carries an ambiguous referent. The concept of balance makes explicit an otherwise latent ambiguity. On the one hand, "copyright" denotes the author's exclusive right of reproduction (among other authorial entitlements). On the other, "copyright" denotes a juridical order of which authorial entitlements are but a part, and of which the limitations imposed on such entitlements are as integral a part. From the standpoint of copyright as an exclusive right of reproduction, limitations appear as external pressures exerted or imposed upon authorial entitlement, as if from a periphery that, if not kept in its place, threatens to minimize or swallow the core. But from the standpoint of copyright as a juridical order of which authors and users are equally integral and balanced parts, limitations are not external but rather essential to the operation of the copyright system. We might say that the concept of balance makes explicit the internal nature of limitations. It underlines and therefore advances the internalization of limitations of authorial entitlement.

This internalization is already clearly visible in *Théberge,* where Justice Binnie grasps copyright exceptions as integral to copyright: "Excessive control by holders of copyrights and other forms of intellectual property may unduly limit the ability of the public domain to incorporate and embellish creative innovation in the long-term interests of society as a whole, or create practical obstacles to proper utilization. This is reflected in the *exceptions to copyright infringement* enumerated in ss. 29 to 32.2, which seek to protect the public domain in traditional ways such as fair dealing for the purpose of criticism or review and to add new protections to reflect new technology, such as limited computer program reproduction and 'ephemeral recordings' in connection with live performances."[4] Thus "exceptions," which one would quite naturally regard as extraordinary or anomalous, or at least as falling outside some general rule, are now rendered as perfectly ordinary or routine, falling squarely within the core of the copyright system.

In *CCH Canadian Ltd. v. Law Society of Upper Canada,* two years after *Théberge,* the Supreme Court of Canada held, famously and unambiguously, that exceptions are rather "user rights" integral to copyright.[5] This landmark affirmation of user rights is but a predictable and natural unfolding of the implications of the concept of balance affirmed in *Théberge. CCH* demonstrates the entrenchment in Canadian copyright jurisprudence of both the proposition that the rights of an author are "limited in nature," and of the corollary that these limits are the indication of the integral role and status of users in copyright law. In 2012, in *SOCAN v. Bell Canada,* Justice Abella affirmed the framing metaphor of balance: "*Théberge,*" she noted, "reflected a move away from an earlier, author-centric view which focused on the exclusive right of authors and copyright owners to control how their works were used in the marketplace."[6]

Authors are not alone in copyright. They must, quite literally, share their work with users. To be a creator—to recall Blackstone's enduring image—is most certainly *not* to have absolute and despotic dominion over one's creation.[7] To create is to share. Because users, too, have rights, the creator cannot keep the work to herself.

Public domain enthusiasm aside, there is actually nothing radically new in this. The judicial authority invoked by Justice Binnie in *Théberge* was none other than the judgment of Willes J. in *Millar v. Taylor.*[8] To assert the copyright balance is by no means to innovate.[9] The proposition that a work of authorship is neither private nor public but rather traversed through and through with both private and public aspects is a familiar one in copyright law. The idea/expression dichotomy and the defense of fair use or fair dealing are clear evidence that what originates in the author is not exclusively the author's. We might say that, in the eyes of copyright law, the creator has a gift, not only in the sense that her work is a deployment of her talents, but also in the sense that aspects of her work are public offerings. The author's gift is in this respect also the public's gift.

Nonetheless, the idea of exceptions somehow "integral" to the system to which they are exceptions begs for further elaboration. The problem is not only that, absent elaboration, a state of both terminological and conceptual ambiguity, threatens to become the rule rather than exception in Canadian copyright jurisprudence (or, for that matter, in *any* copyright jurisprudence seeking to grasp the relation between authors and users as the core of the copyright system). The problem is also that the currently preferred way of accomplishing the integration, the concept of balance, is unequal to the task. In essence, the concept of balance posits the issue of user rights distributively, as a translocation of the relative weights of copyright entitlements from authors to users, from creators to public. Doctrinally, this means that user rights appear, at the level of scope, to widen the fair use or fair dealing defense and to narrow the originality requirement. The challenge presented in and through the concept of user rights, however, is far deeper, engaging issues that transcend the concept of copyright scope.

User rights entail that recurrent and pervasive copying expressly contemplated in copyright legislation is to be interpreted not as a peripheral exception but as a core constituent of the juridical order. Once instances of copying are construed as exercises of right, rather than as excused wrongs, mere "reproduction" (as distinct from reproduction of the work *as a work*) is logically unsustainable, whether normatively or analytically, as the organizing category of copyright law. This, too, is not necessarily new. It reminds us that not all copying is copyright infringement, and that the true paradigm of infringement is the pirate edition, not the copy for personal use. More importantly, it alerts us that the concept of user rights has profound affinities not only with the concept of copyright scope but also with that of copyright subject matter. The task of integrating user rights requires that we conceive a work subject to copyright not as an intangible commodity or metaphysical chattel, but as an act of speech performed by its author. This is not an expansion of the role of scope relative to that of subject matter, as if the latter were to remain untouched and the former nothing more than quantitatively enlarged in a renewed version of the copyright calculus. Rather, the construal of the work as the speech of an author entails a resignification of the relation between scope and subject matter. In the logic of this resignification, user rights are internalized such that scope appears not as a curtailment of subject matter but as an iteration of the nature of subject matter as speech. Thus, for example, fair use or fair dealing—the user's right *par excellence*—is not an exception because it is an immanently driven determination of a work as the speech of an author contemplating another's response.

This does not mean, however, that any and all copyright limitations are or can be internalized. The concept of the work as speech permits us to grasp authors and users as coprotagonists on the copyright stage. But it does not specify for us limitations arising not from within the copyright system but in the wake of encounters between copyright and other recognized juridical interests. What, for example, is the relation between copyright and freedom of expression? Are the claims of a plaintiff as author under copyright law immediately superseded by those of a defendant as citizen under constitutional guarantees of freedom of expression? Is that an "exception" to copyright infringement? What, precisely, is the relation between authorship and citizenship in a liberal democracy?

This final chapter is an effort to locate the copyright system within the larger system of rights of which it is a part. My aim is less to resolve the issues involved than to study the conditions of their possibility; that is, to specify the assumptions that must be made for the questions to arise meaningfully from a rights-based perspective. I argue that we can identify at least four kinds of copyright limitations, of which only one can be regarded as a true exception. There are (a) subject matter limitations, (b) scope limitations, (c) miscellaneous exceptions, and (d) exceptions properly so-called. The upshot of this classification is that "exceptions properly so-called" denote instances where copyright as a juridical order encounters claims recognized in other juridical orders, with the result that the resolution of the ensuing dispute requires reaching beyond or outside the copyright system. We might say that exceptions properly so-called are sites wherein the language of copyright encounters other juridical languages, thereby giving rise to efforts of translation, modes of juridical analysis seeking to articulate, elaborate, and resolve encounters between heterogeneous claims of right.

I first consider the definitions of and distinctions between subject matter limitations, scope limitations, and miscellaneous exceptions. I then discuss aspects of the oft-discussed relation between copyright and human rights as an example of an encounter between copyright and other juridical orders. I suggest by way of conclusion that "proportionality" is the name we give to the efforts of translation that exceptions properly so-called generate. Exceptions are not peripheral phenomena but rather invitations to understand the relatedness of different juridical orders as aspects of a comprehensive system of rights.

Subject Matter Limitations

Subject matter limitations involve the definition of that over which copyright is an entitlement. That is, they are limitations involving the definition of copyright subject matter. For example, the proposition that facts are not copyrightable may be regarded as a limitation, but only in the sense that it defines the specificity of copyright subject matter.[10] It is not that the exclusion of facts from copyright subject matter amounts to an exception to copyright protection. It is rather that facts are not subject to copyright *ab initio*. The mere compilation of facts does not exhibit the skill and judgment (i.e., the originality standard in Canada) or creativity (i.e., the originality standard is the United States) required to give rise to copyright protection.[11] The exclusion of facts from copyright protection is, therefore, a definition in the sense that it establishes a general condition of copyrightability, thereby guarding the entrance, as it were, into the world of copyright. Understood spatially, the limitation is a gate-keeper. In keeping facts out of copyright, the doctrine of originality, as the *sine qua non* of copyright protection, defines copyright subject matter. Originality draws boundaries around copyright. It refuses, so to speak, to grant facts citizenship in the territory it demarcates.

Subject matter limitations are also operative in the distinctions between copyright and other intellectual property regimes. For example, just as facts are not subject to copyright, so are inventions, the subject matter of patent law, not subject to copyright. An invention is not a work. To be sure, there can be no doubt that the invention of a mousetrap requires skill and judgment or creativity. But a mousetrap is not a poem. It lacks the *specific* skill and judgment or creativity required to generate copyright protection. Whatever its nature, the skill and judgment or creativity of inventorship is distinct from the skill and judgment or creativity of authorship. The exclusion of inventions from copyright thus amounts to an exercise in demarcation that defines the specificity of copyright subject matter. As in the case of the exclusion of facts from copyright, the exclusion of inventions is a limitation but not an exception.

Whereas the distinction between works and facts informs us that works require skill and judgment or creativity, the distinction between works and inventions informs us that works require the *specific* skill and judgment or creativity *of an author*. In neither case, however, does the exclusion from copyright protection amount to an exception, in the sense of a deviation from a general rule. On the contrary, to the extent that they define copyright subject matter, the exclusions affirmed through the distinctions establish the very general rule—i.e., that originality gives rise to copyright—deviations from which would amount to exceptions. Once we know that we are dealing with a work rather than a mere fact or an invention, we can then attempt to carve out exceptions; that is, situations in which the work, though as such an instance of originality, will nonetheless not be subject to copyright protection. Subject matter limitations are in this sense conceptually prior to exceptions. They affirm the rule in the absence of which exceptions are impossible.[12]

Scope Limitations

As distinct from subject matter limitations, scope limitations are not about the nature of copyright subject matter but about the nature of the *entitlements* that copyright grants over its subject matter. The distinction between subject matter limitations and scope limitations tracks the distinction between a work and rights in or to the work. If subject matter limitations go to the definition of a *work,* scope limitations go to the definition of the *right.* Copyright is an exclusive right to do certain acts in respect of a work.[13] Scope limitations involve the specification of the particular acts that inhere in the copyright in a work. We might say that whereas subject matter limitations draw boundaries around copyright territory, and impose requirements in the absence of which citizenship will be refused, scope limitations specify the particular entitlements that accompany copyright citizenship once granted.

Because copyright is an exclusive right to do certain acts in respect of a work, a plaintiff in a copyright action must show (a) that she has a work (i.e., that the subject matter in respect of which she makes her claim is indeed a work), and (b) that she has a right (i.e., that the defendant's act in respect of the work is an act to which the plaintiff has an exclusive right). Thus, a defendant seeking to avoid liability can claim either that his impugned act is not an act in respect of a *work,* or that his impugned act does not fall within the scope of the plaintiff's *right* in respect of the work. If the defendant denies that the plaintiff's subject matter is a work, he relies on a subject matter limitation. If he denies that the plaintiff has a right, he relies on a scope limitation.

For example, a defendant who reproduces a phone directory produced by the plaintiff can claim successfully that the directory is not a work, but he could not succeed in claiming that he did not engage in an act of reproduction.[14] He reproduced the plaintiff's product, but this product is not a work subject to copyright. The plaintiff fails for want of subject matter.

Similarly, a defendant who independently authors a poem identical to that of a poem previously authored by the plaintiff can successfully claim that he did not engage in an act of reproduction in respect of the plaintiff's work, but he would not succeed in claiming that the plaintiff's product is not a work.[15] The plaintiff's product is a work, but this product was not reproduced by the defendant. The plaintiff fails for want of an exclusive right in respect of the subject matter he holds.

In the phone directory example, the plaintiff can show reproduction but not subject matter. In the independently created poem example, the plaintiff can show subject matter but not reproduction. In neither case can we speak of an exception—i.e., a situation that would otherwise amount to an infringement of the plaintiff's copyright. Both examples are rather about situations that are not within the plaintiff's copyright to begin with. The defendant does not have to appeal to an exception to avoid liability.

The example about the independently created poem illustrates a scope limitation. The plaintiff fails because his exclusive right of *reproduction* is not an exclusive right of (re-)*creation*. Independent creation by the defendant is not an exception to the plaintiff's right of reproduction, but an act of the defendant's that is *ab initio* outside the scope of the plaintiff's right. Thus, the definition of the right the plaintiff holds as a right of exclusive reproduction specifies the scope of her entitlements in respect of her work. Scope limitations define the plaintiff's right rather than burden it with exceptions. Just as facts are not granted citizenship in the world of copyright, so the preclusion of another person's independent creation is not an incident of copyright citizenship.

Scope Limitations and Exceptions

One would be tempted at this point to assert that if the plaintiff shows both (a) that the subject matter in respect of which she makes her claim is indeed a work, and (b) that the defendant's act in respect of the work is an act of reproduction, then (c) the defendant will be found to have infringed the plaintiff's copyright. But that is not necessarily the case. Considering why that is not necessarily the case will prove instructive in regard to the distinction between scope limitations and exceptions. It will also permit us to cement and develop the interpretation of fair use or fair dealing as a scope limitation rather than as an externally imposed exception to copyright.

Recall that the right of reproduction is a right to reproduce *the work or any substantial part thereof.*[16] Reproductions in respect of the work that are not reproductions of the work or a substantial part thereof do not amount to copyright infringements. A defendant who reproduces *in*substantial parts of the plaintiff's work does not infringe the copyright therein. Thus, even if the plaintiff shows (a) a work *and* (b) an act of reproduction in respect of the work, he still fails to make out his case. Is this an exception to copyright infringement? The answer is no. The reason is that, as in the example of the defendant who recreates but does not reproduce the plaintiff's work, this is an instance of the defendant's act falling *ab initio* outside the plaintiff's copyright. Insubstantial reproductions of the work are not within the plaintiff's right. Once again, what we have here is not an exception but a scope limitation.

The example of insubstantial reproduction reveals that the difference between a scope limitation and an exception involves the generality at which we formulate the plaintiff's right. If the plaintiff's right were defined—without further qualification—as an exclusive right of reproduction in respect of work, then an insubstantial reproduction *would* fall within the plaintiff's copyright, and the defendant would have to invoke an exception to avoid infringement. The exception could be as banal as "except where the reproduction is insubstantial," but the point is that the difference between an exception and a scope limitation goes to the generality (or specificity) of the definition of the right. The defendant who reproduces insubstantially need not rely on an exception because the plaintiff's right is not defined at the highest level of generality (as an exclusive right of reproduction pure and simple), but rather at a lower level of generality (as an exclusive right of *substantial* reproduction). The difference between an exception and a scope limitation is thus about the level of generality at which the right is formulated.[17]

This observation that the distinction between scope limitations and exceptions goes to the generality or specificity of the definition of the right is also applicable to the defense of fair use or fair dealing. Fair use or fair dealing arises as a defense only when the defendant reproduces a substantial part of the plaintiff's work. There is after all no need to invoke fair use or fair dealing in the absence of substantial reproduction. Because fair use or fair dealing comes into play on the basis of a *prima facie* finding of infringement, it is only natural to regard it as an exception. The defendant can avoid liability only to the extent that he can take his act of substantial reproduction out of the general rule that substantial reproduction amounts to infringement. Fair use or fair dealing for the purpose of criticism and review, for example, is one such exception.[18] It absolves the defendant from liability in situations that would otherwise amount to infringement—i.e., in situations to which the general rule would otherwise apply.

Note, however, that, as with the example of insubstantial copying, the proposition that fair use or fair dealing amounts to an exception depends on the level of generality at which the plaintiff's right is formulated. Thus, if we were to say that the plaintiff's right is an exclusive right to reproduce the work or any substantial part thereof *for purposes other than criticism or review,* then the defendant would not have to rely on an exception. Rather, the plaintiff would be unable to show infringement. The case of reproducing the work for purposes of criticism would look the same as the case of reproducing an insubstantial part of the work. We would have written the so-called exception into the definition of the right by lowering the level of generality at which the right is formulated.

Indeed, attentiveness to this issue of the level of generality at which the right is formulated is one way to understand the proposition that exceptions are rather user rights. "Procedurally," the *CCH* Court writes, "a defendant is required to prove that his or her dealing with a work has been fair; however, the fair dealing exception is perhaps more properly understood as an integral part of the *Copyright Act* than simply a defence. Any act falling within the fair dealing exception will not be an infringement of copyright. The fair dealing exception, like other exceptions in the *Copyright Act,* is a user's right. In order to maintain the proper balance between the rights of a copyright owner and users' interests, it must not be interpreted restrictively. As Professor Vaver, *supra,* has explained, at p. 171: 'User rights are not just loopholes. Both owner rights and user rights should therefore be given the fair and balanced reading that befits remedial legislation.'"[19] The point is, in short, that the fact that fair dealing is an exception arising in the *Copyright Act* procedurally as a defense is no reason to relegate it to the periphery of the copyright system. So-called exceptions could have been just as easily written into the definition of the right. They are but ways of defining the scope of the right with greater specificity. The generality at which the definition of the right is formulated in the *Copyright Act* should not be confused with substantive findings about the role and stature of exceptions in the copyright system. The language of user rights is in fact designed to avoid that confusion. It affirms an integrative, rather than a merely residual, formulation and application of the world of so-called exceptions.

It is true, of course, that if the exceptions could have just as easily been incorporated into the definition of the right, then one could plausibly infer that, by neglecting to do so, the legislator sought to minimize their importance in the copyright system. But this view seems at best far-fetched. As the Court reminds us in the above passage, the *Copyright Act* emphatically states (albeit in a section entitled "Exceptions") that fair dealing is not an infringement of copyright.[20] In other words, there is no conclusive finding flowing from the text of the statute that reproducing a work in substantial part for purposes of criticism or review is an infringement of copyright from which defendant may be excused. The words of the statute define fair dealing, along with all other exceptions, not as *excused* infringement but rather as the *absence* of infringement.

Along with the overriding metaphor of "balance," the Court's "user rights" language amounts to an authoritative reinterpretation of the relation between s. 3 of the *Copyright Act* (affirming the copyright owner's rights of exclusion) and ss. 29 to 32.2 (affirming exceptions to the owner's rights). The metaphor of balance dislodges any framing of the relation between s. 3 and ss. 29 to 32.2 in terms of a "core/periphery" metaphor. The idea of balance thus disciplines our thinking about the relation between the right and its exceptions as aspects of a single juridical system. The upshot is that, once internalized as equally constitutive of the core, exceptions appear as *indicia* of the very definition of the author's copyright, limiting its scope *ab initio*. This is why any uses of the copyrighted work that occur outside the scope of the copyright owner's exclusive rights are best grasped as user rights rather than as mere exceptions. The basic point is not that the defendant has acted in a manner deserving to be excused but rather that he has done no wrong to begin with.[21] In short, scope limitations—such as fair use or fair dealing—are not exceptions properly so-called.

Miscellaneous Exceptions

There are limits, however, to the degree to which "exceptions" can be internalized by appeal to the notion of copyright as a system. For example, in what has to be my favorite of all its provisions, the Canadian *Copyright Act* provides that it is not an infringement of copyright for a person to perform a musical work in public without motive of gain at any agricultural or agricultural-industrial exhibition or fair that receives a grant from or is held by its directors under federal, provincial, or municipal authority.[22] Let us call this the "agricultural fairs exception." While it seems natural to treat fair use or fair dealing for purposes of criticism or review as a scope limitation internal to the very definition of the author's copyright, one could hardly escape a sense of awkwardness if one were to extend the same treatment to the agricultural fairs exception.

The reason for that sense of awkwardness is not difficult to identify. It would be hard to think of copyright as a juridical system that does not affirm the permissibility of reproducing a work for purposes of review/comment/criticism or the like. In fact, I cannot think of any jurisdiction that does not have a criticism provision or some variant thereof.[23] This suggests that the permissibility of criticism is constitutive of copyright as such; that is, the right to reproduce another's copyrighted work for purposes of review or criticism is part and parcel of the very concept of copyright. By contrast, the right to use a work in agricultural fairs seems radically external to that concept. The agricultural fairs exception is, to say the least, unusual. This is not at all surprising. Copyright can get on quite well without an agricultural fairs exception. More importantly, the fact that such an exception has found its way into the Canadian *Copyright Act* is by no means sufficient to persuade us that it is of the same stature as the right to deal fairly with another's work for the purpose of criticism or review. The sense of awkwardness has cognitive content: it is a refusal to accept that the agricultural fairs exception could somehow be placed on the same level, relative to core copyright concepts, as the fair use or fair dealing provision can and should be placed.

In *Théberge,* Justice Binnie spoke generally of the exceptions in ss. 29 to 32.2 of the *Copyright Act,* including thereby the agricultural fairs exception in the concept of the copyright balance. Yet we could hardly go astray by suggesting that not all exceptions listed in the *Copyright Act* are of the same kind, and that, as the agricultural fairs exception seems to indicate, the bare fact that an exception has found its way into the *Copyright Act* need not mean that it is "integral" or "internal" to the very definition of the right in the relevant sense. We would likely be forgiven for jesting that the agricultural fairs exception is an exception to Justice Binnie's assertion that the exceptions listed in ss. 29 to 32.2 are integral to the copyright balance. It is not as if agricultural *fair* use is quite the same as fair use.[24]

Consider in this regard the difference between the following two propositions:

(a) An author has the exclusive right to reproduce her work *for purposes other than criticism or review*;
(b) An author has the exclusive right to reproduce her work *for purposes other than performing it in agricultural fairs.*

We need not ascertain precisely the difference between these two propositions in order to identify an elective affinity between copyright subject matter and criticism/review that does not obtain between copyright subject matter and things agricultural. The relation between criticism/review and core copyright concepts is of an entirely different order than that between things agricultural and core copyright concepts. Suffice it to say for present purposes that where such elective affinity is absent, what we have before us is an exception; that is, a limitation that, at the very least *prima facie,* neither is nor can be regarded as internal to the very definition of the author's copyright, and that, therefore, cannot be self-evidently incorporated into the copyright system. On the contrary, the limitation cannot help but strike us as rooted in considerations external to the copyright system. The agricultural fairs exception is, in short, *miscellaneous.*

The idea of a "miscellaneous exception" brings into relief the observation that the internalization of exceptions into the definition of the right under the auspices of the concept of copyright as system has limits. Not every exception can be internalized. Internalization is not only about the level of generality (or specificity) at which the definition of the right is formulated. What precludes the agricultural fairs exception from internalization is not a generality issue, but rather the heterogeneity of the exception relative to core copyright concepts. No level of specificity could undo the absence of an elective affinity between core copyright concepts and things agricultural. The agricultural fairs exception is "miscellaneous" because its heterogeneity resists internalization.

A deeper analysis of this resistance would, as I argued in Chapter 1, reveal that the structuring metaphor of "balance" could not be indifferent to the kind of values it admits into the copyright system, and that it therefore presupposes a qualitative distinction between kinds of values that it itself cannot generate out of a quantitative public interest calculus. It is by no means self-evident, for example, in what way the rights of an author can be intelligibly balanced against agricultural interests. The heterogeneity between authorial interests and agricultural interests is such that it threatens to empty the idea of balancing of any remotely meaningful content.

What matters for present purposes, however, is the bearing that the idea of a miscellaneous exception has on our understanding of the distinction between scope limitations and exceptions. A scope limitation—such as fair use or fair dealing for the purpose of criticism—invites reflection into the relation between authorial interests and the interests asserted in and through the limitation. The limitation prompts us, as it were, to formulate a deeper interpretation of copyright law as a juridical order, one in which the limitation appears rather as an internal or internalized matter of the very definition of the right. By contrast, a miscellaneous exception—such as the agricultural fairs exception—stares at us blankly, so to speak, from the vantage point of its radical externality. A miscellaneous exception is an irreducible residue, a remainder. It is by definition that which resists internalization, less an invitation to deepen our understanding of copyright than to marvel at how the provision affirming it got into the *Copyright Act* to begin with. We might say that, precisely because of its heterogeneity, a miscellaneous exception calls for sociological rather than juridical explanation. It awakens not the jurisprudence but the sociology of copyright. Its radical externality is such that it brings into question the very idea of copyright as a specifically juridical order subject to systematization. In short, it is in fact not so much an "exception," revealing some kind of juridical content, as much as a bare instance of remarkably successful lobbying, likely incapable of formulating itself as a juridical phenomenon.

Exceptions Properly So-Called

With the phrase "exceptions properly so-called," I seek to bring into relief limitations of the author's right that, like miscellaneous exceptions, are external in the sense that they are not capable of integration into the copyright system. At the same time, however, these exceptions are such that, unlike miscellaneous exceptions, they invite specifically jurisprudential reflection into the relation between the nature of the claims they assert and the copyright system. We might say by way of example that seeking to "trump" an author's copyright in the name of another person's freedom of expression raises questions about the relationship between authorship and citizenship in a liberal democracy. Regardless of how we decide a conflict between these interests or rights in any given circumstance, the problem evokes and requires an understanding of the relative roles of copyright and freedom of expression in our juridical system. An exception properly so-called can be said to arise where this investigation of the place of copyright in our juridical system requires that an author's copyright give way in certain circumstances to an interest or principle other than authorship. The resulting limitation of the right is, of course, external to copyright. Unlike the agricultural fairs exception, however, the exception is much more than merely miscellaneous in that it calls for specifically jurisprudential reflection rather than sociological explanation.[25]

Exceptions properly so-called are thus the nexus of an encounter between copyright and other juridical interests. As such, they present two immediate and related analytical challenges. Because an exception properly so-called is externally imposed, the first of these challenges is to think through the distinction between "internal" and "external" in regard to copyright. The second is to formulate the parameters whereby conflicts between copyright interests and other juridical interests can be resolved.

The concept of an encounter between copyright and other juridical interests is by no means new, whether in legal practice or legal scholarship.

There is a growing body of scholarship, for example, approaching the nexus between copyright and human rights, attempting both to guide and to interpret jurisprudential developments in the area.[26] My purpose here is to set forth a line of thought exploring the conditions for the possibility of systematic study of the relation between copyright and human rights generally. In short, I want to inquire about what is in the "and" in the phrase "copyright and human rights." This inquiry will permit us to distinguish between the inside and the outside of copyright, as well as to suggest a structure through which the encounter between claims arising in distinct legal regimes can take place. This structure, as we shall see, is the idea of "proportionality." Exceptions properly so-called are invitations to apply the structure of proportionality to mediate claims arising in distinct legal regimes.

What's in the "and" in "Copyright and Human Rights"?

The view I want to develop is that the word "and" in the phrase "copyright and human rights" expresses both an aspiration and an imperative. The aspiration is that encounters between these two separate legal regimes can be juridically resolved through reasoned discussion, rather than ideologically dissolved through mere choice between radically incomparable values. The imperative is to formulate the conditions for the possibility of a juridical resolution, as opposed to an ideological dissolution.

It will come as no surprise that, if one had to select three words that appear very frequently in discussions of the relationship between copyright and human rights, one would likely wind up, first, with the word "balance," and then with the words "internal," and "external."[27] The word "balance" (or "balancing") is, of course, a familiar metaphor. The metaphor is in this context intended to capture something about the procedure to be followed when we are faced with an encounter between copyright, on the one hand, and human rights, on the other. The metaphor tells us that if we find ourselves in a situation where A's copyright, for example, conflicts with B's freedom of expression, "balancing" is what we need to do to resolve the conflict.

There is of course nothing *prima facie* wrong with this habitually recommended procedure. On the contrary, the command or wish to balance already expresses the aspiration that "balancing" is indeed possible. But the metaphor is in and of itself insufficient for the task, and in fact obscures it. The entire problem contained in the phrase "copyright and human rights" is whether these two separate legal regimes can be meaningfully reduced to a common denominator that would make the very thought of weighing them on a balance possible to begin with. In that context, the word "balancing" is at best unhelpful because it assumes the entire problem away. It assumes (1) that copyright and human rights have weights; (2) that these so-called weights are somehow commensurable; and (3) that we can actually place these measurements on some kind of balance that would presumably give us an answer. To put it otherwise, the "balancing" metaphor conceals a plethora of assumptions that require elaboration before the very topic of "copyright and human rights" can begin to make sense as a topic, as an area of investigation. Even if we accept its language, balancing must be the conclusion, rather than the starting point, of any discussion of the human rights/copyright nexus. The entire question is whether balancing—whatever it means—is possible.

Nor can we fail to note that the words "internal" and "external" are also metaphors. They evoke images of physical location, efforts to ascertain *where* the encounter between copyright and human rights takes place. Does it take place *inside* copyright, such that apparent conflicts between copyright and freedom of expression can be resolved through the judicious application of copyright doctrine? If that is the case, then the question to be resolved is how freedom of expression considerations are to be grasped as part and parcel of the copyright system, perhaps as scope limitations analogous to fair use or fair dealing. Or does the encounter between copyright and freedom of expression take place *outside* copyright, such that conflicts must be resolved by subjecting copyright to external pressures? If that is the case, then the question to be resolved is how freedom of expression considerations can be grasped as giving rise to exceptions properly so-called, inviting us to formulate the conditions for the possibility of such externally rooted limitations of copyright interests. Whichever the case, the inside/outside metaphor tells us how to do what needs to be done: we are to approach the copyright/freedom of expression nexus either by applying copyright doctrine (if freedom of expression is always already inside copyright), by externally burdening copyright (if freedom of expression is outside copyright), or perhaps by doing a little bit of each (if—you will forgive the jest—we seek a balanced and pragmatic outcome that we have magically arrived at elsewhere).

But just as the balancing metaphor has its difficulties, so does the inside/outside metaphor have its own difficulties. One of these is that in order to make the required determinations about whether we are inside or outside copyright at any given time, we in fact need to know what copyright is. Just as the balancing metaphor carries the danger of distracting us away from the task of formulating the conditions for the possibility of balancing to begin with, so does the inside/outside metaphor distract us away from the task of formulating a view of what it means to be inside or outside copyright. This is no small task either. It is not unusual, for example, to find discussion of the internalization (or lack thereof) of freedom of expression concerns into copyright.[28] Such discussion indicates that the distinction between inside and outside is rather fluid, and that just because we happen to think that we are outside at any given point, this does not mean that we may not find, at the very next moment, that we are in fact already inside. One person's inside, we may say, is another's outside, and in this squabble between outsiders and insiders one can lose one's bearings pretty quickly.

Of course, it is tempting to disregard this entire inside/outside issue as a red herring having no significant practical import. Does it really matter whether we find ourselves inside or outside copyright, even if we knew what these metaphors mean? It seems, however, that it *does* matter a great deal. For when we put the two metaphors together, the metaphor of balance and the metaphor of inside and outside, we find that the kind of balancing that is appropriate in any given case depends on whether we are inside or outside, so that, on penalty of uselessly applying copyright doctrine when we should actually bring external pressure to bear on copyright, we must—whether we like it or not—try to make sense of what these widespread metaphors are trying to tell us. The nature of the defendant's impugned act, for example, would have significantly different juridical status depending on whether it is framed as an "internal" fair use or fair dealing matter or as an "external" freedom of expression issue. The body of scholarship seeking to work through the freedom of expression/copyright nexus can be seen as an ongoing discussion whether copyright law has the internal resources to accommodate freedom of expression concerns.[29]

With this inside/outside conundrum in mind, then, I suggest the following procedure. I want to discuss briefly three cases unrelated to copyright in the hopes of extracting from them lessons regarding the meaning of the words "internal" and "external." I will then return to the copyright/freedom of expression nexus, and to the metaphor of "balancing." While the path I suggest is admittedly circuitous, it will permit us to appreciate inside/outside issues in unrelated case law, and thus to apply that appreciation to the copyright context.

Inside and Outside

The first case I have in mind is a classic nuisance case: *Fontaineblau H. Corp. v. Forty-Five Twenty-Five Inc.*[30] The dispute involves two Miami Beach hotels. Plaintiff Eden Roc Hotel complains that defendant Fontaineblau Hotel wants to construct an addition of fourteen stories to its current building. The result of this building up will be that during the winter months from around two o'clock in the afternoon and through the remainder of the day, the shadow of the addition will extend over the cabana, swimming pool, and sunbathing areas of the Eden Roc, rendering the beach unsuited for the enjoyment of Eden Roc guests. The Court held in favor of the defendant. The building up by the defendant may result in injury to the plaintiff's business interests but it does not amount to an infringement of the plaintiff's property right. The plaintiff's action is but an attempt to reach into the defendant's property, as it were, seeking to prevent the defendant from exercising its own property rights.

I take this case to illustrate a radically internal standpoint. This is because, juridically speaking, there is no need to appeal to anything outside property law to generate a solution to the problem the case presents. The Court decides in favor of the defendant's right to build up. This right of the defendant—nothing less than a right to occupy space in or on one's own property—is so fundamental to ownership that one would indeed be truly hard put to find anything in the plaintiff's property right that would be sufficient to trump the defendant's building up project. Were the plaintiff able to rely on its own property right in order to deny the defendant the possibility of occupying space on the defendant's own land, the defendant's so-called property would be all but meaningless. In fact, the case is such that, in the circumstances, the plaintiff has no right whatsoever to speak of. To be sure, the plaintiff owns an adjacent piece of land and operates a hotel, including a beach, on that land. But his property right does not entail a guarantee that direct sunlight reach that beach, and so the defendant's building up project cannot plausibly be characterized as some kind of trespass or nuisance. There is not even a balancing of rights here, as if we had to decide between equally recognized claims or interests. There is simply a determination on the basis of property law alone, that the plaintiff has no cause of action. The property game, so to speak, cannot even get off the ground, as one of the players here just does not have the right equipment to play. Thus, the case illustrates a radically internal standpoint in that we need nothing other than property itself to resolve the dispute.

My second example is another nuisance case, *Appleby v. Erie Tobacco Inc.*[31] Here the plaintiff complains that the defendant, who manufactures tobacco on neighboring land, is interfering with the plaintiff's right to a reasonable enjoyment of his own property because of the absolutely intolerable smell that the tobacco manufacturing process produces. The smell is such that the plaintiff, who is in no way especially sensitive to smells, cannot live on his own property. The Court found in favor of the plaintiff, who obtained an injunction ordering the defendant to stop producing the smell.

This case also illustrates a radically internal standpoint. But it is in one important respect different from the building up case. In *Fontainebleau* the plaintiff had no right to stand on, and so he lost against the defendant's fundamental right to occupy space, to build up. There was no need to balance rights as one of the parties had nothing, so to speak, to put on the balance. But in the tobacco smell case both parties have something to stand on. The plaintiff has a right to the normal enjoyment of his property. It is this right that is being infringed by the smell that renders such enjoyment impossible. The defendant has a competing right—namely, the right to manufacture tobacco on his property. Thus, we have an encounter between two otherwise legitimate and recognized claims. Balancing is indeed required. But this balancing is still internal. It is a balancing *within* the law of property rather than between property and some other legal regime. What we have is a conflict between property rights that is in principle soluble through the prism of property law, to which both litigants are necessarily subject, because each and both have, after all, asserted a property right. It is as if the litigants had made things easy for us because the very structure of their dispute already gives us the basic concept that is equally applicable to both and that would give rise to the resolution of the dispute. They both present themselves as property owners, and so it is only fitting to ask property law to resolve the conflict.

Thus, we might say that if in the building up case the game of property did not get off the ground because one of the parties did not have the equipment required to play, in the tobacco smell case the game *does* get off the ground, and the winner is determined in accordance with the rules of the property game. The plaintiff's general or ordinary use of his property prevails over what, *in the circumstances,* is the defendant's particular or extraordinary use.[32] We might say that the plaintiff's basic right to reasonable enjoyment of his property is prior to the defendant's wish to use his property in a manner that produces intolerable smells incompatible with the plaintiff's ordinary use.[33] Regardless of result, however, the point here is that property law need not reach outside itself in order to make the determination.

Things would be different, of course, and more complex, if the parties to the action were, so to speak, playing different games, each of which games could or would give rise to a recognized claim in respect to the same set of events. In that case, it would not be feasible to suggest that the resolution of the conflict could take place within either game. Rather, the conflict would raise a question about the external relation of the games to each other, or of the litigants to each other as legitimate representatives of each of the games. This is the situation I have in mind for our third example.

The third case is a famous 1976 Supreme Court of Canada decision, *Harrison v. Carswell.*[34] Here we have an employee, Sophie Carswell, of a business located at a shopping center. Sophie Carswell is legally on strike, and she is exercising her right to be on strike by picketing outside her place of work along with eleven other persons. But although she is outside her place of work, she is still on shopping center property. She is picketing in one of the public areas of the privately owned shopping center. When the shopping center owner asks her to leave, she refuses to do so on the grounds that she is exercising her right to picket. The issue in the case is whether she is trespassing.

It is tempting, of course, to see this as a simple property case, and to say that Sophie Carswell is clearly trespassing, in that she is on another's property without that other's consent.[35] But that would be to underestimate the complexity of the case. It would be to lose sight of the very heart of the case, which is an encounter between rights or claims, each *prima facie* valid in its own sphere. The case is interesting because, unlike the previous two cases we examined briefly above, it forces us to think through a relationship between heterogeneous claims.[36] It is clear that, from the standpoint of property law, the shopping center owner is exercising a valid and legitimate claim. It is equally clear that the picketer is involved in a legal picket, exercising a valid and legitimate right as a matter of labor or employment law. What is unclear is the interaction between the separate legal regimes. This is a case of a paradigmatic external encounter.

Before moving on to discuss this encounter further, however, it will prove fruitful at this point to develop analogies between the three aforementioned examples and examples involving copyright law and doctrine.

Copyright Analogues

The three previous examples permit us to draw some conclusions about the distinction between internal and external standpoints. Specifically, the difference between the third example (about the picket on the shopping center) and the first two (about building up and about tobacco smell) tells us that the inside/outside location metaphor can be grasped as a distinction between the kinds of considerations required to resolve a given dispute. Thus, the first two cases required nothing more than considerations drawn from property law. The third case, however, called for considerations extraneous to property. A dispute is inside or internal to a given legal regime when the claims made by the disputants can be apprehended through a common referent. We are, metaphorically speaking, inside a given legal regime when the claims made by the disputants can be resolved through a set of shared considerations. The considerations are shared because each and both of the litigants appeal to them. In the first two examples above, both litigants appear as property owners.

What does this tell us about the inside and outside of copyright?

I want to suggest that the copyright analogue to the internal standpoint is present in cases that turn either on the defense of independent creation or on the idea/expression dichotomy. As we noted, the defense of independent creation provides that a defendant cannot be held liable in copyright where he can show that his work, though identical to or substantially similar to the plaintiff's, was independently created. To make out a defense of independent creation is to make out a claim that the defendant's work is not copied. The defense establishes that the identity or substantial similarity between the defendant's work and the plaintiff's is a mere coincidence, and not an actionable wrong.

A defendant's appeal to the defense of independent creation in a copyright case can be interpreted in two complementary ways. On the one hand, as we observed, the defendant's claim is that the plaintiff's copyright is a right of reproduction, not a right of independent (re-)creation. The point is that the defendant's act of independent creation does not fall within the scope of the plaintiff's copyright. The defense of independent creation amounts not to an exception externally burdening the plaintiff's copyright but rather to an affirmation of its internal limitations. On the other hand, as we noted in Chapter 2, the defendant's appeal to the defense of independent creation challenges what we might regard as the coherence of the plaintiff's allegation. It is as if the defendant were saying: "Look here, plaintiff, you claim rights arising from your authorship, but so do I. My work is not copied from yours but independently created. I too am an author in my own right." In saying that he, too, is an author, the defendant is facing the plaintiff with the very same considerations that give rise to the plaintiff's copyright to begin with. He is not asking us to look at anything other than the very ground of copyright itself to resolve the dispute. He is only demanding that the plaintiff not be permitted to deploy her authorship to reach into the defendant's (just as, we may add, the defendant in *Fontainebleau* argued successfully that the plaintiff cannot be allowed to deploy the plaintiff's property right to reach into the defendant's property and prevent the defendant from building up.) Thus, whether viewed as an affirmation of the limits of the plaintiff's copyright, or as an affirmation of the defendant's own authorship, the defense of independent creation arises on radically internal grounds.

We can say the same thing, albeit in a different sense, about idea/expression dichotomy cases. In these cases, we have a plaintiff who has suffered a harm or loss of some sort, but who cannot point to a right that has been infringed. In *Fontainebleau,* the hotel owner whose beach is now detrimentally covered by a shadow has no right as a matter of property law to prevent the defendant from building up. Similarly, in idea/expression cases, the author of a work has no right as a matter of copyright law to prevent a defendant from using ideas contained in that work—from building, so to speak, another work expressing the very same ideas. One way to grasp this along the same lines as the defense of independent creation is to say that although the defendant has made use of an idea in the plaintiff's work, the defendant has nonetheless expressed this idea anew in her own work—so that, indeed, the defendant is once again saying, in paradigmatically internal fashion, "I too am an author in my own right."

Fair use or fair dealing for the purpose of criticism cases are, by contrast, similar to the tobacco smell case described above. In fair use or fair dealing for the purpose of criticism cases, or in transformative use more generally, we have rights—or claims recognized by copyright—on both sides. The defendant here has not independently created a work that happens to be identical to the plaintiff's. Nor has he taken only ideas from the plaintiff's work. On the contrary, the defendant has in fact reproduced a substantial part of the plaintiff's work. Thus the plaintiff's action cannot be dismissed on the grounds that his claim does not sound as a matter of copyright law. At the same time, however, the defendant is not devoid of copyright claims of her own, claims that themselves sound in copyright law. In cases involving fair use or fair dealing for the purpose of criticism, as we noted in Chapter 2, the defendant claims that, as a matter of copyright law, the legitimacy and validity of his act is, like the legitimacy and validity of the plaintiff's own right, intelligible as a matter of authorship. This, then, is also a case where the defendant can say "I too am an author in my own right"—with the difference, of course, that he does indeed make use of plaintiff's copyrighted expression and can do so only so long as this is reasonably necessary for the allowable purpose. Because authorship remains the common referent, however, this case too is an instance of an internal standpoint. It has the same structure as the tobacco smell case, in which the shared identity of the litigants as property owners orients the resolution of the dispute.

Though it is at best difficult to find property law analogues, nonuse and personal use as I have formulated and interpreted them in Chapters 3 and 5 respectively, are also instances of an internal standpoint. Nonuse involves the distinction between a work and its material form, along with the claim that noncommunicative use of the material form of a work is not actionable because it is not use of the work as a work. Personal use similarly involves the definition of the work as a communicative act, along with the claim that enjoyment of the work in the absence of recommunication is not actionable because, again, it is not a use of the work as a work. In both situations the denial of liability is internal in the sense that, albeit not in reliance on the defendant's authorship, it proceeds from copyright considerations in respect to the definition of copyright subject matter and copyright scope.

Proportionality

Not so in a third kind of copyright case, where the considerations necessary to resolve the dispute must move beyond copyright law in that the defendant relies on other legally recognized rights such as, for example, freedom of expression.[37] In this kind of case, the defendant says not "I too am an author in my own right" but "I am a person whose freedom of expression is at stake." The true copyright and freedom of expression case arises where the defendant cannot avail herself of copyright considerations, even if we are at times accustomed to saying that the defendant could win a transformative use case by appealing to freedom of expression, or even if we are at times fond of saying that transformative use incorporates or internalizes freedom of expression concerns.[38]

Let us return to *Harrison,* the picketing case, for some guidance about this. Writing for the majority, Justice Dickson held that, as she was on another's property without that other's consent, the defendant Sophie Carswell was clearly trespassing. Writing in dissent, Justice Laskin refused to make a finding of trespass. He underlined, *inter alia,* (a) the importance of public access to the very functioning of the shopping center as a shopping center, (b) the fact that the defendant was not only a member of the public but also an employee involved in a labor dispute with a tenant of the shopping center, (c) the fact that the defendant's picket proceeded peacefully pursuant to a lawful strike, and (d) the fact that the peaceful picketing took place in "public areas" and "without obstruction of the sidewalk or incommoding of others."[39] His point in emphasizing these factors was to say that in the circumstances the picketing actually produced a rather minimal impairment of the shopping center owner's property right. While there can be no doubt that the defendant's unauthorized presence on shopping centre property was an impairment of sorts, it is equally clear that the impairment was minimal—that is, that the picket did not interfere with the operation of the shopping center as a shopping center. By contrast, imposing an injunction on the picketer that she refrain from picketing as and where she picketed would amount to a substantial impairment of her right to picket.[40] Lorraine Weinrib and Ernest Weinrib make the point succinctly in their discussion of *Harrison* as an example of "private law proportionality": "[g]ranting the owner the power to proscribe picketing in the shopping centre would cut more deeply into the picketer's freedom of expression than would the permissibility of picketing cut into the owner's proprietary rights."[41] In these circumstances, Justice Laskin held for the defendant.

It is important to emphasize that Justice Laskin's ruling does not mean that he would necessarily hold for freedom of expression rather than property, picket rather than trespass, in different circumstances. On the contrary, he explicitly held that "[t]he character of a shopping centre, such as the one involved here, is one thing, and the nature and place of activities carried on there are something else. I would agree that it does not follow that because unrestricted access is given to members of the public to certain areas of the shopping centre during business hours, those areas are available at all times during those hours and in all circumstances to any kind of peaceful activity by members of the public, regardless of the interest being promoted by that activity and regardless of the number of members of the public who are involved. The Court will draw lines here as it does in other branches of the law as may be appropriate in the light of the legal principle and particular facts."[42] My point here is not to speculate as to the specific circumstances, such as the nature of the interest being promoted, the number of picketers and the exact location of the picket on the public areas of a shopping center, that would, in Laskin's analysis, transform picketing into trespass or vice versa. Rather, my point is to highlight the methodology deployed by Justice Laskin, which we may summarize as follows: encounters between heterogeneous claims of right require an assessment of the gravity of the impairment to which each of the rights, in the specific circumstances of any given case, would be subjected through the exercise of the other right. The less impaired right is the right that should give way in those circumstances.

This approach is rightly regarded as an instance of "proportionality" analysis.[43] The basic assumption of the approach is that while the claims made by the litigants in this kind of case are external to each other, in the way that copyright and freedom of expression are external to each other as separate legal regimes, this very externality requires that the separate legal regimes be conceptualized as internal to a larger system of rights. The point is that if a jurisprudential analysis of the conflict is possible, then this possibility necessarily appeals to the coherence of a system of rights in which the separate legal regimes must be assumed as subsumed.[44]

There can be no doubt that this approach would face many difficulties. But that is no basis to lose sight of the perhaps equally daunting difficulties posed by a refusal to think through the possibility of reasoning about certain kinds of heterogeneous claims. Such a refusal entails two related assumptions that are after all far from self-evident:

1. that we can reason cogently about conflict *only* where the conflict is between parties that share fundamental assumptions—basically, that is, that we can reason about the first and second cases offered above, but not about the third;
2. that there is no such thing as a system of rights—that is, that we cannot advance beyond the acknowledgment that what we have is a collection of heterogeneous and incommensurable claims arising from distinct legal regimes struggling for supremacy in the absence of rational or reasonable mediation.

Of course, neither of these assumptions is necessarily untrue—but neither is self-evident either. They are both deeply skeptical about the possibility that the copyright/human rights nexus has anything to teach. Yet it is equally plausible to doubt the skepticism itself, and the assumptions it seems to hold dear. Once those assumptions are no longer regarded as self-evident, it is only natural to consider the conditions required for the formulation of a meaningful copyright/human rights nexus. The question to be posed would be: What would have to be true for it to be the case that conflicts between copyright and human rights would be juridically resolved rather than ideologically dissolved? The answer, I think, is the twofold idea of a system of rights of which copyright and human rights are each a part, and of proportionality as the link between the separate legal regimes that constitute the system. Thus, the aspiration and imperative found in the "and" in the phrase "copyright and human rights" are the aspiration and imperative of a system of rights held together through proportionality.

An "Idea of Reason"

To recapitulate, subject matter limitations cannot be appropriately regarded as exceptions. Subject matter limitations—such as the exclusion of facts from copyright protection—are in fact conceptually prior to exceptions. By imposing the conditions that must be met for copyright protection to arise, subject matter limitations frame the baseline, deviations from which will amount to exceptions.

The originality requirement, the idea/expression dichotomy, the doctrine of merger and the concept of nonuse are subject matter limitations. Originality establishes copyright subject matter as a speaking in one's own words. The idea/expression dichotomy sustains this speaking as a form of expression, as distinct from the content expressed. The doctrine of merger excludes instances of communication that, because they flow necessarily or too closely from the substance expressed, cannot be suitably regarded as a person's own speech. Merged communications, in other words, are not original in the requisite sense. Nonuse distinguishes the speaking from the material form in which it is embodied, and excludes that material form from the field of copyright subject matter. All four subject matter limitations thus flow from the principle of independent creation: an author's work is not a copy but a speaking in her own words.

Scope limitations—such as transformative use—cannot be appropriately regarded as exceptions either. Whereas subject matter limitations define the nature of the work subject to copyright, scope limitations define the nature of the copyright entitlements to the work. Scope limitations, that is, define the rights that copyright grants over its subject matter. It is true that scope limitations specify situations in which copyrightable subject matter is not subject to copyright. Nonetheless, it would be incorrect to regard them as exceptions. To do so is to assume that, in the absence of exceptions, the entitlement over copyright subject matter would be absolute, so that any scope limitation—such as the definition of the right as a right of *substantial* reproduction—is to be regarded as exceptional. But that is precisely the point. Copyright entitlement is by no means absolute. The absence of limitations is not the baseline from which scope limitations carve away situations in which the copyright holder's entitlement is artificially curtailed. On the contrary, scope limitations define the very nature of the right, and therefore the boundaries constitutive of the copyright holder's entitlement *ab initio*.

In defining the nature of the right, scope limitations track its subject matter in the sense that they preserve and sustain its nature as speech. That originality is a speaking in one's own words entails the lawfulness of responses arising from the author's audience. This entailing is but a manifestation of the proposition that a plaintiff cannot claim authorship rights inconsistent with the possibility of the defendant's own authorship. The defense of independent creation—which is but a corollary of the originality requirement—is the clearest instance of this proposition in copyright doctrine. It tells us that the principle of independent creation is a principle equally applicable to all. The principle thus frames a work as an interpersonal reality in a twofold sense: as directed toward another and as subject to the equal rights of that other. Thus, originality, the idea/expression dichotomy and transformative use double up, so to speak, as both subject matter and scope limitations. Originality carries within itself the defense of independent creation; the idea/expression dichotomy grants the plaintiff's rights over her expression while preserving the conditions of the defendant's authorship in the free availability of ideas; and transformative use circles back, as it were, preserving the conditions of the defendant's authorship while at the same time granting her rights in respect of her own original expression.

Merger and nonuse are pure subject matter limitations. Merger is a corollary of originality. It functions not to include but to exclude from copyright, thus telling us what is not, rather than what is subject to copyright. From a copyright perspective, merged expression is a fact, not a work. Because it functions to exclude, merger does not give rise to further determinations at the level of scope in order to preserve and sustain equality imperatives. The exclusion functions to eject merged material from copyright concern. Nonuse is similar. It excludes a work's material form from copyright concern. From a copyright perspective, a work's material form is a material object, not a work. It may give rise to property relations but not to copyright scope determinations.

Personal use can be characterized as both a subject matter and a scope limitation. Like nonuse, it is not a use of the work as a communicative act. That is, it involves no publication of the work. But whereas nonuse pertains to material that has been refused entry into the field of copyright, personal use pertains to material that is frankly within the field of copyright. Thus it is not so much that personal use involves absolutely no use of the work, as much as that the nature of its use does not fall within the purview of the author's exclusive right to communicate and recommunicate the work. From this point of view, personal use is a scope limitation. At the same time, however, because in personal use the defendant's use is not of the plaintiff's form of expression, in the sense that no publication of the work is at issue, personal use is not use of copyright subject matter. From this point of view, it is a subject matter limitation. It is, we might say, use of expression only as idea, not as form but as content. Because it does not recommunicate the work, it is, like nonuse, not subject to fair use or fair dealing analysis.

Subject mater limitations and scope limitations thus concurrently define copyright both as an exclusive right to perform a communicative act—i.e., to publish a work—and as a systemic set of juridical relations entailed in that right as a relation between persons. As distinct from limitations, exceptions are situations in which acts in respect of copyright subject matter falling within copyright scope do not give rise to liability. There are basically two kinds of exceptions, miscellaneous exceptions and exceptions properly so-called. Yet miscellaneous exceptions are exceptions only in a very limited sense. They are exceptions in that they do indeed preclude liability arising from acts in respect of copyright subject matter falling within copyright scope. But their miscellaneous character is such that they appear less as juridical phenomena than as merely grafted attachments that, as such, call for sociological rather than jurisprudential explanation. The agricultural fairs exception, for example, prompts more questions about its history than about its fundamental import for our understanding of copyright.

By contrast, exceptions properly so-called do call for jurisprudential explanation. They are exceptions to the extent that they preclude liability arising from acts in respect of copyright subject matter falling within copyright scope. Yet this preclusion of liability is not a matter of mere attachment by grafting but rather an occasion to elaborate the relation between copyright and other juridical interests affirmed through the exception. Thus, if subject matter and scope limitations concurrently define copyright, exceptions properly so-called point toward the relation between copyright and other rights in the comprehensive system of rights of which it is a part. These exceptions are "properly so-called" in that the limitations they affirm can be construed as juridical phenomena.

Finally, proportionality is the structure that permits reflection into the nature of exceptions properly-so-called less as peripheral phenomena than as indicia of encounters between juridical orders. Exceptions are nodal points, as it were, giving rise to efforts of translation aspiring to elucidate the relationship between diverse juridical orders as aspects of a comprehensive language of rights. Of course, this comprehensiveness is itself an aspiration. It is an "idea of reason"—a starting point for an interminable task: to cultivate an understanding of exceptions as hinges in a jurisprudence animated by the idea of a system of rights.

BY WAY OF CONCLUSION

A Note on Copyright Citizenship

Feist Publications Inc. v. Rural Telephone Service Co. Inc. and *CCH Canadian Ltd. v. Law Society of Upper Canada* accomplish a transition from sweat of the brow to creativity or skill and judgment as originality standards.[1] The implications of this transition are truly momentous. I have argued that it remains incomplete, and I have charted the direction to be followed if its implications are to be fully developed.

Originality is a distinction between uncopyrightable and copyrightable subject matter. It guards the entrance into copyright territory. The most basic implication of the transition from sweat of the brow to creativity or skill and judgment is that raw facts are not subject to copyright protection. Not the labor of fact collection but the work of authorship summons copyright into operation. The transition from sweat of the brow to creativity or skill and judgment is thus a transition from labor to authorship.

Both *Feist* and *CCH* propose the transition in the name of balance. Yet balance is both insufficient and counterproductive as a category grounding the transition. It is insufficient because the distinction between labor and authorship is a qualitative distinction between kinds of value. Balance, however, as its name indicates, is a way to think quantitatively about the distribution of value. We might say that balance asks "how much?" questions, whereas the transition from sweat of the brow to creativity or skill and judgment is a "what?" question. Balance is insufficient to generate originality because it in fact presupposes originality as the principle that makes the balance intelligible as a copyright-significant balance to begin with. We just can't possibly tell what to put or what not to put on the balance by looking at it. Thus, ironically enough, nothing in the concept of balance can tell us why facts are not copyright-significant.

Balance is counterproductive because it implies a conception of the public domain as a countervailing weight against the author's weight, and because it therefore necessarily construes the weight granted to the public—the public's weight, so to speak—as a weight that would otherwise remain with the author. Author and public thus literally burden each other. Each insists that the other be regarded as a mere exception. Each posits a general rule rendering the other as a kind of residual carve-out necessary to sustain breathing space in an otherwise suffocating arrangement. The situation strikes me as even worse than trying to determine what to put on a balance by looking at it. It is more like trying to operate a balance in the absence of gravity—an unhappy marriage, perhaps, in which each of the participants is willing to grant the other nothing more than what is absolutely necessary for cohabitation to continue without becoming totally insufferable. Balance is not a juridical category but a sociological euphemism for the copyright wars.

While the theory of copyright as balance may not be as serviceable as it wishes to be, copyright practice suggests from within itself the parameters of its own self-understanding. The effort to derive authorship from balance is ill-fated, but the presence in both *Feist* and *CCH* of the principle of authorship as the irreducible *sine qua non* of copyright protection is unambiguous. Exegesis of originality doctrine, and of the principle of independent creation at its heart, brings authorship *per se* (neither value-creation nor value-distribution) forcefully into relief as the central organizing principle of copyright law. A work of authorship now appears as first and foremost a communicative act, and the rights attendant on it are to be disciplined by the requirement that they be consistent with the equal authorship of each and all. As a copyright law matter, an author speaks in a context ensuring conditions for dialogue. The principle of independent creation thus offers speech in place of value, equality in place of efficiency, and dialogue in place of balance as metaphors structuring copyright interpretation. The idea/expression dichotomy and the defense of fair use or fair dealing affirm and elaborate the dialogical core of copyright law. The free availability of ideas and of expression itself in certain circumstances serves as a necessary condition guaranteeing the autonomy of authors to respond to and develop each other's utterances without requiring each other's authorization. Analysis of the specificity of copyright vis-à-vis patent and trademark in the great intellectual property triptych confirms the resonance of this construal of copyright as dialogue.

The concept of the work as a communicative act also brings in its wake a distinction between a work and its material form. An author's exclusive right in respect of her work is not an exclusive right to any and all uses of her work's material from. Precisely as a communicative act, a work gives rise to rights in respect of its specifically communicative use. Noncommunicative use of the material form of a work is thus not within the purview of an author's copyright. The accounting forms in *Baker v. Selden,* as well as the use of digital images as thumbnails in *Kelly v. Arriba Soft Corp.,* are among the most dramatic and helpful examples of a general category that I have called nonuse.[2] The category underlines the proposition that copyright protects not any and all value but rather the specific value of a work of authorship as a communicative act. It thus captures doctrinally the lawfulness of merely technical, noncommunicative use without subjecting the defendant to a fair use analysis.

This conception of the work as a communicative act also indicates the normative basis of copyright protection. The descriptive narrative of copyright as dialogue is also a justificatory narrative. Because a work of authorship is a communicative act, an infringement of the rights attendant on it is a disposing of another's authorial speech in the absence of authorization. Copyright infringement is compelled speech. The fact that an author has already published a work neither does nor can mean that its republication is now free as the air to common use. Most deeply at stake in copyright protection is the integrity of an author's choice whether to publish or not. The act of publication is an affirmation of that prerogative, not an abandonment of it. Publication is an act of public address, not a making public in the sense of a divesting oneself of the subject mater of protection. Copyright is about authorship, not privacy.

Focusing copyright protection on the integrity of the author's publication choice opens up the public domain not as a burden or countervailing weight imposed on the author's entitlement but rather as necessarily constitutive of its juridical intelligibility. The entirety of copyright doctrine arises as a definition (and therefore a limitation) of copyright subject matter as the speech of a person addressed to others reciprocally entitled to respond. Because a work is a communicative act, rights attendant on it must (a) be confined to specifically communicative uses of the work, and (b) be consistent with the communicative rights of others. The public domain thus arises not as a contingent calculation focused on the creation and distribution of value but as a necessary aspect of the autonomy and equality of the authorship of each and all. Copyright limitations are user rights rather than mere exceptions. Equality, not market failure, anchors the public domain. Exceptions properly so-called, arising from the encounter between copyright and other recognized juridical orders, would in this vein be dealt with under the rubric of proportionality analysis.

While at once descriptive and justificatory, the dialogue narrative is neither entirely. Its descriptive aspect is rather a rendering of copyright doctrine as a coherent whole from the standpoint of the foundational principle of independent creation. Its justificatory aspect is thus simultaneously critical of existing practices at odds with that coherence. Thus, for example, the concept of the work as a communicative act would extend protection to computer programs only to the extent that they could be regarded as communicative, and only in respect of communicative uses, if any. Under the dialogue model, computer programs as tools would not be subject to copyright protection any more than Selden's accounting forms were in *Baker*. Protecting computer programs is not any less a distortion of copyright principles than would be the protection of raw facts. The fact that computer programs have a great deal of value does not mean that, as tools, they originate in an act of authorship.[3]

Similarly, the concept of the work as a communicative act cannot tolerate the "derivative work right." Generally speaking, a derivative work is a work based upon another.[4] The derivative work right is thus a right granted to the author of a primary work against the author of the derivative work.[5] Thus, for example, a Harry Potter story written by a Harry Potter fan (i.e., an instance of "fan fiction"), or a sequel or prequel, may attract liability. Because it is inseparable from recognition of the defendant's authorship as irreducibly integral to the copyright system, the concept of the work as a communicative act requires elimination of the exclusive right to prepare derivative works. From the standpoint of copyright as dialogue, fan fiction, to stay with that example, is not an actionable use of another's work but a lawful response to that other's work. Fan fiction is the cultural space where fans become interlocutors. Because the lawfulness of fan fiction under the dialogue model is thus rooted in normative and juridical attentiveness to the defendant's own authorship, this pattern of reasoning can be readily applied to varied instances of mimicry, such as sampling in rap music, and appropriation art more generally. Of course, this does not mean that any and all instances of appropriation are lawful, as they would still need to be subjected to fair use analysis. But it does mean that, because it skews the analysis unilaterally toward consideration of the plaintiff's authorship, the derivative work right is inconsistent with the dialogical core of copyright.[6]

Examining the case of translation under existing copyright law will serve to sketch the point briefly. On the one hand, an unauthorized translation is an infringement of the copyright in the original. To translate is to copy. On the other, the act of translation generates its own copyright. To translate is to author. Unauthorized copying of a translation thus amounts to simultaneous infringement of two copyrights: that of the author of the original, and that of the author of the translation. From a copyright perspective, the conceptual challenge is that translation is an instance wherein the very act of (unauthorized) authorship is an infringing act. To author is to copy.

This is no mere convergence of authorship and copying, as in author B's review and criticism of author A's work. It is rather a veritable coincidence of authorship and copying, so much so that existing copyright law premises the lawfulness of the translator's authorship, and hence the copyright it generates, on the permission to translate granted by the author of the original.[7] In other words, the translator is she whose authorship is derivative not only in the sense that (a) her work is based upon another's, but also in the sense that (b) the lawfulness of her authorship, and thus the recognition of its juridical significance, is mediated through another's permission. Thus, the derivative work right entails the concept of derivative authorship.

But it is that concept that is necessarily inconsistent with copyright as dialogue. Derivative authorship is an oxymoron. Independent creation, idea/expression dichotomy, and transformative use each affirm and elaborate the equality of authors as a matter of copyright law. An author is always among others: he cannot assert his authorship in a manner rendering the authorship of others unlawful. The concept of the derivative work right is therefore inconsistent with the foundational principle of independent creation. Authorship is the irreducible fulcrum that generates and sustains the claim of right to which copyright responds. It cannot be derivative any more than, as a copyright law matter, speaking in one's own words requires another's permission. Either a translator is an author in her own right, in which case her work generates its own copyright and cannot require permission, or a translator is *not* an author in her own right, in which case her (unauthorized) activity infringes the copyright in the original and can have no independent protection under copyright. No other construal is intelligible.

Unlike fan fiction, which uses the work of another in one's own, translation is not a speaking in one's own words but a rendering of another's words in another language. Unauthorized translation is therefore infringing. This does not mean that imagining how an author would have spoken in another language partakes of the mechanical commonplaceness of "mere" copying. It means, rather, that the dignity of translation is of a different order than that of authorship: translation does not generate its own copyright. To translate a novel is not to author one. The labor of translation is not a work of authorship. On this view, what grounds a copyright action against unauthorized copying of a translation is the copyright in the original. The protection of translation is thus thoroughly derivative. At stake is the authorship of the original, not the (so-called) derivative authorship of the translation.

Bluntly put, there is no such thing as a derivative *work:* a work of authorship cannot require another's permission to claim the copyright it rightfully generates.[8] Melville Nimmer famously stated that the derivative work right is "completely superfluous."[9] It is also self-contradictory and, therefore, normatively untenable.

The category of nonuse, to highlight something that the dialogue narrative would introduce into rather than exclude from existing practices, is not, of course, a traditional copyright category, yet it is firmly anchored in the principle of independent creation. The distinction between a work and its material from is at the heart of nonuse. Analysis of independent creation makes available the observation that multiple works can occupy the same material form. A work cannot be equated with its material from. The category of nonuse makes explicit the clear implication that use of the material form is not use of the work. Nonuse is a prophylactic, as it were, preventing the reification of a communicative act as a thing.

Nonetheless, some may regard the suggestion of the nonuse category as unnecessary. Recent case law, of which *Arriba Soft* is an example; recognizes, expands, and develops fair use beyond the confines of transformative use of another's work in one's own. In this vein, transformative use comes to signify not only creative incorporation of a work in another but rather use of a work for a different purpose.[10] Thus, Arriba Soft's use of Kelly's photographs, albeit as straightforward reproductions, is nonetheless transformative. Judge Chin's recent historic finding in *Authors Guild, Inc. v. Google, Inc.* that the massive digitization involved in the Google Books Project is lawful as fair use is another example.[11] One would not wish to rain on a parade that one would rather enthusiastically join. Yet the celebration cannot help but ring warning bells in my mind reminiscent of Mark Rose's magnificent exposure of the striking reversal at the heart of the great literary property debate over two centuries ago: a finding of fair use comes at the cost of an admission (or assumption) that the reproductions involved are *prima facie* infringing. I can hardly avoid the quip that *Authors Guild* is but the proprietary *Millar v. Taylor* with a pleasing overlay of *Donaldson v. Becket.*[12] No doubt the movement from a Google settlement (licensing the Google Books Project) to a fair use finding is more than welcome, as it signals a movement away from a permission culture, in which lawful copying is rather licensed copying.

Still, a fair use culture is not all it is cracked up to be.[13] The gigantic public interest weight of the Google Books Project is not the kind of force one can mobilize frequently in the name of lawful copying. The category of nonuse strikes me as a more succinct way to capture doctrinally (as an implication of the principle of independent creation) the lawfulness of merely technical, noncommunicative reproduction incidental to the operations of digital technology.

Speaking more generally, the concept of the work as a communicative act entails a dislocation of copying or reproduction as the central organizing principle of copyright law. Grasped from the standpoint of the foundational principle of independent creation, copyright is not an exclusive right of reproduction but an exclusive right of publication. The formulation is by no means unprecedented. Quite the contrary: it is the expansion of copyright to include any and all uses of a work as *prima facie* wrongful that, historically speaking, is the real novelty.[14] Nothing in Lord Mansfield's "copy," to put it bluntly, encompassed mere reproduction as unlawful. Nor, of course, are recurrent fears arising in response to proposals for significant minimizations of copyright protection by any means unprecedented. The abolition of perpetual copyright in *Donaldson,* however, did not spell the death of publishing any more than *Feist* and *CCH* spelled the death of fact collection, or than *Authors Guild* is at all likely to usher the collapse of culture as we know it. On the contrary, we seem to have forgotten that the dignity of authorship is inseparable from the dignity of the copy, as the former is quite literally impossible in the absence of the latter.

In essence, the transition from the balance model to the dialogue model of copyright law requires a shift in the way we conceptualize copyright subject matter. The balance model centers its attention on the tangible/intangible distinction. It sees copyright law as the provision of artificial fences designed to solve the production and distribution of works of authorship conceived as a public goods problem. The insufficiencies of the model are thus rooted in its starting point: the intangibility of a work of authorship tells us nothing about its specificity. Facts, too, are intangible, yet categorically excluded from copyright. The dialogue model, by contrast, centers its attention on the distinction between a thing (whether tangible or intangible) and an act. It sees copyright as juridical protection of the integrity of an author's choice whether to publish or not. Its starting point is thus the specificity of a work of authorship as a communicative act. Facts are not subject to protection because they do not owe their origin to an act of authorship. Albeit intangible, they are nothing but things.

The fundamental implication of this shift from the tangible/intangible to the thing/act distinction is most obviously discernible in the way each model conceptualizes the nature of exclusion in copyright law, and thus the nature and role of the public domain. In the balance model, a work of authorship is a fenced-in or propertized intangible. It matters little that this fencing-in is understood as a state-granted monopoly. What matters is that it is understood as a mimicking of proprietary exclusion. Copyright subject matter is thus imagined as a self-contained entity, a thing, limits to which come from its outside, so to speak, as challenges to its producer's otherwise despotic dominion. To limit is to trespass. In the dialogue model, by contrast, an author's right to exclude others from his choice to speak or not speak is instead, and necessarily, a mode of inclusion. Speech contemplates audiences and interlocutors. It has within itself, by its very nature as address, the principles of its own self-limitation. To posit the inherent dignity of authorship is simultaneously to posit the public domain. In the world of copyright, an author is no sovereign despot in an inverted world of commodities. She is rather a citizen among others in the great Republic of Letters.

NOTES

INTRODUCTION

1. Friedrich Nietzsche, *Beyond Good and Evil,* trans. Walter Kaufmann (New York: Random House, 1966), Aphorism 97: "What? A great man? I always see only the actor of his own ideal."
2. Aristotle, *Politics,* book I, 1253a, trans. Benjamin Jowett in *The Complete Works of Aristotle, The Revised Oxford Translation*, ed. Jonathan Barnes (Princeton: Princeton University Press, 1984).
3. Feist Publications Inc. v. Rural Telephone Service Co. Inc. 499 U.S. 340 (1991), 361.
4. See, for example, Dan L. Burk, "Law and Economics of Intellectual Property: In Search of First Principles," *Annual Review of Law and Social Science* 8 (2012): 397–414, 400.
5. On the idea/expression dichotomy, see Nichols v. Universal Pictures Corporation 45 F.2d 119 (2d Cir. 1930), 121; Moreau v. St. Vincent [1950] Ex. C.R. 198 (Can. Ex. Ct.), 203.
6. See Kelly v. Arriba Soft Corp. 336 F. 3d 811 (9th Cir. 2003), 818.
7. I could not resist invoking this image of Benjamin Kaplan's here, even though he deploys it from a different point of view. See Benjamin Kaplan, *An Unhurried View of Copyright* (Clark, New Jersey: The Law Book Exchange, Ltd., 2008), 64. This is a reprint of the James S. Carpentier Lectures delivered by Professor Kaplan at the Columbia University School of Law in March, 1966.
8. See, for example, Feist Publications v. Rural Telephone, 346: "[A]ssume that two poets, each ignorant of the other, compose identical poems. Neither work is novel yet both are original and, hence, copyrightable."
9. On fair use/fair dealing, see Campbell v. Acuff-Rose Music, Inc. 510 U.S. 569 (1994); CCH Canadian Ltd. v. Law Society of Upper Canada, 2004 SCC 13.
10. Baker v. Selden, 101 U.S. 99 (1879).
11. On merger, see Herbert Rosenthal Jewelry Corp. v. Kalpakian, 446 F.2d 738 (9th Cir. 1971).
12. Samuel Warren and Louis D. Brandeis, "The Right to Privacy," *Harvard Law Review* 4 (1890): 193–220.

13. Edgar Allan Poe, "The Purloined Letter," in *Complete Stories and Poems of Edgar Allan Poe* (New York: Doubleday, 1984), 125–138, 136.
14. Jorge Luis Borges, "Pierre Menard, Author of the *Quixote*," in *Labyrinths: Selected Stories and Other Writings,* ed. Donald A. Yates and James E. Irby, trans. James E. Irby (New York: New Directions Publishing, 1964), 36–44, 42.
15. See Sigmund Freud, *The Ego and the Id,* trans. James Strachey (New York: W.W. Norton, 1960).
16. Immanuel Kant, "On the Wrongfulness of Unauthorized Publication of Books," in *Practical Philosophy*, trans. and ed. Mary J. Gregor (Cambridge, UK: Cambridge University Press, 1996), 27–35.

1. THE POVERTY OF VALUE

1. See Copyright Act, R.S.C. 1985, c. C-42, s. 5 (Can.); Copyrights, 17 U.S.C. § 102 (2006); CCH Canadian Ltd. v. Law Society of Upper Canada, 2004 SCC 13; Feist Publications Inc. v. Rural Telephone Service Co. Inc. 499 U.S. 340 (1991).
2. Feist Publications v. Rural Telephone, 345.
3. CCH v. Law Society of Upper Canada, para. 16.
4. Ibid., para. 15: "There are competing views on the meaning of 'original' in copyright law . . . [t]his approach is consistent with the 'sweat of the brow' or 'industriousness' standard of originality . . . [o]ther courts have required that a work must be creative to be 'original' . . ." Internal citations omitted. Feist Publications v. Rural Telephone, 354: "Without a doubt, the 'sweat of the brow' doctrine flouted basic copyright principles."
5. For discussion of Feist as an affirmation of an emerging global originality standard, see Daniel Gervais, "Feist Goes Global: A Comparative Analysis of the Notion of Originality in Copyright Law," *Journal of the Copyright Society of the U.S.A.* 49 (2002): 949–981. See also Jane C. Ginsburg, "The Concept of Authorship in Comparative Copyright Law," *DePaul Law Review* 52 (2002–2003): 1063–1092.
6. See, for example, Walter v. Lane, [1900] A.C. 539, 545. See also Kelly v. Morris (1866), L.R. 1 Eq 697.
7. See Feist Publications v. Rural Telephone, 354; CCH v. Law Society of Upper Canada, para. 23.
8. CCH v. Law Society of Upper Canada, para. 22.
9. Feist Publications v. Rural Telephone, 349–350.
10. CCH v. Law Society of Upper Canada, para. 23.
11. See, for example, Norman Siebrasse, "Copyright in Facts and Information: *Feist Publications* Is Not, and Should Not Be, The Law in Canada," *Canadian Intellectual Property Review* 11 (1994): 191–202.

12. Consider, for example, MacMillan v. Cooper, [1924] 93 L.J.P.C. 113, 116–117.
13. University of London Press Ltd. v. University Tutorial Press Ltd., [1916] 2 Ch. 601; Walter v. Lane.
14. Feist Publications v. Rural Telephone, 347.
15. Ibid., 344, 345, 347, 347, 347, 349, 349. Internal quotations and citations omitted.
16. Ibid., 347.
17. Ibid., 354.
18. Ibid.
19. Ibid., 349. Internal citations omitted.
20. Ibid. See also U.S. Const. art. I, § 8, cl. 8.
21. U.S. Const. art. I, § 8, cl. 8.
22. Feist Publications v. Rural Telephone, 349–350. Internal citations omitted. See also Computer Assocs. v. Altai, 982 F. 2d 693 (1992), 696: "The author's benefit, however, is clearly a 'secondary' consideration."
23. Alfred C. Yen, "The Legacy of Feist: Consequences of the Weak Connection between Copyright and the Economics of Public Goods," *Ohio State Law Journal* 52 (1991): 1343–1378, 1369; Norman Siebrasse, "A Property Rights Theory of the Limits of Copyright," *University of Toronto Law Journal* 51 (2001): 1–61, 57; Siebrasse, "Copyright in Facts and Information."
24. Feist Publications v. Rural Telephone, 347.
25. For comparisons of Canadian fair dealing, UK fair dealing and US fair use, see Giuseppina D'Agostino, "Healing Fair Dealing? A Comparative Copyright Analysis of Canada's Fair Dealing to U.K. Fair Dealing and U.S. Fair Use," *McGill Law Journal* 53 (2008): 311–363.
26. CCH v. Law Society of Upper Canada, para. 48: "Before reviewing the scope of the fair dealing exception under the *Copyright Act,* it is important to clarify some general considerations about exceptions to copyright infringement. Procedurally, a defendant is required to prove that his or her dealing with a work has been fair; however, the fair dealing exception is perhaps more properly understood as an integral part of the *Copyright Act* than simply a defence. Any act falling within the fair dealing exception will not be an infringement of copyright. The fair dealing exception, like other exceptions in the *Copyright Act,* is a user's right. In order to maintain the proper balance between the rights of a copyright owner and users' interests, it must not be interpreted restrictively."
27. See Matthew Rimmer, "Canadian Rhapsody: Copyright Law and Research Libraries," *Australian Academic and Research Libraries* 25 (2004): 193–213.
28. Following *CCH,* the Supreme Court of Canada has amply confirmed user rights as a permanent and central component of its understanding of copyright law. See Alberta v. Canadian Copyright Licensing Agency, 2012

SCC 37; Entertainment Software Association v. SOCAN, 2012 SCC 36; Re: Sound v. MPTAC, 2012 SCC 38; Rogers Communications Inc. v. SOCAN, 2012 SCC 35; SOCAN v. Bell Canada, 2012 SCC 36. For commentary, see Michael Geist, ed., *The Copyright Pentalogy: How the Supreme Court of Canada Shook the Foundations of Canadian Copyright Law* (Ottawa, ON: University of Ottawa Press, 2013).

29. CCH v. Law Society of Upper Canada, paras. 1, 2.
30. Ibid., paras. 36, 73.
31. Ibid., paras. 24, 48.
32. Ibid., para. 24.
33. Feist Publications v. Rural Telephone, 345.
34. See, for example, Daniel J. Gervais and Elizabeth Judge, *Intellectual Property: The Law in Canada* (Toronto, ON: Carswell, 2005), 23: "But it seems that the Supreme Court [of Canada] chose a 'middle-path' only in appearance. Canada instead has taken on a standard essentially identical to those of our American neighbours and to the Continental systems." See also Daniel J. Gervais, "Canadian Copyright Law Post-CCH," *Intellectual Property Journal* 18 (2004): 131–167; Teresa Scassa, "Recalibrating Copyright Law? A Comment on the Supreme Court of Canada's Decision in CCH Canadian Ltd. v. Law Society of Upper Canada," *Canadian Journal of Law and Technology* 3 (2004): 89–100, 91. For comparative discussion of originality in Canada pre-*CCH*, see Yo'av Mazeh, "Canadian Originality and The Tension Between the Commonwealth and The American Standards for Copyright Protection: The Myth of Tele-Direct," *Intellectual Property Journal* 16 (2003): 561–598.
35. University of London Press v. University Tutorial Press, 609.
36. Ibid., 608–609.
37. Sheldon v. Metro-Goldwyn Pictures Corp. 81 F. 2d 49 (2d Cir. 1936), 54.
38. University of London Press v. University Tutorial Press, 609.
39. Ibid.
40. Ibid. Emphasis added.
41. Ibid.
42. Ibid.
43. Ibid.
44. Ibid. Emphasis added.
45. Ibid.
46. Ibid.
47. Ibid., 608.
48. Ibid., 609–610. Emphasis added.
49. David Vaver, *Copyright Law* (Toronto, ON: Irwin Law, 2000), 148.
50. Consider in this regard International News Service v. Associated Press, 248 U.S. 215 (1918), 239: "[D]efendant, by its very act, admits that it is taking

material that has been acquired by complainant as the result of organization and the expenditure of labor, skill, and money, and which is salable by complainant for money, and that defendant in appropriating it and selling it as its own is endeavoring to reap where it has not sown."

51. Walter v. Lane, 545. Strictly speaking, use of the phrase "sweat of the brow" to denote Lord Halsbury's judgment is anachronistic. The phrase describes a school of thought with respect to the originality requirement, but the word "original" did not find its way into the English *Copyright Act* until 1911, eleven years after *Walter.* Still, in the pre-1911 jurisprudence, including *Walter,* the debate about copyrightability took place through inquiry into the meaning of the word "author." See Robert Howell and Ysolde Gendreau, "Qualitative Standards for Protection of Literary and Artistic Property," in *Contemporary Law: Canadian Reports to the 1994 International Congress of Comparative Law, Athens, 1994* (Cowansville, QC: Yvon Blais, 1994), 518, 521–522, 542–545.
52. See, for example, Kelly v. Morris.
53. Walter v. Lane, 546.
54. Ibid., 553.
55. Ibid.
56. Ibid., 554.
57. Ibid.
58. Ibid., 555.
59. Ibid. Emphasis added.
60. Ibid., 560.
61. Ibid.
62. Ibid., 560–561.
63. Ibid., 561. Emphasis added.
64. Ibid.
65. Ibid.
66. Ibid. Emphases added.
67. Ibid., 562.
68. Ibid., 549.
69. See, for example, Siebrasse, "Copyright in Facts and Information." Consider also CCH Canadian Ltd. v. Law Society of Upper Canada, 2002 FCA 187, para. 59.
70. Sayre v. Moore, 1 East 361, 102 Eng. Rep. 139 (Eng. K.B.) (1785), 139.
71. CCH v. Law Society of Upper Canada (FCA), para. 59: "Admittedly, the public interest in the dissemination of works may be a policy reason to impose a high standard of 'creativity' as a prerequisite to copyright protection. There is also the concern that overprotection of certain works will thwart social and scientific progress by precluding persons from building upon earlier works. However, I would suggest that copyright monopolies

are better controlled through the avenues that Parliament has established than through the imposition of an arbitrary and subjective standard of 'creative spark' or 'imagination.' As will be discussed below, a fair interpretation of user rights can counteract the apparent imbalance potentially generated by a low threshold (see Vaver, *Copyright Law, supra,* at pages 169–70). For example, the fair dealing provisions of the *Act* provide a mechanisms [*sic*] whereby user rights are better considered."

72. See, for example, Yen, "The Legacy of Feist."
73. CCH v. Law Society of Upper Canada, para. 25. Emphasis added.
74. Ibid., para. 24.
75. I borrow the fulcrum image from Justice Bastarache's judgment in Euro-Excellence Inc. v. Kraft Can. Inc., 2007 SCC 37, para. 84. The "axiom" characterization is from Feist Publications v. Rural Telephone, 352.
76. See Dianne Zimmerman, "It's an Original!(?) In Pursuit of Copyright's Elusive Essence," *Columbia Journal of Law and Arts* 28 (2005): 187–212.

2. ORIGINALITY AS SPEAKING IN ONE'S OWN WORDS

1. On the copyright wars, see for example, W. F. Patry, *Moral Panics and the Copyright Wars* (New York: Oxford University Press, 2009).
2. International News Service v. Associated Press 248 U.S. 215 (1918), 250 (Brandeis J.).
3. Copyright Act, R.S.C. 1985, c. C-42 s. 5 (Can.): "[C]opyright shall subsist . . . in every *original* literary, dramatic, musical and artistic work." Emphasis added.
4. Patent Act, R.S.C. 1985, c. P 4, s. 2 (Can.): "'[I]nvention' means any *new* and useful art." Emphasis added.
5. Feist Publications Inc. v. Rural Telephone Service Co. Inc. 499 U.S. 340 (1991), 345–346.
6. University of London Press Ltd. v. University Tutorial Press Ltd., [1916] 2 Ch. 601, 609.
7. CCH Canadian Ltd. v. Law Society of Upper Canada, 2004 SCC 13, para. 16: "For a work to be 'original' within the meaning of the *Copyright Act,* it must be more than a mere copy of another work. At the same time, it need not be creative in the sense of being novel or unique. What is required to attract copyright protection in the expression of an idea is an exercise of skill and judgment."
8. Feist Publications v. Rural Telephone, 345: "Original, as the term is used in copyright, means only that the work was independently created by the author (as opposed to copied from other works) and that it possesses at least some minimal degree of creativity."

9. Ibid., 347.
10. Ibid., 349.
11. On the appropriate role of comparisons between works in the originality inquiry, see Agustin Waisman, "May Authorship Go Objective?" *Journal of Intellectual Property Law & Practice* 4 (2009): 583–591.
12. See Patent Act, s. 2: "'[I]nvention' means any *new* and useful art." Emphasis added; Ibid., s. 28.2(1)(a): "The subject-matter . . . must not have been disclosed . . . in such a manner that the subject-matter became available to the public in Canada or elsewhere."
13. See Free World Trust v. Électro Santé Inc., [2000] 2 S.C.R. 1024, paras. 25–26; Hayden Mfg. Co. v. Canplas Indus. Ltd., [1998] 98 C.P.R. (3d) 17, paras. 11–16; Omark Indus. (1960) Ltd. v. Gouger Saw Chain Co., [1965] 1 Ex. C.R. 457, paras. 82–83.
14. See, for example, Free World Trust, paras. 25–26; Beloit Can. Ltd. v. Valmet Oy, [1986] 8 C.P.R. (3d) 289, 297. See also Kalman v. Kimberly-Clark Corp. 713 F.2d 760 (Fed. Cir. 1983), 771: "[Anticipation requires that] each element of the claim in issue is found, either expressly described or under the principles of inherency, in a single prior art reference, or that the claimed invention was previously known or embodied in a single prior art device or practice."
15. Jorge Luis Borges, "Pierre Menard, Author of the *Quixote*," in *Labyrinths: Selected Stories & Other Writings*, ed. Donald A. Yates and James E. Irby, trans. James E. Irby, (New York: New Directions Publishing, 1964), 36–44.
16. Ibid., 38–39.
17. Ibid., 39.
18. Ibid., 39. Last two emphases added.
19. Menard produced a work substantially similar to that of Cervantes, and he had access to Cervantes's work. This convergence of substantial similarity and access gives rise to a *prima facie* finding of infringement. If, as Menard proposed, however, the identity between his work and that of Cervantes were a mere coincidence, then Menard's work is original for copyright purposes. Strictly speaking, it is as an independent creation. There can be no doubt, of course, that Menard would have a hard time proving this in court!
20. Borges, "Pierre Menard," 43.
21. See, for example, Herbert Rosenthal Jewelry Corp. v. Kalpakian, 446 F.2d 738, 742 (9th Cir. 1971); Francis Day & Hunter Ltd. v. Bron (trading as Delmar Publishing Co.), [1963] Ch. 587, 627; Preston v. 20th Century Fox Can. Ltd., [1990] 33 C.P.R. (3d) 242, paras. 65–68.
22. See Francis Day, 598; Rosenthal Jewelry Corp., 738; Preston, para. 10.
23. On establishing infringement and the role of independent creation, see Francis Day, 627: "Even complete identity of the two works may not be

conclusive evidence of copying, for it may be proved that it was impossible for the author of the alleged infringing work to have had access to the copyright work. And, once you have eliminated the impossible (namely, copying), that which remains (namely, coincidence) however improbable, is the truth; I quote inaccurately, but not unconsciously, from Sherlock Holmes."

24. Patent Act, s. 28.2(a); s. 54. See, for example, Harris v. Rothwell (1887), 35 Ch. D. 416 (C.A.), 429; Woven Plastic Products Ltd. v. British Ropes Ltd., [1970] F.S.R. 47 (C.A.), 58; Kirin-Amgen Inc. v. Hoechst Marion Roussel Ltd., [2004] UKHL 46, 52, 158–159; applied in Canada in Bridgeview Mfg. Inc. v. 931409 Alberta Ltd., 2010 FCA 188, 35–36. See also David Vaver, *Intellectual Property Law,* 2nd ed. (Toronto, ON: Irwin Law, 2011), 320.
25. See R. v. Stewart, [1988] 1 S.C.R 963.
26. There can be no doubt, of course, that technology is in another sense a part of culture widely conceived. The point here, however, is the distinction between person-object relations and person-person relations. See Jurgen Habermas, "Labor and Interaction: Remarks on Hegel's Jena *Philosophy of Mind,*" in *Theory and Practice,* trans. John Viertel (Boston: Beacon Press, 1973), 142–169.
27. Patent Act, s. 27(3).
28. Patent Act, s. 2: "'[I]nvention' means any new and *useful* art." Emphasis added.
29. On the contrary, functionality can disqualify purported creations from copyright protection. See, for example, Delrina Corp. v. Triolet Sys. Inc., [2002] 17 C.P.R. (4th) 289; Computer Assocs. Int'l Inc. v. Altai Inc. 982 F.2d 693 (2d Cir. 1992); Hollinrake v. Truswell, [1894] 3 Ch. 420; Baker v. Selden, 101 U.S. 99 (1879).
30. Moreau v. St. Vincent, [1950] Ex. C.R. 198 (Can. Ex. Ct.), 203. Emphasis added.
31. Ibid.
32. Ibid.
33. Nichols v. Universal Pictures Corporation 45 F.2d 119 (2d Cir. 1930), 122.
34. Ibid.
35. Ibid.
36. Ibid.
37. Ibid.
38. Ibid., 121, 122.
39. Ibid., 121.
40. See, for example, Moreau v. St. Vincent, 203: "Every one may freely adopt and use the ideas but no one may *copy* his literary work without his consent." Emphasis added.
41. "Nor does she [the plaintiff] fare better," Hand J. adds, "as to her characters. It is indeed scarcely credible that she should not have been aware of

those stock figures, the low comedy Jew and Irishman. The defendant has not taken from her more than their prototypes have contained for many decades. If so, obviously so to generalize her copyright, would allow her to cover what was not original with her. *But we need not hold this as a matter of fact, much as we might be justified. Even though we take it that she devised her figures out of her brain de novo, still the defendant was within its rights.*" See Nichols v. Universal Pictures, 122. Emphasis added.

42. See Pierson v. Post 3 Cai. R. 175 (N.Y. Sup. Ct. 1805). For commentary, see Carol M. Rose, "Possession as the Origin of Property" in Carol M. Rose, *Property and Persuasion: Essays on the History, Theory, and Rhetoric of Ownership* (Boulder, CO: Westview Press, 1994), 11–24; Peter Benson, "The Idea of Property in Private Law" in *The Oxford Handbook of Jurisprudence and Philosophy of Law,* ed. Jules Coleman and Scott Shapiro (Oxford, UK: Oxford University Press, 2002), 752. I discuss Pierson v. Post in detail in Chapter 4.
43. Nichols v. Universal Pictures, 122.
44. Ibid., 121.
45. I hesitate because the doctrine of merger seems to contemplate the possibility that ideas may be "possessed" or "occupied." The doctrine provides that "[i]f an idea can be expressed in only one or in a very limited number of ways, then copyright of that expression will be refused for it would give the originator of the idea a virtual monopoly on the idea. In such a case it is said that the expression merges with the idea and thus is not copyrightable." See Delrina Corporation v. Triolet Systems Inc. (1993), 47 C.P.R. (3d) 1 (Ont. Gen. Div.), 41. See also Morrissey v. Procter & Gamble Company, 379 F.2d 675 (1st Cir. 1967); and Herbert Rosenthal Jewelry v. Kalpakian. It is as if the law of copyright refuses protection precisely at the point where expression most closely resembles exclusive "possession" or "occupation" of an idea. Thus it is not so much that ideas cannot be occupied but rather that where they can be occupied, there will be no copyright. To be sure, the difficulties involved in occupying an idea may be a reason why the law refuses to copyright ideas. Nonetheless, the doctrine of merger suggests that the problem of occupation, considered as an evidentiary problem, cannot be the whole of the story.
46. See, for example, Jessica Litman, "The Public Domain," *Emory Law Journal* 39 (1990): 965–1023; and Alfred C. Yen, "Restoring the Natural Law: Copyright as Labor and Possession," *Ohio State Law Journal* 51 (1990): 517–559. See also Norman Siebrasse, "A Property Rights Theory of the Limits of Copyright," *University of Toronto Law Journal* 51 (2001): 1–61.
47. Copyrights, 17 U.S.C. § 107 (2006). Emphasis added.
48. Copyright Act, R.S.C. 1985, c. C-42 s. 29, 29.1, 29.2.
49. For a view that the fair dealing purposes in the Canadian *Copyright Act* are, too, illustrative, see Ariel Katz, "Fair Use 2.0: The Rebirth of Fair Dealing in Canada," in *The Copyright Pentalogy: How the Supreme Court of Canada Shook*

the Foundations of Canadian Copyright Law, ed. Michael Geist (Ottawa, ON: University of Ottawa Press, 2013), 93–156.

50. See, for example, CCH v. Law Society of Upper Canada, para. 50.
51. Ibid., paras. 53–60.
52. Beloff v. Pressdram Ltd., [1973] F.S.R. 33, 60: "[the] fairness [of the dealing] must be judged in relation to that purpose."
53. CCH v. Law Society of Upper Canada, paras. 56–60.
54. Théberge v. Galerie d'Art du Petit Champlain inc., 2002 SCC 34, para. 32. Emphasis added.
55. Campbell v. Acuff-Rose Music Inc. 510 U.S. 569 (1994), 579. Emphasis added, internal citations omitted.
56. Ibid.
57. See, for example, Gideon Parchomovsky, "Fair Use, Efficiency, and Corrective Justice," *Legal Theory* 3 (1997): 347–378, 371: "[O]nly authors, but not copycats, should be entitled to the fair use privilege." On transformativeness in fair use, Melville B. Nimmer and David Nimmer, *Nimmer on Copyright* § 13.05[A][1][b] (2012); Laura A. Heymann, "Everything is Transformative: Fair Use and Reader Response," *Columbia Journal of Law and the Arts* 31 (2008): 445–466; Paul Edward Geller, "A German Approach to Fair Use: Test Cases for TRIP's Criteria for Copyright Limitations," *Journal of the Copyright Society of the U.S.A.* 57 (2010): 901–919. On fair use generally, see Neil Netanel, "Making Sense of Fair Use," *Lewis & Clark Law Review* 15 (2011): 715–771; Pamela Samuelson, "Unbundling Fair Uses," *Fordham Law Review* 77 (2009): 2537–2621.
58. On equality and bilaterality in private law, see generally Ernest J. Weinrib, *The Idea of Private Law* (Oxford, UK: Oxford University Press, 2012); Alan Brudner (with Jennifer M. Nadler), *The Unity of the Common Law,* Second Edition (Oxford, UK: Oxford University Press, 2013); Arthur Ripstein, *Force and Freedom: Kant's Legal and Political Philosophy* (Cambridge, MA: Harvard University Press, 2009). On equality in intellectual property, see generally Wendy J. Gordon, "A Property Right in Self-Expression: Equality and Individualism in the Natural Law of Intellectual Property," *Yale Law Journal* 102 (1993): 1533–1609. See also Seana Valentine Shiffrin, "Lockean Arguments for Private Intellectual Property," in *New Essays in the Legal and Political Theory of Property,* ed. Stephen Munzer (Cambridge, UK: Cambridge University Press, 2001), 138–167.
59. CCH v. Law Society of Upper Canada, para. 49.
60. Trade-marks Act, R.S.C. 1985, C. T 13, s. 2: "'[T]rade-mark' means (a) a mark that is used by a person for the purpose of distinguishing or so as to distinguish wares or services manufactured, sold, leased, hired or performed by him from those manufactured, sold, leased, hired or performed by others."

61. Mattel, Inc. v. 3894207 Can. Inc., [2006] 1 S.C.R. 772, para. 75, quoting Western Clock Co. v. Oris Watch Co., [1931] Ex. C.R. 64, 67: "Distinctiveness is of the very essence and is the cardinal requirement of a trade-mark." "A non-distinctive trade-mark, " as David Vaver puts it, "is a contradiction in terms." David Vaver, *Intellectual Property Law,* 2nd ed., 464.
62. Even where trademark law imposes liability for a defendant's nonconfusing use, it does so only where such use is—to track the language of Section 22 of the Canadian statute—"likely to have the effect of depreciating the value of the goodwill" attaching to the plaintiff's trademark; only, that is, by reference to the role of the trademark in signifying the plaintiff to the marketplace. Trade-marks Act, s. 22(1). See, for example, Veuve Clicquot Ponsardin v. Boutiques Cliquot Ltée, [2006] S.C.R. 824. For commentary on trademark liability, including liability for nonconfusing use, see Mark McKenna, "The Normative Foundations of Trademark Law," *Notre Dame Law Review* 89 (2007): 1839–1916.
63. See (albeit a passing off decision) the formulation in Reckitt & Colman Ltd. v. Borden Inc., [1990] 1 All E.R. 873, 880: "[H]e must establish a goodwill or reputation attached to the goods or services which he supplies in the mind of the purchasing public by association with the identifying "get-up" (whether it consists simply of a brand name or a trade description, or the individual features of labelling or packaging) under which his particular goods or services are offered to the public, such that the get-up is recognised by the public as distinctive specifically of the plaintiff's goods or services."
64. CCH v. Law Society of Upper Canada, para. 16: "What is required to attract copyright protection in the expression of an idea is an exercise of skill and judgment."
65. See, for example, Abercrombie & Fitch Co. v. Hunting World Inc. 537 F.2d 4 (2d Cir. 1976).

3. THE WORK AS A WORK

1. Baker v. Selden, 101 U.S. 99 (1879).
2. A.V. v. iParadigms LLC, 562 F.3d 630 (4th Cir. 2009), 640: "iParadigms' use of these works was completely unrelated to the expressive content and was instead aimed at detecting and discouraging plagiarism."
3. Baker v. Selden, 100.
4. Ibid., 104–105.
5. Ibid.
6. Ibid., 105.
7. Ibid.

8. Ibid., 103.
9. Were this otherwise, "everybody who made a rabbit pie in accordance with the recipe of Mrs. Beeton's Cookery Book would infringe the literary copyright in that book." See Cuisenaire v. S.W. Imports Ltd., [1969] S.C.R. 208, para. 9, quoting Cuisenaire v. Reed, [1963] V.R. 719. 735. In Baker v. Selden, 102–103, the Court provides several examples:

    > A treatise on the composition and use of medicines, be they old or new; on the construction and use of ploughs, or watches, or churns; on the mixture and application of colors for painting or dyeing; or on the mode of drawing lines to produce the effect of perspective—would be the subject of copyright; but no one would contend that the copyright of the treatise would give the exclusive right to the art or manufacture described therein. . . . The difference between the two things, letters patent and copyright, may be illustrated by reference to the subjects just enumerated. Take the case of medicines. Certain mixtures are found to be of great value in the healing art. If the discoverer writes and publishes a book on the subject (as regular physicians generally do), he gains no exclusive right to the manufacture and sale of the medicine; he gives that to the public. If he desires to acquire such exclusive right, he must obtain a patent for the mixture as a new art, manufacture, or composition of matter. He may copyright his book if he pleases, but that only secures to him the exclusive right of printing and publishing his book. So of all other inventions and discoveries.

10. Baker v. Selden, 103. Emphasis added.
11. Ibid., 104.
12. Ibid., 102.
13. Ibid., 104.
14. Ibid. Emphasis added.
15. Ibid., 103. Emphasis added.
16. On the word "copy" as a term of art, see Millar v. Taylor, 98 E.R. 201 (K.B.) (1769), per Lord Mansfield: "I use the word 'copy,' in the technical sense in which that name or term has been used for ages, to signify an incorporeal right to the sole printing and publishing of somewhat intellectual, communicated by letters." I discuss Millar v. Taylor in detail in Chapter 5.
17. Nichols v. Universal Pictures Corporation 45 F.2d 119 (2d Cir. 1930), 121.
18. See Morrissey v. Procter & Gamble Co., 379 F.2d 675 (1st Cir. 1967), 678–679; Herbert Rosenthal Jewelry Corp. v. Kalpakian, 446 F.2d 738 (9th Cir. 1971), 742.

19. Pamela Samuelson, "The Story of *Baker v. Selden:* Sharpening the Distinction Between Authorship and Invention," in *Intellectual Property Stories*, ed. Jane C. Ginsburg and Rochelle C. Dreyfuss (New York: Foundation Press, 2006), 189.
20. See Computer Assocs. v. Altai, 982 F. 2d 693 (2nd Cir. 1992), 707, discussing aspects of *Baker* as "the cornerstone for what has developed into the doctrine of merger."
21. Benjamin Kaplan, *An Unhurried View of Copyright* (Clark, New Jersey: The Law Book Exchange, Ltd., 2008), 33. This is a reprint of the James S. Carpentier Lectures delivered by Professor Kaplan at the Columbia University School of Law in March, 1966.
22. Baker v. Selden, 103.
23. Ibid.
24. Ibid., 100–101. Emphasis added.
25. Ibid., 104.
26. In her magisterial treatment of *Baker* in "Why Copyright Law Excludes Systems and Processes from the Scope of Its Protection," *Texas Law Review* 85 (2007): 1921–1977, Pamela Samuelson anchors the case in the patent/copyright distinction and forcefully demonstrates that it cannot be reduced to the idea/expression dichotomy. See also Pamela Samuelson, "The Story of *Baker v. Selden.*" In "Why Copyright Law Excludes," Samuelson notes at 1936 that

    > While *Baker* is principally known for its powerful statements about what copyright does not protect, it is grounded in a positive conception of that which copyright does and should protect, namely, original works of authorship that convey information by explaining or describing it, and works that display or depict an aesthetic or ornamental appearance (e.g., works of fine art). It is the language that an author uses to explain, describe, or express whatever ideas or useful arts she may have discovered or created that copyright protects, along with the artistic way in which an author draws or illustrates those ideas or useful arts that copyright protects.

    As I understand it, Samuelson's view is that *Baker* denies copyright in Selden's forms because they are aspects of the accounting system. This view precludes a distinction between the forms as works, subject to copyright, and the forms as tools, excluded from copyright protection. Interpreted in that way, *Baker* cannot ground a use-driven concept of copyright premised on the distinction between a work and its material form. Samuelson quotes at 1934 as follows from *Baker:*

    > Where the [useful] art [a work] teaches cannot be used without employing the methods and diagrams used to illustrate the book, or

> such as are similar to them, such methods and diagrams are to be considered as necessary incidents to the art, and given therewith to the public . . . for the purpose of practical application.

The ellipsis stands for the following italicized phrase: "and given therewith to the public; *not given for the purpose of publication in other works explanatory of the art, but* for the purpose of practical application." Baker v. Selden, 103. Emphasis added. There is no doubt that from Samuelson's perspective the phrase is indeed hardly significant. My reading of *Baker* turns on the significance of that phrase.

27. Kelly v. Arriba Soft Corp. 336 F. 3d 811 (9th Cir. 2003), 815.
28. For a different view see Matthew Sag, "Copyright and Copy-Reliant Technology," *Northwestern University Law Review* 103 (2009): 1607–1682.
29. For a different view, see Maurizio Borghi and Stavroula Karapapa, "Non-Display Uses of Copyright Works: Google Books and Beyond," *Queen Mary Journal of Intellectual Property* 1 (2011): 21–52; Maurizio Borghi and Stavroula Karapapa, *Copyright and Mass Digitization* (Oxford: Oxford University Press, 2013).
30. Kelly v. Arriba Soft, 816.
31. Ibid., 818.
32. Ibid.
33. See Public Relations Consultants Association Ltd v. Newspaper Licensing Agency Ltd and others, [2013] UKSC 18, [2013] 2 All ER 852. On browsing and implied license or authorization, see Sunny Handa, *Copyright Law in Canada* (Markam, ON: Butterworths, 2002), 292–294; Barry B. Sookman, *Computer, Internet and Electronic Commerce Law* (Toronto, ON: Carswell, 2000), 3-213; Roger T. Hughes and Susan J. Peacock, *Copyright and Industrial Design,* 2nd ed. (Markam, ON: Butterworths, 1991), 499. See also Glen A. Bloom and Thomas J. Denholm, "Research on the Internet: Is Access Copyright Infringement?," *Canadian Intellectual Property Review* 12 (1996): 337–365.
34. Canadian Ass'n of Internet Providers v. Society of Composers, Authors, & Music Publishers of Canada, [2004] 2 S.C.R. 427, para. 116. See also Euro-Excellence Inc., [2007] S.C.C. 37, para. 81. In Canadian Ass'n of Internet Providers, the Supreme Court of Canada defined caching as follows, para. 23:

> When an end user visits a Web site, the packets of data needed to transmit the requested information will come initially from the host server where the files for this site are stored. As they pass through the hands of an Internet Service Provider, a temporary copy may be made and stored on its server. This is a cache copy. If another user wants to visit this page shortly thereafter, using the same Internet Service Provider, the information may be transmitted to the subsequent user either directly from the Web site or from what is kept in

the cache copy. The practice of creating "caches" of data speeds up the transmission and lowers the cost. The subsequent end user may have no idea that it is not getting the information directly from the original Web site. Cache copies are not retained for long periods of time [*sic*] since, if the original files change, users will get out-of-date information. The Internet Service Provider controls the existence and duration of caches on its own facility, although in some circumstances it is open to a content provider to specify no caching, or an end user to program its browser to insist on content from the original Web site.

35. Ibid., para. 115.
36. Copyright Act, R.S.C. 1985, c. C-42 s. 3.(1) (Can.).
37. Ibid. On the move from two-dimensional form (e.g., a drawing) to three-dimensional form (e.g., a doll or model) as copyright infringement, see King Features Syndicate Inc. v. O. & M. Kleeman Ltd., [1941] A.C. 417 (H.L.).
38. See Catnic Components Ltd. v. Hill & Smith Ltd., [1978] F.S.R. 405 (Ch. Div.); Burnaby Machine & Mill Equipment Ltd. v. Berglund Industrial Supply Co. 81 C.P.R. (2d) 251 (1984); Rucker Co. v. Gavel's Vulcanizing Ltd. 7 C.P.R. (3d) 294 (1985). For discussion, see Daniel Gervais and Elizabeth F. Judge, *Intellectual Property: The Law in Canada* (Toronto, ON: Thomson Carswell, 2005), 597–600 (suggesting an implied license solution); Robert J. Tomkowicz, "Copyrighting Chocolate: *Kraft Canada Inc. v. Euro-Excllence,*" *Intellectual Property Journal* 20 (2007): 423–425 (suggesting "a limited judicial doctrine of copyright misuse" rooted in the purpose of the *Copyright Act*). See also Robert J. Tomkowicz and Elizabeth F. Judge, "The Right of Exclusive Access: Misusing Copyright to Expand the Patent Monopoly," *Intellectual Property Journal* 19 (2006): 351–391.
39. Consider Energy Absorption Systems Inc. v. Y. Boissoneault & Fils Inc. 30 C.P.R. (3d) 420 (F.C.T.D.) 275 (1990) where defendant is found to have infringed the plaintiff's patent by making and selling the plaintiff's invention, and also to have infringed the plaintiff's copyright by reproducing in the defendant's operation manual diagrams contained in the plaintiff's manual for the use of the invention.
40. Consider Copyrights, 17 U.S.C. § 113(b) (2006), providing that copyright in a work portraying a useful article does not extend to the useful article portrayed. Consider also Bastarache J. in Euro-Excellence Inc. v. Kraft Canada Inc., 2007 SCC 37, para. 103, dismissing the plaintiff's claim that otherwise lawful importation into Canada of chocolate bars is rendered unlawful as copyright infringement arising from importation of copyrighted works imprinted as logos on the chocolate bar wrappers:

> The above does not imply that the Côte D'Or or Toblerone logos are not copyrightable works. Quite the opposite: the logos have been properly registered and there is no reason to dispute the trial judge's conclusions that the logos meet the Act's originality threshold and are therefore copyrightable works. KCI [Kraft Canada Inc.], as holder of those copyrights in Canada, would surely succeed in an action for copyright infringement against a defendant who produced and distributed posters of the logos, for example. However, it is necessary to ensure that this legitimate copyright protection is not illegitimately leveraged into protection for a market in consumer goods.

"Can a chocolate bar," Bastarache J. asks (rhetorically) in the first sentence of his judgment, "be copyrighted because of protected works appearing on its wrapper?" See Euro-Excellence, para. 57.

41. On the distinction between reproduction and infringement see Jessica Litman, "Revising Copyright Law for the Information Age," in *Digital Copyright*, ed. Jessica Litman (Amherst, NY: Prometheus Books, 2001), 171–191; Ernest Miller and Joan Feigenbaum, "Taking the Copy Out of Copyright," in *DRM'01 Revised Papers from the ACM CCS-8 Workshop on Security and Privacy in Digital Rights Management*, ed. Tomas Sander (London: Springer-Verlag, 2002), 233–224; Sarah Stadler, "Copyright as Trade Regulation," *Pennsylvania Law Review* 155 (2007): 899–960; Jessica Litman, "Lawful Personal Use," *Texas Law Review* 85 (2007), 1871–1920; Paul Edward Geller, "Beyond the Copyright Crisis: Principles for Change," *Journal of the Copyright Society of the U.S.A.* 55 (2008): 165–199; Maurizio Borghi, "Copyright and Truth," *Theoretical Inquiries in Law* 12 (2011): 1–27.
42. See, for example, Compagnie Générale des Établissements Michelin-Michelin & CIE v. Nat'l Auto, Aerospace, Transp. & Gen. Workers Union of Can., [1997] 2 F.C. 306.

4. INFRINGEMENT AS COMPELLED SPEECH

1. Glynn S. Lunney, Jr, "Examining Copyright's Incentives-Access Paradigm," *Vanderbilt Law Review* 49 (1996): 483–571.
2. See Robert P. Merges, *Justifying Intellectual Property* (Cambridge, MA: Harvard University Press, 2011), 3. Speaking of intellectual property generally, Merges writes: "Every time I play the archaeologist and go looking for utilitarian footings of the field, I come up empty. Try as I might, I simply cannot justify our current IP system on the basis of verifiable

data showing that people are better off with IP law than they would be without it. Maximizing utility, I have come to see, is not a serviceable first-order principle of the IP system. It is just not what IP is really all about at the deepest level." On empirical validation issues of the model, see also Jessica Silbey, *The Eureka Myth: Creators, Innovators, and Everyday Intellectual Property* (Stanford, CA: Stanford Law Books, 2014); Dan L. Burk, "Law and Economics of Intellectual Property: In Search of First Principles," *Annual Review of Law and Social Science* 8 (2012): 397–414, 410; Diane Leenheer Zimmerman, "Copyrights as Incentives: Did We Just Imagine That?," *Theoretical Inquiries in Law* 12 (2011): 29–58, 53–54; Seana V. Shiffrin, "The Incentives Argument for Intellectual Property Protection" in *Intellectual Property and Theories of Justice*, ed. A. Gosseries, A. Marciano, and A. Strowel (London and New York: Palgrave Macmillan, 2008), 94–105; Stephen Breyer, "The Uneasy Case for Copyright: A Study of Copyright in Books, Photocopies, and Computer Programs," *Harvard Law Review* 84 (1970): 281–355.

3. Feist Publications Inc. v. Rural Telephone Service Co. Inc. 499 U.S. 340 (1991), 347.
4. Immanuel Kant, "On the Wrongfulness of Unauthorized Publication of Books" in *Practical Philosophy*, ed. and trans. Mary J. Gregor (Cambridge, UK: Cambridge University Press, 1996), 27–35, 34.
5. Immanuel Kant, "The Metaphysics of Morals," *Practical Philosophy*, ed. and trans. Mary J. Gregor (Cambridge, UK: Cambridge University Press, 1996), 353–603, 437.
6. Kant, "On the Wrongfulness of Unauthorized Publication," 34. Emphasis in original. For reasons that need not concern us here, Kant's concept of a "discourse to the public"—which he offers as a definition specifically of a "book"—is narrower than our concept of a copyrightable "work."
7. See Kant, "On the Wrongfulness of Unauthorized Publication," 35 note *.
8. On Kant and copyright, see Jonathan Peterson, "Liberalism and the Public Interest in Art," unpublished PhD thesis, University of Toronto (2008); Maria Chiara Pievatolo, "Publicness and Private Intellectual Property in Kant's Political Thought" in *Law and Peace in Kant's Philosophy*, ed. Valerio Rohden, Ricardo R. Terra, Guido A. de Almeida, and Margit Ruffing (Berlin: Walter de Gruyter, 2008), 631–642; Kim Trieger-Bar-Am, "Kant on Copyright: Rights of Transformative Authorship," *Cardozo Arts & Entertainment Law Journal* 25 (2008): 1059–1103; Maurizio Borghi, "Copyright and Truth," *Theoretical Inquiries in Law* 12 (2011): 1–27; Anne Barron, "Kant, Copyright and Communicative Freedom," *Law and Philosophy* 31 (2012): 1–48; Laura Biron, "Public Reason, Communication and Intellectual Property," in *New Frontiers in the Philosophy of Intellectual Property*, ed. Annabelle Lever (Cambridge, UK: Cambridge University Press, 2012), 225–260. See

also Rita Risser, "Determinism, Creative Works and Proprietorship," *The Monist* 93 (2010): 353–367.

9. Section 3(1) of the Canadian *Copyright Act* provides that "For the purposes of this Act, 'copyright,' in relation to a work, means the sole right . . . *if the work is unpublished, to publish the work or any substantial part thereof* . . .": Copyright Act, R.S.C. 1985, c. C-42 s. 3.(1) (Can.). Emphasis added. See also Copyrights, 17 U.S.C. § 104 (a) (2006): "Unpublished Works—The works specified by sections 102 and 103, while unpublished, are subject to protection under this title. . . ."
10. Samuel Warren and Louis D. Brandeis, "The Right to Privacy," *Harvard Law Review* 4 (1890): 193–220.
11. For discussion and development of wider views of privacy, see Lisa Austin, "Privacy and the Question of Technology," *Law & Philosophy* 22 (2003): 119–166; Michael Birnhack, "A Quest for a Theory of Privacy: Context and Control," *Jurimetrics: The Journal of Law, Science and Technology* 51 (2011): 447–479. For a political theorist's view, see Annabelle Lever, *On Privacy* (London: Routledge, 2011).
12. See West Virginia State Board of Education v. Barnette, 319 U.S. 624 (1943) (U.S. Supreme Court overturning a law compelling public school children to salute the flag and recite the Pledge of Allegiance).
13. Pierson v. Post, 3 Cai. R. 175 (N.Y. 1805); Nichols v. Universal Pictures Corporation 45 F.2d 119 (2d Cir. 1930).
14. The phrase is Judge Livingston's, writing in dissent in Pierson v. Post, 181.
15. Pierson v. Post, 178: "[T]he mortal wounding of such beasts, by one not abandoning his pursuit, may, with the utmost propriety, be deemed possession of him."
16. That a reasonable prospect of capture is sufficient to constitute possession is the rule stated by Livingston J. in his dissent. Ibid., 182: "[P]roperty in animals *ferae naturae* may be acquired without bodily touch or manucaption, provided the pursuer be within reach, or have a reasonable prospect (which certainly existed here) of taking what he has thus discovered an intention of converting to his own use."
17. Ibid., 179–180. For commentary on *Pierson,* see Peter Benson, "Philosophy of Property Law," in *The Oxford Handbook of Jurisprudence and Philosophy of Law*, ed. Jules Coleman and Scott Shapiro (Oxford: Oxford University Press, 2002), 752; and Carol M. Rose, "Possession as the Origin of Property," in *Property and Persuasion: Essays on the History, Theory, and Rhetoric of Ownership* (Boulder, CO: Westview Press, 1994), 11–24.
18. Pierson v. Post, 178.
19. See Ferguson v. Miller, 1 Cow. 243 (N.Y. Sup. Ct. 1823); The Tubantia, [1924] All E.R. 615 (Pr. & Ad. Div.); Parker v. British Airways Board, [1982] 1 All E.R. 834 (C.A.); Clift et al. v. Kane et al. 5 Nwfld. L.R. 327 (1870).

20. See Bruce Ziff, *Principles of Property Law, Sixth Edition* (Toronto, ON: Carswell, 2014), 145–146; James W. Harris, *Property and Justice* (Oxford: Clarendon Press, 1996), 81–84. See also Alan Brudner, *The Unity of the Common Law*, Second Edition (Oxford: Oxford University Press, 2013), 118–119; Arthur Ripstein, *Force and Freedom: Kant's Legal and Political Philosophy* (Cambridge, MA: Harvard University Press, 2009), 96–98; Ernest J. Weinrib, "Poverty and Property in Kant's System of Rights," *Notre Dame Law Review* 78 (2003): 795–828, 809. Kant's discussion is in Immanuel Kant, "The Metaphysics of Morals," 401–421.
21. See Nichols v. Universal Pictures Corporation, 121.
22. Ibid.
23. See, for example, Burk, "Law and Economics of Intellectual Property," 399–401.
24. See Alfred Chueh-Chin Yen, "The Legacy of Feist: Consequences of the Weak Connection Between Copyright and the Economics of Public Goods," *Ohio State Law Journal* 52 (1991): 1343–1378, 1373–1374.
25. Feist Publications v. Rural Telephone, 362–363, 364.
26. Ibid., 346, quoting Burrow-Giles Lithographic Co. v. Sarony 111 U.S. 53 (1884), 58.
27. Ibid., 347.
28. Ibid., 361.
29. Ibid., 346.
30. See Warren and Brandeis, "The Right to Privacy," 193.
31. This is not necessarily to say that copyright law does not or should not draw distinctions between unpublished and published works. Copyright law frequently considers the unpublished or published status of a work under the rubric of fair use or fair dealing. My point is not that such distinctions should be foreclosed but that they should be construed, if at all, as flowing not from qualitatively distinct interests, but from the diverse ways in which different circumstances—including the circumstance that a work is either unpublished or published—may impinge upon authorship interests. The right of first publication is an aspect of an author's copyright, not her privacy. It should therefore be interpreted as such. For examples of judicial treatments of the unpublished/published distinction, see Harper & Row v. Nation Enterprises, 471 U.S. 539 (1985); A.V. v. iParadigms LLC, 562 F.3d 630 (4th Cir. 2009); Beloff v. Pressdram Ltd., [1973] 1 All E.R. 241; Lion Laboratories Ltd. v. Evans, [1984] 3 W.L.R. 539; Hyde Park Residence Ltd. v. Yelland, [2000] 3 W.L.R. 215. One can hardly fail to mention in this context a recent remark of the Supreme Court of Canada: "Although certainly not determinative, if a work has not been published, the dealing may be *more fair* in that its reproduction with acknowledgment could lead to a wider public dissemination of the work—one of the goals

of copyright law." See CCH Canadian Ltd. v. Law Society of Upper Canada, 2004 SCC 13, para. 58. Emphasis added. For commentary on unpublished works and fair use, see Robert Spoo, "'Ah, you publishing scoundrel!' A Hauntological Reading of Privacy, Moral Rights, and the Fair Use of Unpublished Works," *Law and Literature* 25 (2013): 85–102; Kenneth D. Crews, "Fair Use of Unpublished Works: Burdens of Proof and the Integrity of Copyright," *Arizona State Law Journal* 31 (1999): 1–93; Benjamin E. Marks, "Copyright Protection, Privacy Rights, and the Fair Use Doctrine in the Post-*Salinger* Decade," *NYU Law Review* 72 (1997): 1376–1419; Stephen B. Thau, "Copyright, Privacy, and Fair Use," *Hofstra Law Review* 24 (1995): 179–221. For commentary on unpublished works and fair dealing, see Robert Burrell and Alison Coleman, *Copyright Exceptions: The Digital Impact* (Cambridge, UK: Cambridge University Press, 2005), 45–48. On aspects of the history of the unpublished/published work distinction, see Sunny Handa, *Copyright Law in Canada* (Markham, ON: Butterworths, 2002), 107–112; Ronan Deazley, *On the Origin of the Right to Copy: Charting the Movement of Copyright Law in Eighteenth-Century Britain 1695–1775* (Oxford, UK and Portland, OR: Hart Publishing, 2004), 69–74.

32. Warren and Brandeis, "The Right to Privacy," 193.
33. Ibid.
34. Ibid.
35. Ibid., 194.
36. Ibid., 195.
37. Ibid.
38. Ibid.
39. Ibid. Emphasis added.
40. Ibid.
41. Ibid.,196.
42. Ibid., 206.
43. Ibid., 196.
44. Ibid., 197. Emphasis added.
45. Ibid.
46. Ibid.
47. Ibid., 196.
48. Ibid., 197.
49. Ibid., 198.
50. Ibid., 207.
51. Ibid., 200.
52. Ibid. Emphasis added.
53. Ibid. Emphasis added.
54. Ibid. Emphases in original.
55. The United States retained perpetual common law protection of unpublished works until the *Copyright Act* of 1976, which treated published

and unpublished works under the same statutory scheme of protection. See Copyrights, 17 U.S.C. §§ 102 and 301 (1976). The UK and Canada abandoned the common law protection of unpublished works in the UK Copyright Act, 1911 (sections 3, 17 and 31) and the Canadian Copyright Act, 1921 (sections 5, 9 and 44) providing instead a statutory guarantee of perpetual protection for such. The statutory guarantee of perpetual protection for unpublished works was abandoned in the UK in the *European Union Directive on Term of Copyright,* EU Directive 93/98, Art. 1(1), adopted by the UK on January 1, 1996, and in Canada in Bill C-32, *An Act to Amend the Copyright Act,* 2d sess., 35th Parl., 1996–1997, s. 6.

56. See Wheaton v. Peters, 33 U.S. 591 (1834); Donaldson v. Beckett, 4 Burr. 2408 (H.L.) (1774); Millar v. Taylor, 98 E.R. 201 (K.B.) (1769). Warren and Brandeis cite Yates J.'s dissent from Millar v. Taylor in "The Right to Privacy," 198, note 2.
57. Warren and Brandeis, "The Right to Privacy," 201–202.
58. See Robert C. Post, "Rereading Warren and Brandeis: Privacy, Property, and Appropriation," *Case Western Reserve Law Review* 42 (1990): 647–680, 655 (noting that the reading of *Prince Albert v. Strange* offered by Warren and Brandeis is "strained and historically sterile").
59. Warren and Brandeis, "The Right to Privacy," 202.
60. Ibid., 205.
61. Ibid.
62. Ibid., 206.
63. Ibid.
64. Neil M. Richards, "The Puzzle of Brandeis, Privacy, and Speech," *Vanderbilt Law Review* 63 (2010): 1295–1352, 1296: "Their short article is considered by scholars to have established not just the privacy torts but the field of privacy law itself;" citing Harry Kalven, Jr., "Privacy in Tort Law—Were Warren & Brandeis Wrong?," *Law and Contemporary Problems* 31 (1966): 326–339, 327: "The Right to Privacy" is "the most influential law review article of all."
65. Post, "Rereading Warren and Brandeis," 648.
66. Ibid., 658: "The argument from authority was important to Warren and Brandeis because they were concerned to cast the right to privacy as a mere extension of existing common law principles and so avoid the charge of 'judicial legislation.'"

5. THE PUBLIC DOMAIN AS DIALOGUE

1. See Jane C. Ginsburg, "A Tale of Two Copyrights: Literary Property in Revolutionary France and America," in *Of Authors and Origins: Essays in Copyright Law*, ed. Brad Sherman and Alain Strowel (Oxford: Clarendon Press, 1994).

2. See William Fisher, "Theories of Intellectual Property" in *New Essays in the Legal and Political Theory of Property*, ed. Stephen R. Munzer (Cambridge, UK: Cambridge University Press, 2001), 169 (describing "optimal balance" as the "most popular" approach to intellectual property theory). On the copyright wars, see, for example, W. F. Patry, *Moral Panics and the Copyright Wars* (New York: Oxford University Press, 2009). On copyright maximalism and copyright minimalism see Neil Netanel, "Copyright and a Democratic Civil Society," *Yale Law Journal* 106 (1996): 283–387. On copyright politics, see Jessica Litman, *Digital Copyright* (Amherst, NY: Prometheus Books, 2006). For examples of work outside the incentive model, see Wendy J. Gordon, "A Property Right in Self-Expression: Equality and Individualism in the Natural Law of Intellectual Property," *Yale Law Journal* 102 (1993): 1533–1609; Justin Hughes, "The Philosophy of Intellectual Property," *Georgetown Law Journal* 77 (1988): 287–366, 303–304; Roberta Kwall, *The Soul of Creativity: Forging a Moral Rights Law for the United States* (Stanford, CA: Stanford Law Books, 2010), 23, 53; Alfred Yen, "Restoring the Natural Law: Copyright as Labor and Possession," *Ohio State Law Journal* 51 (1990): 517–559; Shyamkrishna Balganesh, "The Obligatory Structure of Copyright Law: Unbundling the Wrong of Copying," *Harvard Law Review* 125 (2012): 1664–1690. Seana Valentine Shiffrin, "Lockean Arguments for Private Intellectual Property," in *New Essays in the Legal and Political Theory of Property*, ed. Stephen Munzer (Cambridge, UK: Cambridge University Press, 2001), 138–167; Lior Zemer, "The Making of a New Copyright Lockean," *Harvard Journal of Law and Public Policy* 29 (2006): 891–947; Kim Treiger-Bar-Am, "Kant on Copyright: Rights of Transformative Authorship," *Cardozo Arts & Entertainment Law Journal* 25 (2008): 1059–1103; Anne Barron, "Kant, Copyright and Communicative Freedom," *Law and Philosophy* 31 (2012): 1–48; Maurizio Borghi, "Copyright and Truth," *Theoretical Inquiries in Law* 12 (2011): 1–27; Maurizio Borghi and Stavroula Karapapa, "Non-Display Uses of Copyrighted Works: Google Books and Beyond," *Queen Mary Journal of Intellectual Property* 1 (2011): 21–52; Robert P. Merges, *Justifying Intellectual Property* (Cambridge, MA: Harvard University Press, 2011).
3. See U.S. Const. art. I, § 8, cl. 8: "The Congress shall have Power . . . to promote the Progress of Science and useful Arts, by securing for limited Times to Authors and Inventors the exclusive Right to their respective Writings and Discoveries." For discussion of plausible noninstrumentalist readings of the clause see Yen, "Restoring the Natural Law," 530–531; Mark McKenna and Brett Frischmann, "Intergenerational Progress," *Wisconsin Law Review* (2011): 123–139.
4. 1710, 8 Anne., c. 19 (Eng.).
5. See, for example, Carys J. Craig, "Locke, Labour and Limiting the Author's Right: A Warning against a Lockean Approach to Copyright Law," *Queen's*

Law Journal 28 (2002): 1–60, 41–43; Dennis S. Karjala, "Harry Potter, Tanya Grotter, and the Copyright Derivative Work," *Arizona State Law Journal* 38 (2006): 17–40, 22.

6. Donaldson v. Beckett, 1 Eng. Rep. 837 (1774, H.L.).
7. Millar v. Taylor, 98 Eng. Rep. 201 (K.B.) (1769).
8. A couple of examples will suffice: J. Boyle, *The Public Domain: Enclosing the Commons of the Mind* (New Haven: Yale University Press, 2008); Christophe Geiger, "Promoting Creativity Through Copyright Limitations: Reflections on the Concept of Exclusivity in Copyright Law," *Vanderbilt Journal of Entertainment and Technology Law* 12 (2010): 515–548.
9. Jessica Litman, "Lawful Personal Use," *Texas Law Review* 85 (2007): 1871–1920, 1882.
10. See, for example, William M. Landes and Richard A. Posner, *The Economic Structure of Intellectual Property Law* (Cambridge, MA: Harvard University Press, 2003), 167.
11. See, for example, Dan L. Burk, "Law and Economics of Intellectual Property: In Search of First Principles," *Annual Review of Law and Social Science* 8 (2012): 397–414, 411.
12. See U.S. Const. art. I, § 8, cl. 8.
13. On the "literary property debate," see, for example, Ronan Deazley, *On the Origin of the Right to Copy: Charting the Movement of Copyright Law in Eighteenth-Century Britain 1695–1775* (Oxford: Hart Publishing, 2004); Brad Sherman and Lionel Bently, *The Making of Modern Intellectual Property Law* (Cambridge, UK: Cambridge University Press, 2008), 9–42; Mark Rose, *Authors and Owners: The Invention of Copyright* (Cambridge, MA: Harvard University Press, 1993). See also Simon Stern, "From Author's Right to Property Right," *University of Toronto Law Journal* 62 (2012): 29–91.
14. 1710, 8 Anne., c. 19 (Eng.).
15. Rose, *Authors and Owners,* 111–112. Elsewhere, Rose writes:

    > "The London booksellers failed to secure perpetual copyright, but their arguments did develop the representation of the author as a proprietor, and this representation was very widely disseminated. Moreover, the Lords' decisions did not touch the basic contention that the author had a property in the product of his labor. Neither the representation of the author as a proprietor nor the representation of the literary work as an object of property was discredited. Nor, I suspect, could these contentions have been discredited at this point in history: too many and too powerful economic and social ideological forces were at work. So long as society was and is organized around the principles of possessive individualism, the notion that the author has the same kind of property right in his work as

any other laborer must and will recur." Mark Rose, "The Author as Proprietor: Donaldson v. Becket and the Genealogy of Modern Authorship," *Representations* 23 (1988): 51–85, 69–70.

16. Feist Publications Inc. v. Rural Telephone Service Co. Inc. 499 U.S. 340 (1991); CCH Canadian Ltd. v. Law Society of Upper Canada, 2004 SCC 13.
17. Feist Publications v. Rural Telephone, 349, 350.
18. CCH v. Law Society of Upper Canada, paras. 22–24.
19. Walter v. Lane, [1900] A.C. 539 (H.L.), 545: "I should very much regret it if I were compelled to come to the conclusion that the state of the law permitted one man to make profit and to appropriate to himself the labour, skill, and capital of another . . . In the view I take of this case I think the law is strong enough to restrain what to my mind would be a grievous injustice. The law which I think restrains it is to be found in the Copyright Act. . . ."
20. In the United States the duration of copyright protection is life plus seventy years, see Copyrights, 17 U.S.C. § 302 (2010). In Canada, it is life plus fifty years, see Copyright Act, R.S.C. 1985, c. C-42, s. 6 (Can.). The Statute of Anne, by contrast, allowed for a maximum term of twenty-eight years.
21. For discussion of technical protection measures, see Pamela Samuelson and Jason Schultz, "Should Copyright Owners Have to Give Notice About their Use of Technical Protection Measures?," *Journal of Telecommunications and High Technology Law* 6 (2007): 41–75; Margaret J. Radin, "Regime Change in Intellectual Property: Superseding the Law of the State with the 'Law' of the Firm," *University of Ottawa Law & Technology Journal* 1 (2003–2004): 173–188; Carys J. Craig, "Digital Locks and the Fate of Fair Dealing in Canada: In Pursuit of 'Prescriptive Parallelism'," *The Journal of World Intellectual Property* 13 (2010): 503–539.
22. The phrase "fair use as market failure" is Wendy Gordon's. See Wendy J. Gordon, "Fair Use as Market Failure: A Structural and Economic Analysis of the Betamax Case and Its Predecessors," *Columbia Law Review* 82 (1982): 1600–1657. For a deployment of the concept of fair use as market failure in the direction of a minimization of the public domain, see Tom W. Bell, "Fair Use vs. Fared Use: The Impact of Automated Rights Management on Copyright's Fair Use Doctrine," *North Carolina Law Review* 76 (1998): 557–619. For Gordon's own rejection of that view, see Wendy J. Gordon and Daniel Bahls, "The Public's Right to Fair Use: Amending Section 107 to Avoid the 'Fared Use' Fallacy," *Utah Law Review* 3 (2007): 619–658; Wendy J. Gordon, "Excuse and Justification in the Law of Fair Use: Transaction Costs Have Always Been Only *Part* of the Story," *Journal of the Copyright Society of the U.S.A.* 50 (2002–2003): 149–197.

23. With thanks to Arthur Ripstein for the phrasing that the public domain is "what it is too expensive to charge for."
24. Rose, "The Author as Proprietor," 51.
25. Rose, *Authors and Owners,* 107. See also, Deazley, *On the Origin of the Right to Copy,* 220: "The London booksellers, in arguing for the existence of the perpetual right had developed, over time, a convincing, accessible and necessary theory of literary property. This remains their legacy. The London monopolists, while they may have not won the battle of the booksellers, won the war of words." And also Sherman and Bently, *The Making of Modern Intellectual Property Law,* 40: " . . . [T]he literary property debate is also noteworthy in that the literary property which was recognized in the 1710 Statute of Anne was indirectly confirmed and reinforced. Once there had been doubts as to whether it was an institution which should be supported and encouraged by the law, but over the course of the debate the legal status of literary property was placed beyond doubt (or as good as). While the legislation that preceded the literary property debate—the Statute of Anne, the Engravers' Act of 1775—and the decisions that grew up around these played a role in the normalization of literary property, the mere fact that literary property was discussed so widely and in so much detail had the effect that its normative status was effectively rendered incontestable."
26. Millar v. Taylor, 229. Internal quotation marks omitted.
27. Ibid., 230.
28. Ibid., 233. Internal quotation marks omitted.
29. Ibid., 234.
30. Compo Co. Ltd. v. Blue Crest Music et al., [1980] 1 S.C.R. 357, 372–373.
31. Millar v. Taylor, 232.
32. Ibid., 233.
33. Deazley, *On the Origin of the Right to Copy,* 218, 222.
34. C. B. MacPherson, *The Political Theory of Possessive Individualism: Hobbes to Locke* (Oxford: Oxford University Press, 2011).
35. Deazley, *On the Origin of the Right to Copy,* 226.
36. Benjamin Kaplan, *An Unhurried View of Copyright* (Clark, New Jersey: The Law Book Exchange, Ltd., 2008), 12–13. This is a reprint of the James S. Carpentier Lectures delivered by Professor Kaplan at the Columbia University School of Law in March, 1966.
37. Millar v. Taylor, 250–251. At this point Mansfield LCJ had been on the court for thirteen years. He was appointed Lord Chief Justice in November 1756. Deazley, *On the Origin of the Right to Copy,* 175.
38. Millar v. Taylor, 251.
39. Ibid.
40. Ibid. Internal quotation marks omitted.
41. Ibid.

42. Ibid., 253. Emphasis added.
43. Ibid., 252. Emphasis added.
44. The Canadian *Copyright Act* defines "publication" as making copies available to the public. Copyright Act, R.S.C. 1985, c. C-42 s. 2.2(1) (Can.): "For the purposes of this Act, 'publication' means (*a*) in relation to works, (i) making copies of a work available to the public, (*b*) in relation to sound recordings, making copies of a sound recording available to the public, (*c*) the performance in public, or the communication to the public by telecommunication, of a literary, dramatic, musical or artistic work or a sound recording, or (*d*) the exhibition in public of an artistic work."
45. Millar v. Taylor, 230. Emphasis added.
46. Ibid.
47. Ibid., 232.
48. International News Service v. Associated Press 248 U.S. 215 (1918), Brandeis J., 250.
49. Millar v. Taylor, 230.
50. See R. v. Stewart, [1988] 1 S.C.R. 963, para. 35: "Confidential information is not of a nature such that it can be converted because if one appropriates confidential information without taking a physical object, for example by memorizing or copying the information or by intercepting a private conversation, the alleged owner is not deprived of the use or possession thereof. Since there is no deprivation, there can be no conversion. The only thing that the victim would be deprived of is the confidentiality of the information." See also Pocklington Foods Inc. v. Alberta (Provincial Treasurer), [1995] A.J. No. 280 (ABQB), para. 49: "In English and Canadian law an action for conversion cannot succeed unless tangible property has been converted to the plaintiff's use."
51. Millar v. Taylor, 251.
52. Ibid.
53. Ibid.
54. The Canadian Copyright Act defines infringement as doing what only the copyright owner has the right to do. Copyright Act, s. 27(1): "It is an infringement of copyright for any person to do, without the consent of the owner of the copyright, anything that by this Act only the owner of the copyright has the right to do."
55. Millar v. Taylor, 251. Emphasis added.
56. Ibid.
57. Ibid., 252.
58. See Rose, *Authors and Owners*, 86–87; Deazley, *On the Origin of the Right to Copy*, 144–145, 177–178; Sherman and Bently, *The Making of Modern Intellectual Property Law*, 19–20; See also Stern, "From Author's Right," 73–76.

59. Compo v. Blue Crest, 373: "The legislation speaks for itself and the actions of the appellant must be measured according to the terms of the statute." Bishop v. Stevens, [1990] 2 S.C.R. 467, para 18: "Analysis of these arguments must begin by emphasizing that copyright law is purely statutory law . . . First and foremost, then, this case is a matter of statutory interpretation."
60. Millar v. Taylor, 229. Emphasis added.
61. Ibid., 232.
62. Ibid., 235.
63. Ibid., 231.
64. Ibid.
65. Ibid., 230, Yates J.: "It was argued, that invention and labour are the means of acquiring property; and that literary compositions are the objects of the author's sole pains and labour; therefore they have the sole right in them. If this argument is confined to the manuscript, it is true; it is the object only of his own labour, and is capable of a sole right of possession. But it is not true, if extended to his ideas . . . To extend this argument, beyond the manuscript, to the very ideas themselves, seems to me very difficult, or rather quite wild."
66. Ibid., 229. Internal quotations omitted.
67. Ibid., 235.
68. In his reflection on Warren and Brandeis's "The Right to Privacy," Robert Post notes that the central thrust of the iconic article is "to disentangle privacy from property, and the subsequent influence of the piece rests in great measure upon its success in that effort." See Robert C. Post, "Rereading Warren and Brandeis: Privacy, Property, and Appropriation," *Case Western Reserve Law Review* 42 (1990): 647–680, 648. The shift from the tangible/intangible distinction to the object/act distinction in Lord Mansfield's judgment in Millar v. Taylor strikes me as an analogous striving (albeit not as self-aware as that of Warren and Brandeis in respect of privacy) to disentangle copyright from property. In Lord Mansfield's hands, however, the disentangling remains admittedly ambiguous, perhaps not least because he retains, understandably yet infelicitously, the word "property" to describe his "copy." According to Mark Rose, Lord Mansfield's judgment displays a "mingling of propriety and property" in which the "justness of the author's receiving the profits of his labors" and the "fitness that he should control the use of his name and the release of his work" reinforce and validate each other: "the personal interests moralized the economic claim" in the very same dynamic whereby "the property claim gave legal weight to the personal interests." Thus, in Rose's view of Lord Mansfield's judgment, the author's personal interest in privacy, for example, serves to justify but also becomes submerged under the rubric of copyright as

property. From this point of view, when Warren and Brandeis invoke the copyright law of unpublished works in order to disentangle privacy from property, they are encountering, as Rose puts it, the "task to untie the knot that Mansfield had tied a century and a half earlier." It is as if, as archaeologists of the common law, Warren and Brandeis had to retrieve from within propertized copyright the privacy interests that Lord Mansfield had grafted onto it. In my view, Rose's incisive reading exaggerates the reified "property" and overlooks the speech-based "copy" in Lord Mansfield's judgment. Lord Mansfield's achievement is to have anchored an understanding of copyright able to integrate the law of unpublished and published works under the single rubric of the specificity of copyright as the law of unauthorized publication. The move from proprietary to communicative discourse, and thus from the tangible/intangible to the object/act distinction, is the *sine qua non* of this foundational achievement. There can be no doubt that this move remained and remains incomplete, but this need not motivate Rose's sense that Lord Mansfield crafted, whether implicitly or otherwise, "a representation of the work itself as a commodity." See Rose, *Authors and Owners,* 82, 139–140. On the contrary, from the point of view of a speech-based construal of Lord Mansfield's achievement, it becomes clear that Warren and Brandeis tied quite a knot of their own. They regressed behind Lord Mansfield's understanding by leaving the propertization of the law of published works intact, and by invoking the law of unpublished works only to obfuscate it under the mantle of privacy. In my view, the emancipation of copyright from property emerges with luminous clarity in Immanuel Kant's brief 1785 essay, "On the Wrongfulness of Unauthorized Publication of Books" in Mary J. Gregor, trans. and ed., *Practical Philosophy* (Cambridge, UK: Cambridge University Press, 1996). Announced in the very first two paragraphs of the essay, the critical move from the tangible/intangible distinction to the object/act distinction is the heart of Kant's radically nonproprietary, speech-based account of the wrongfulness of unauthorized publication.

69. Consider use of sheet music not for its musicality but as wallpaper. This use is not technical in the tool-like sense of *Baker* or *Arriba Soft,* but it is still an instance of nonuse: it reproduces the material form of the work but not the work as a work.

70. See Litman, "Lawful Personal Use," 1883: "Courts confronting novel claims of infringement sought to locate the allegedly infringing behavior on the continuum between exploitation and enjoyment, in order to preserve copyright owners' control over exploitation while denying them control over individual reading, listening, playing, and viewing." See also, generally, Stavroula Karapapa, *Private Copying* (London: Routledge, 2012);

Ashley M. Pavel, "Reforming Reproduction: The Case for Personal Use Copies," *Berkeley Technology Law Journal* 24 (2009): 1615–1645.

71. On the distinction between repeating and learning, publishing and reading, see Johann Gottlieb Fichte, "Proof of the Illegality of the Unauthorized Reprinting of Books: An Argument and a Parable" (1793), Graham Mayeda translation in *University of Ottawa Law and Technology Journal* 5 (2008), 171–197. See also Martha Wondmansee's translation, "Proof of the Illegality of Reprinting: A Rationale and a Parable," available at www.case.edu/affil/sce/authorship/Fichte,_Proof.doc. For commentary, see Maurizio Borghi, "Owning Form, Sharing Content: Natural-Right Copyright in the Digital Environment," in *New Directions in Copyright Law,* vol. 5, ed. Fiona Macmillan (Cheltenham, UK: Edward Elgar, 2007), 197; Mario Biagioli, "Genius against Copyright: Revisiting Fichte's Proof of the Illegality of Reprinting," *Notre Dame Law Review* 86 (2011): 1847–1867; Graham Mayeda, "Commentary on Fichte's 'The Illegality of the Unauthorized Reprinting of Books': An Essay on Intellectual Property During the Age of Enlightenment," *University of Ottawa Law and Technology Journal* 5 (2008): 141–170.
72. Research and private study, to recall two of the three fair dealing purposes in the Canadian *Copyright Act* not requiring the defendant's authorship, would also fall under this rubric. To the extent that education, the third nonauthorial fair dealing purpose, transcends criticism, review, research, and private study, it could also fall under this rubric, but only on the assumption that the learning purposes of the end user are determinative. See *Alberta v. Canadian Copyright Licensing Agency,* 2012 SCC 37.

6. COPYRIGHT AND THE SYSTEM OF RIGHTS

1. Théberge v. Galerie d'Art du Petit Champlain Inc., 2002 SCC 34.
2. Ibid., para. 30.
3. Ibid., para. 31.
4. Ibid., para. 32. Emphasis added.
5. CCH Canadian Ltd. v. Law Society of Upper Canada, 2004 SCC 13, para. 48.
6. Society of Composers, Authors and Music Publishers of Canada v. Bell Canada, 2012 SCC 36, para. 9, referring to Bishop v. Stevens, [1990] 2 S.C.R. 467, 478–479. Bell Canada is one five Canadian Supreme Court of Canada cases known as the "copyright pentalogy." For commentary on the pentalogy, see the collection of essays in Michael Geist, ed., *The Copyright Pentalogy: How the Supreme Court of Canada Shook the Foundations of Canadian Copyright Law* (Ottawa, ON: University of Ottawa Press, 2013).

7. William Blackstone, *Commentaries on the Laws of England* (Oxford: Clarendon Press, 1765–1769), Book 2, Chapter 1, p. 2: " . . . the right of property; or that sole and despotic dominion which one man claims and exercises over the external things of the world, in total exclusion of the right of any other individual in the universe."
8. Théberge v. Galerie d'Art , para. 30.
9. On the history of balance in Canadian copyright see, for example, Saleh Al-Sharieh, "Birth, Retreat and Renaissance: The Lifecycle of Balance under the Canadian Copyright Law," *The Journal of World Intellectual Property* 10 (2007): 225–258.
10. See Feist Publications Inc. v. Rural Telephone Service Co. Inc. 499 U.S. 340 (1991), 344–345, stating that "[t]he most fundamental axiom of copyright law is that no author may copyright his ideas or the facts he narrates," quoting Harper & Row, Publishers, Inc. v. Nation Enterprises 471 U.S. 539 (1985), 556. Internal quotation marks omitted. See also CCH v. Law Society of Upper Canada, para. 22.
11. CCH v. Law Society of Upper Canada, para. 16; Feist Publications v. Rural Telephone, 345.
12. See Bruce Chapman, "Defeasible Rules and Interpersonal Accountability" in *The Logic of Legal Requirements: Essays on Defeasibility*, ed. Jordi Ferrer Beltran and Giovanni Battista Ratti (Oxford: Oxford University Press, 2012), 401–415.
13. See s. 3(1) Canadian Copyright Act, R.S.C. 1985, c. C-42. See also ss. 16–27 ("Rights of Copyright Owner") of the UK Copyright, Designs and Patents Act, 1988 c. 48; and Copyrights, 17 U.S.C. § 106 (2006).
14. See Feist Publications v. Rural Telephone; see also Hollinrake v. Truswell, [1894] 3 Ch. 420.
15. See Sheldon v. Metro-Goldwyn Pictures Corp., 81 F.2d 49, 54 (2d Cir. 1936). See also Kilvington Bros. Ltd. v. Goldberg et al. (1957), 8 D.L.R. (2d) 768.
16. "For the purposes of this Act, 'copyright,' in relation to a work, means the sole right to produce or reproduce the work or any substantial part thereof . . .": Canadian Copyright Act, s. 3(1). See also s. 16(3)(a) of the UK Copyright, Designs and Patents Act: "References in this Part to the doing of an act restricted by the copyright in a work are to the doing of it (a) in relation to the work as a whole or any substantial part of it . . ." In the U.S., infringement requires a showing of substantial similarity. See, for example, Arnstein v. Porter 154 F.2d 464 (2nd Cir. 1946).
17. See Frederick Schauer, "Exceptions," *University of Chicago Law Review* 58 (1991): 871–899.
18. See s. 29.1 of the Canadian Copyright Act. See also the references to "fair dealing" in s. 29 ("Research and private study") and s. 30 ("Criticism,

review, and news reporting") of the UK *Copyright Act,* and Copyrights, 17 U.S.C. § 107 (2006) ("Limitations on exclusive rights: Fair Use").

19. CCH v. Law Society of Upper Canada, para. 48.
20. For example, "[f]air dealing for the purpose of criticism or review *does not infringe copyright* . . .": section 29.1 of the Canadian Copyright Act (emphasis added).
21. See, for example, Christophe Geiger, "Fundamental Rights, a Safeguard for the Coherence of Intellectual Property Law?," *IIC: International Review of Intellectual Property and Competition Law* 35 (2004): 268–280; Christophe Geiger, "Drafting the Appropriate and Balanced Scope of Copyright Protection in the European Union: What Language Can Contribute to the Debate" in *Language and Copyright,* ed. Ysolde Gendreau and Abraham Drassinower (Montreal, QC: Carswell, 2009). But see also Annette Kur, "Of Oceans, Islands, and Inland Water: How Much Room for Exceptions and Limitations under the Three-step Test?," *Richmond Journal of Global Law and Business* 8 (2009): 287–350.
22. See Copyright Act, s. 32.2(2). To fall within the exception, the otherwise infringing performance in public of a musical work "at any agricultural or agricultural-industrial exhibition or fair that receives a grant from or is held by its directors under federal, provincial or municipal authority" must take place "without motive of gain." The US Copyright Act has a similar, but not equivalent provision. See Copyrights, 17 U.S.C. § 110(6) (2006).
23. See, for example, Paul Geller, "A German Approach to Fair Use: Test Cases for TRIPs Criteria for Copyright Limitations?," *Journal of the Copyright Society of the U.S.A.* 57 (2010): 901–919.
24. I am not one to resist a word play. With thanks to Mayo Moran for pointing it out.
25. Further examples of relations between copyright and other interests inviting juridical reflection may include, *inter alia,* Section 32.1(1) of the Canadian Copyright Act, providing that it is not an infringement to do certain acts pursuant to the *Access to Information Act,* the *Privacy Act,* the *Cultural Property Export and Import Act,* and the *Broadcasting Act.* See also Jonathan Griffiths, "Pre-empting Conflict: A Re-examination of the Public Interest Defence in UK Copyright Law," *Legal Studies* 33 (2013): 1–27, rendering the UK public interest exception as a way of articulating the relation between copyright and other juridically recognized interests, and providing access to information as an example.
26. The literature is vast and growing. See, for example, the essays in Paul L. C. Torremans, ed., *Copyright and Human Rights: Freedom of Expression—Intellectual Property—Privacy* (The Hague: Kluwer Law International, 2004) and in the enhanced edition of this volume, Paul L. C. Torremans, ed., *Intellectual Property and Human Rights, Enhanced Edition of Copyright and Human Rights* (The

Hague: Kluwer Law International, 2008); Geiger, "Fundamental Rights"; Laurence R. Helfer, "Human Rights and Intellectual Property: Conflict or Coexistence?," *Minnesota Intellectual Property Review* 5 (2003): 47–61; P. Bernt Hugenholtz, "Copyright and Freedom of Expression in Europe," in *Expanding the Boundaries of Intellectual Property: Innovation Policy for the Knowledge Society*, ed. Rochelle Cooper Dreyfuss, Dianne Leenheer Zimmerman, and Harry First (Oxford: Oxford University Press, 2001), 343; François Dessemontet, "Copyright and Human Rights" in *Intellectual Property and Information Law: Essays in Honour of Herman Cohen Jehoram*, ed. Jan Kabel and Gerard Mom (The Hague: Kluwer Law International, 1998), 113.

27. See, for example, Paul L. C. Torremans ed., "Copyright as a Human Right" in *Copyright and Human Rights*, 1; Michael D. Birnhack, "Copyrighting Speech: A Trans-Atlantic View," in *Copyright and Human Rights*, ed. Paul L. C. Torremans, 37.
28. See, for example, Birnhack, "Copyrighting Speech," 45–46 (discussing the shortcomings of refusing to take an external view of the conflict between copyright and freedom of expression). See also Neil Netanel's discussion of the issue in "First Amendment Constraints on Copyright after Golan v. Holder," *UCLA Law Review* 60 (2013): 1084–1128; Rebecca Tushnet, "Copy this Essay: How Fair Use Doctrine Harms Free Speech and How Copying Serves It," *Yale Law Journal* 114 (2004): 535–589; Seana Shiffrin, "The Incentives Argument for Intellectual Property Protection" in *Intellectual Property and Theories of Justice,* ed. A. Gosseries, A. Marciano and A. Strowel (London: Palgrave McMillan, 2008), 94–105; A. Couto, "Copyright and Freedom of Expression: A Philosophical Map" in *Intellectual Property and Theories of Justice,* ed. A. Gosseries, A. Marciano and A. Strowel (London: Palgrave McMillan, 2008), 160–187.
29. See, for example, Robert Burrell and Alison Coleman, *Copyright Exceptions: The Digital Impact* (Cambridge, UK: Cambridge University Press, 2005); Neil W. Netanel, *Copyright's Paradox* (Oxford: Oxford University Press, 2008); David L. Lange and H. Jefferson Powell, *No Law: Intellectual Property in the Image of an Absolute First Amendment* (Stanford, CA: Stanford Law Books, 2009).
30. Fontaineblau H. Corp. v. Forty-Five Twenty-Five Inc., 172 So.2d 248 (Fla. App., 1936). The discussion of nuisance case law that follows draws from Ernest Weinrib, *The Idea of Private Law* (Cambridge, MA: Harvard University Press, 1995), 190–196.
31. Appleby v. Erie Tobacco Co. (1910), 22 O.L.R. 533 (Div. Ct.).
32. I say "in the circumstances" because it is by reference to circumstances that the generality or particularity of a use can be determined. Thus, in a locality devoted to tobacco factories, it would be the plaintiff's wish to be free from smells produced thereby that would be the more particular or extraordinary use. See Weinrib, *The Idea,* 193 and case law cited therein.

33. See Weinrib, *The Idea*, 192: "A conspicuous example of the relevance of the ordinary is the plaintiff's right to be free from 'inconvenience materially interfering with the ordinary comfort physically of human existence.' This formulation, applied on a case-by-case basis, protects so basic an aspect of use that its denial would amount to a deprivation of the possibility of treating what one owns as property. The idea is that property, as a juridical expression of the agent's freedom, entails the possibility of uses that serve 'the ordinary purposes of life.' Uses incompatible with the ordinary purposes of life are comparatively particular, and cannot, therefore, represent a generally shared standard. For instance, the pungent smells emanating from a tobacco factory constitute an interference with the neighbors' use of their properties, because it would be inconsistent with property, as something that all property owners had an equal right to use and enjoy, to have a property regime in which everyone always had to tolerate another's unpleasant smells." Internal citations omitted.
34. Harrison v. Carswell, [1976] 2 S.C.R. 200.
35. This is basically the approach adopted by Justice Dickson, writing for the majority in Harrison v. Carswell, 219: "Anglo-Canadian jurisprudence has traditionally recognized, as a fundamental freedom, the right of the individual to the enjoyment of property and the right not to be deprived thereof, or any interest therein, save by due process of law. The Legislature of Manitoba has declared in *The Petty Trespasses Act* that any person who trespasses upon land, the property of another, upon or through which he has been requested by the owner not to enter, is guilty of an offence. If there is to be any change in this statute law, if A is to be given the right to enter and remain on the land of B against the will of B, it would seem to me that such a change must be made by the enacting institution, the Legislature, which is representative of the people and designed to manifest the political will, and not by the Court."
36. This is basically the approach adopted by Justice Laskin, writing in dissent in Harrison v. Carswell, 209: "The respondent picketer in the present case is entitled to the privilege of entry and to remain in the public areas to carry on as she did (without obstruction of the sidewalk or incommoding of others) as being not only a member of the public but as being as well, in relation to her peaceful picketing, an employee involved in a labour dispute with a tenant of the shopping centre, and hence having an interest, sanctioned by law, in pursuing legitimate claims against her employer through the peaceful picketing in furtherance of a lawful strike."
37. See, for example, Ashdown v. Telegraph Group Ltd., [2001] 4 All E.R. 618. See also HRH Prince of Wales v. Associated Newspapers Ltd, [2006] EWHC 522, [2006] ECDR 20 (Ch), [2008] Ch 57 (CA). For comment and analysis of Ashdown, see Michael D. Birnhack, "Acknowledging the Conflict between

Copyright Law and Freedom of Expression under the Human Rights Act," *Entertainment Law Review* (2003): 24–34. Writing in 2004, Ysolde Gendreau referred to Ashdown as "the high point of judicial analysis on the relationship between the freedom of expression of the [United Kingdom] Human Rights Act and copyright law." See Ysolde Gendreau, "Copyright and Freedom of Expression in Canada," in *Copyright and Human Rights*, ed. Paul L. C. Torremans, 21. For recent commentary and analysis of Ashdown and post-Ashdown developments, see Griffiths, "Pre-empting Conflict."

38. See, for example, Netanel's discussion of the issue in "First Amendment Constraints on Copyright."
39. See the Harrison v. Carswell passage quoted in note 36. See also ibid., 208–209: "If it was necessary to categorize the legal situation which, in my view, arises upon the opening of a shopping centre, with public areas of the kind I have mentioned (at least where the opening is not accompanied by an announced limitation of the classes of public entrants), I would say that the members of the public are privileged visitors whose privilege is revocable only upon misbehaviour (and I need not spell out here what this embraces) or by reason of unlawful activity. Such a view reconciles the interests of the shopping centre owner and of the members of the public, doing violence to neither and recognizing the mutual or reciprocal commercial interests of shopping centre owner, business tenants and members of the public upon which the shopping centre is based."
40. Relevant passages from the Harrison v. Carswell decision include, 209: "The shopping centre owner has no overriding or even coequal interest to serve in intervening in the labor dispute and, if anything, is acting as surrogate of the struck tenant in a situation where the latter has not and probably could not claim redress or relief." And 212: "Illustrations were given during the course of argument of situations which might put the respondent's [i.e., Sophie Carswell's] activity in a different light relative to the place of picketing and to the object of picketing and which, correlatively, might provide some redeeming interest of the shopping centre owner in exercising control over the public areas . . . In the present case it is the respondent who has been injured rather than the shopping centre owner."
41. Lorraine Weinrib and Ernest Weinrib, "Constitutional Values and Private Law in Canada" in *Human Rights in Private Law*, ed. Daniel Friedmann and Daphne Barak-Erez (Oxford: Hart Publishing, 2002), 43–72, 61.
42. Harrison v. Carswell, 212.
43. On the distinction between proportionality and "private law proportionality," see Weinrib and Weinrib, "Constitutional Values." But see also David M. Beatty, "Proportionality," Chapter 5 of *The Ultimate Rule of Law* (Oxford: Oxford University Press, 2004). On proportionality and copyright, see,

for example, Torremans, "Copyright as a Human Right." See also Justine Pila, "Pluralism, Principles and Proportionality in Intellectual Property," *Oxford Journal of Legal Studies* 34 (2014): 181–200. On defeasibility, exceptions and proportionality, see Chapman, "Defeasible Rules," 413, n. 29: "Under proportionality analysis, for example, the force of each claim is measured according to how high it is *on its own scale* and this is compared to how high the other claim is *on its scale.* The claim with the higher proportionate claim on its own scale 'outweighs' the other. But there is no common (commensurable) space in which both scales operate (as in the more usual cost-benefit or utilitarian analysis that turns on a commensurable cardinality across the two scales)." Emphases in original. See also Bruce Chapman, "Incommensurability, Proportionality and Defeasibility," *Law, Probability and Risk* 12 (2013): 259–274.

44. I see this view of the concept of a coherent system of rights as a fundamental condition of the possibility of jurisprudence (both as theory and as practice) as a version of Immanuel Kant's concept of law as an "idea of reason." See Immanuel Kant, "On the Common Saying: That May be Correct in Theory, But It is of No Use in Practice," in *Practical Philosophy*, trans. and ed. Mary J. Gregor (Cambridge, UK: Cambridge University Press, 1996), 273–310. For discussion, see Ernest Weinrib, "Law as a Kantian Idea of Reason," *Columbia Law Review* 87 (1987): 472–508; Arthur Ripsten, *Force and Freedom: Kant's Legal and Political Philosophy* (Cambridge, MA: Harvard University Press, 2009), 198–204; Ernest Weinrib, "Private Law and Public Right," *University of Toronto Law Journal* 61 (2011): 191–211.

BY WAY OF CONCLUSION

1. Feist Publications Inc. v. Rural Telephone Service Co. Inc. 499 U.S. 340 (1991); CCH Canadian Ltd. v. Law Society of Upper Canada, 2004 SCC 13.
2. Baker v. Selden, 101 U.S. 99 (1879); Kelly v. Arriba Soft Corp. 336 F. 3d 811 (9th Cir. 2003).
3. On *Baker* and computer program protection see Pamela Samuelson, "Why Copyright Law Excludes Systems and Processes from the Scope of Its Protection," *Texas Law Review* 85 (2007): 1921–1977. See also Pamela Samuelson, "The Uneasy Case for Software Copyrights Revisited," *George Washington Law Review* 79 (2010): 1746–1782.
4. Copyrights, 17 U.S.C. § 101 (2006): "A 'derivative work' is a work based upon one or more preexisting works, such as a translation, musical arrangement, dramatization, fictionalization, motion picture version, sound recording, art reproduction, abridgment, condensation, or any other form in which a work may be recast, transformed, or adapted." With thanks to

Jessica Silbey and Mark McKenna for helpful discussion of the concept of derivative work.

5. Ibid. § 106(2): "[T]he owner of copyright . . . has the exclusive rights . . . to prepare [and to authorize the preparation of] derivative works based upon the copyrighted work."
6. On derivative works see Pamela Samuelson, "The Quest for a Sound Conception of Copyright's Derivative Work Right," *Georgetown Law Journal* 101 (2013): 1505–1564; Daniel Gervais, "The Derivative Right: Or Why Copyright Law Protects Foxes Better than Hedgehogs," *Vanderbilt Journal of Entertainment and Technology Law* 15 (2013): 785–855; Rebecca Tushnet, "Payment in Credit: Copyright Law and Subcultural Creativity," *Law & Contemporary Problems* 70 (2007): 135–174; Dennis S. Karjala, "Harry Potter, Tanya Grotter, and the Copyright Derivative Work," *Arizona State Law Journal* 38 (2006): 17–40.
7. Copyrights, 17 U.S.C. § 103(a): "[P]rotection for a work employing preexisting material in which copyright subsists does not extend to any part of the work in which such material has been used unlawfully."
8. Thus, if assuming a narrowly construed reproduction right, one were to define translation as authorship rather than copying, then translation would not require authorization from the author of the original. See Stowe v. Thomas, 23 F. Cas. 201 (C.C.E.D. Pa. 1853) (No. 13,514). The derivative work right first appeared in the U.S. Copyright Act in 1976.
9. Melville B. Nimmer and David Nimmer, *Nimmer on Copyright* § 8.09 [A] (2012): "Countless woks are 'inspired by' or 'based on' copyrighted works and, in that lay sense, constitute 'derivative works.' But unless the product is substantially similar to its forbear, it remains nonactionable." Internal citations omitted.
10. See Maurizio Borghi and Stavroula Karapapa, *Copyright and Mass Digitization,* Chapter 2, "Technological Transformative Use" (Oxford: Oxford University Press, 2012); Neil Netanel, "Making Sense of Fair Use," *Lewis & Clark Law Review* 15 (2011): 715–771.
11. Authors Guild, Inc. v. Google, Inc. 954 F. Supp. 2d 282 (S.D.N.Y. 2013). .
12. Millar v. Taylor (1769), 98 Eng. Rep. 201 (K.B.); Donaldson v. Beckett, 1 Eng. Rep. 837 (1744, H.L.).
13. On fair use ambivalence, see Rebecca Tushnet, "Copy This Essay: How Fair Use Doctrine Harms Free Speech and How Copying Serves It," *Yale Law Journal* 114 (2004): 535–590; Anthony Reese, "The Story of Folsom v. Marsh: Distinguishing Between Infringing and Legitimate Uses (Copyright)," in *Intellectual Property Stories*, ed. Jane C. Ginsburg and Rochelle Cooper Dreyfuss (New York: Foundation Press, 2006), 259.
14. See Jessica Litman, "Lawful Personal Use," *Texas Law Review* 85 (2007): 1871–1920.

INDEX